COGNITION

Theory, Research,
Promise

Constance Scheerer Photograph

MARTIN SCHEERER   1900—1961

COGNITION

Theory, Research, Promise

PAPERS READ AT THE
MARTIN SCHEERER MEMORIAL MEETINGS
ON COGNITIVE PSYCHOLOGY,
UNIVERSITY OF KANSAS,
MAY, 1962.

edited by Constance Scheerer

HARPER & ROW, PUBLISHERS
*New York, Evanston,
and London*

COGNITION: *Theory, Research, Promise*

A-O

Library of Congress Catalog Card Number: 64-10111

CONTENTS

v

PREFACE

Martin Scheerer died on October 19, 1961.

Almost at once there was a deeply felt need on the part of many people to perpetuate the contributions of Martin Scheerer—both intellectually and personally—to a generation of American psychologists, and a meeting was planned which would accomplish this aim. The participant speakers who came together in May of 1962 were either colleagues or former students of Martin Scheerer; all were friends as well. As someone observed shortly after he died, "Martin taught colleagues, learned from students, and was a friend to both."

In the words of Erik Wright, the meetings were designed to be sessions that "Martin himself would have enjoyed attending." The field chosen was the most fitting one, Cognitive Psychology, to which Martin Scheerer had made so many contributions over the years. Speakers were given considerable freedom under the topic; no one was discouraged from presenting a purely theoretical paper, or from following an outline of present research with speculations as to future directions.

The meetings were held at the University of Kansas on May 7, 8, and 9, 1962. The papers are presented here in the order in which they were read. So that none of the work mentioned herein should appear to be wrongly dated, it should be stressed that the research referred to in the various papers is of very recent completion, is still in progress, or is part of larger, still ongoing experiments; hence the words "now," "currently," "at present," etc. have not been deleted from the text.

Most heartfelt thanks and appreciation are here expressed to
Drs. Anthony J. Smith, M. Erik Wright, and Jay Jackson of the
University of Kansas Psychology Department for their tireless
work in corresponding with participants, planning schedules, and
otherwise making the numerous detailed and difficult arrangements for setting up the meetings at which these papers were
presented.

A special debt of gratitude is also owed to Dr. Gardner Murphy
of The Menninger Foundation for his guidance and interest in
this volume.

C.S.

CONTRIBUTORS

SOLOMON E. ASCH is Professor of Psychology at Swarthmore College. He is the author of *Social Psychology* and of numerous articles in the fields of learning, thinking, and perception. He formerly taught in the Graduate Faculty of the New School for Social Research, and at Harvard University. He has been twice a Fellow of the Guggenheim Foundation and was for two years a member of the Institute for Advanced Study at Princeton. His fields of interest are social and experimental psychology.

JOHN CERASO is Assistant Professor of Psychology in the Department of Experimental and Clinical Psychology of the Graduate School of Education, Yeshiva University. Before going to Yeshiva he was research assistant to Solomon Asch and Wolfgang Köhler. His main interests in research have involved problems in associative learning and retention, with major emphasis on the phenomena of retroactive and proactive inhibition.

RILEY W. GARDNER is director of The Menninger Foundation's Cognition Project. He has published a number of papers and monographs on his clinical and experimental research, including a series on individual differences in perception, attention, concept formation, learning, remembering, etc., and their relations to defense mechanisms and intellectual abilities. He is also a faculty member of The Menninger School of Psychiatry.

FRITZ HEIDER holds a University Distinguished Professorship in Psychology at the University of Kansas. After three years at the University of Hamburg, Germany, he taught at Smith College until he came to Kansas in 1947. Twice holder of a Guggenheim Award, he is author of *The Psychology of Interpersonal Relations*. During the past academic year, he was at Duke University as a William Preston Few Professor of Psychology.

SHELDON J. KORCHIN is now Professor of Psychology at the University of California at Berkeley. From 1961 to 1963, he was Chief of the Section on Stress of the National Institute of Mental Health in Bethesda. He spent the year 1960–1961 as Fulbright Professor at the University of Genoa, Italy, and has taught at Harvard, Princeton, and Chicago. His has been a long-time concern with the problems of personality and cognition.

JOSEPH LYONS is currently a research psychologist at the Veterans Administration Hospital in Lexington, Kentucky. He spent the past academic year as Senior Research Fellow at the University of Louvain, Belgium, working on problems of expression and social perception. He formerly worked as chief psychologist and staff psychologist in the Veterans Administration Hospitals in Indianapolis and Topeka.

C. KERMIT PHELPS is Chief of the Psychology Service of the Veterans Administration Hospital in Kansas City, Missouri, Assistant Professor at the University of Kansas, and also Lecturer and Consultant at Rockhurst College, the University of Kansas City, the College of St. Teresa, and St. Mary College. He has spent the past ten years on some phase of research pertaining to problems of the brain-injured. At present he is active in group work with mentally retarded and dull-normal children.

IRVIN ROCK is Professor of Psychology in the Department of Experimental and Clinical Psychology of the Graduate School of Education, Yeshiva University. Previously a member of the Graduate Faculty of the New School for Social Research, he has published numerous articles in the field of perception, such as a recent work on the Moon Illusion, and in the field of human learning and memory, including one-trial learning.

RONALD TAFT is Reader in Psychology at the University of Western Australia. He spent the year 1962 at the Educational Testing Service at Princeton, where he worked on cognitive styles and personality. He is co-author, with Sarbin and Bailey, of *Clinical Inference and Cognitive Theory*.

SEYMOUR WAPNER, Professor and Chairman of the Department of Psychology at Clark University, is author of numerous articles on perception. He is co-author, with Heinz Werner, of *Perceptual Development*; co-editor, with Bernard Kaplan, of *Perspectives in Psychological Theory*; and one of the collaborators in *Personality Through Perception*.

HERMAN A. WITKIN has been since 1952 in the Department of Psychiatry at the State University of New York College of Medicine of New York City, where he is Professor and Director of the Psychology Laboratory. He is also director of the program of research training in psychiatry, a two-year post-residency program for psychiatrists. He is co-author of two books, *Personality Through Perception* and *Psychological Differentiation*.

COGNITION

Theory, Research,
Promise

MARTIN SCHEERER

FRITZ HEIDER

University of Kansas

ALL OF US WHO HAVE COME TOGETHER here today have known Martin Scheerer as friend and colleague and teacher—for Martin these were never separate roles. Each of us has warm and vivid memories of him that will remain an important part of our lives.

Roger Barker once said something about Martin that seemed so right that I will take it as my starting point. He said that there were many ways in which we could think of Martin as the ideal of what a professor should be: He loved his teaching and was deeply involved with individual students. He was a man of ideas who did experimental work and made important advances in his own field. And along with all this, he played his full part in the department and the university. There are few of us who measure up in all these ways as Martin did.

An amazingly large proportion of the younger generation of American psychologists who studied with him here and elsewhere recognize their contact with him as an important step in their intellectual growth, and look back with affection on their relationship with him. Martin had the rare capacity of making every contact a collaboration. He gave his students the experience of seeing ideas come into being and grow, and of finding their own places in the world of ideas. The friendships that came from these collaborations, from his own student days on, have been deep and enduring. And through his students, as well as through his own work, he has had an important influence on the development of psychology in this country.

1

Martin's colleagues at the University of Kansas bear witness to his contribution to the life of the department.

But what I want to do here is to trace something of Martin's own intellectual development as I have known it from the time when we were first together at the University of Hamburg, especially stressing those early times.

At that time, around 1928, William Stern was head of the department, Heinz Werner taught there, and Cassirer was head of the Department of Philosophy. There were close connections between the departments of psychology and philosophy. Martin and I met casually on different occasions, at seminars of Stern and Cassirer, and we were often together at after-lecture sessions in cafés, with groups that had lively discussions. I remember how struck and attracted I was when I first noticed him at a seminar as he argued brilliantly and excitedly, full of humor, his dramatic gestures bringing life to the abstractions of our discussion.

He was working on his thesis at the time and none of us knew much about it. The rumor was that it was of great proportions, and that Stern and Cassirer thought highly of it. And we knew that Martin had had firsthand contact with Gestalt psychology in Berlin, and that his thesis was a critique of Gestalt psychology from the Hamburg point of view.

Thus, at that time the two important influences on Martin's thinking were, on the one hand, Berlin Gestalt psychology, and on the other hand, the Hamburg kind of philosophy or psychology which was a mixture of Stern's personalism, Werner's developmental psychology, and Cassirer's neo-Kantianism.

In 1930 I came to this country, but Martin and I continued to keep in touch with each other. His thesis was published in 1931 as a book of 400 pages; and it is still an interesting book. It was called *Die Lehre von der Gestalt* or *The Theory of the Gestalt*.

Essentially, Martin said that Gestalt theory is too behavioristic, though that may sound strange. What he meant was that Gestalt psychology reduces psychological phenomena to processes which are essentially like physical processes; that it neglects the dimension of meaning, the act character of psychological phenomena; that it confuses intentionality with processes of inorganic nature.

For instance, he said that physical equilibrium is not the same as cognitive equilibrium; when one talks about cognition a new dimension enters. Gestalt neglects the totality and basic subjectivity of experience in considering the natural science frame of reference as primary. In short, he was concerned with the polarity, nature vs. person, and he blamed Gestalt psychology for reducing person to nature. If one reads this book again today, one is reminded of existentialist and phenomenological writers, and it is significant that in recent years Martin had been greatly interested in them.

In 1930 he started teaching at Hamburg. He found special stimulation in a seminar on thinking which he gave jointly with Werner.

In the summer of 1931 I got a long letter in which he discussed some of the objections that I had raised to his thesis—for example, that it was too extreme and that it did not quite do justice to Gestalt psychology. Already in this letter he wrote about going to America, and he described the general mood that prevailed in Hamburg. There was a feeling of impending catastrophe which stirred even people who had been quite nonpolitical in their outlook up to that point.

The catastrophe came in 1933. Stern and Werner wrote during that time about the breakup of the Hamburg department but I heard nothing directly from Martin between 1933 and 1936—only vague rumors that he was somewhere in the south of France. We could only wonder whether the catastrophe had swallowed him up.

Then came a long letter in February, 1936, from New York. He wrote that he had become very much concerned about the relation between science and politics, and the relation between psychology and sociology. He said, "You will be surprised; I am a changed man. I have given up transcendental philosophy and idealism, though I believe that it is a very fruitful and necessary stage in the training of a scientist. But one must not remain at that stage. The critique of knowledge must be revised in the face of facts like war, revolution, etc. Also, today I would not be so radical in my critique of Gestalt psychology."

One might say that this was the third important influence on Martin's thinking—after Berlin psychology and Hamburg philosophy it was German fascism which opened the eyes of many previously nonpolitical people to certain ugly realities and possibilities—and this not only influenced his theoretical thinking, but also led to his passionate and compassionate concern for justice and freedom.

He kept in touch, as closely as he could, with the colleagues of his Hamburg days, and sent material help as soon as the channels were open for him to do so, welcoming them as they came to this country.

It was very fortunate, and indeed, one might say inevitable, that in America Martin became associated with Kurt Goldstein. Goldstein, too, was close to Gestalt psychology on the one hand, and to Hamburg philosophy on the other. He was a cousin of Cassirer, who had made frequent visits to the clinic where Goldstein had demonstrated to him a great number of the cases of brain injury now famous in the literature.

Goldstein's distinction between concrete and abstract behavior was of great interest to Cassirer, who, in turn, probably helped give this distinction a broader meaning.

However, while Goldstein had, like Martin, absorbed Gestalt psychology and neo-Kantianism, he also was familiar with clinical problems. Martin steeped himself in this new experience during the years 1936–1939 when he worked at Montefiore Hospital. This was another important source of Martin's thinking—and we all know how creatively he used his earlier training in this new field.

The work with Goldstein preceded his New York teaching when he passed on his own synthesis of old and new to his students of City College, Brooklyn, and the New School, and through them—and through his own publications—fed it into the stream of American psychological thinking.

Then in 1947 came the establishment of the new department here at K.U. and we naturally thought of trying to induce Martin to come to Kansas. I had known Martin in large cities, in Hamburg and during visits to New York, and for some reason I had come to think of him as a city man. When we first corresponded about the possibility of his coming to Kansas I was not sure that he would be happy in a small city in the Midwest with wheat fields about, and I wrote him this. His answer relieved these doubts—*he liked wheat fields*, he wrote—and so came his visit and the decision to move to Kansas. The years here have proved how completely the country and K.U. became his home. Here he wrote the article on cognitive theory in the *Handbook of Social Psychology* and developed his theory of memory in the book, *Memory and Hypnotic Age Regression*, which he published with Reiff. We cannot express the extent of our debt to him for the years that he gave to the work that is so important to all of us.

AN ORGANISMIC-
DEVELOPMENTAL APPROACH
TO THE STUDY OF
PERCEPTUAL AND OTHER
COGNITIVE OPERATIONS[1]

SEYMOUR WAPNER

Clark University

I HAVE TAKEN AS MY TOPIC an overall description of the experimental-theoretical research program in perception which Heinz Werner and I initiated some dozen years ago. Our research program, originally directed toward the analysis of perception and referred to as the sensory-tonic field theory of perception, has expanded over the years. Working with a number of colleagues,[2] our approach, now broadly characterized as organismic-developmental, has evolved through a continual intertwining of theory,

[1] With few exceptions, the Clark investigations reported here are supported by PHS Grant MH-348, or by PHS Grant MY-2262, from the National Institute of Mental Health. I wish to thank Dr. Bernard Kaplan for his helpful comments on an early draft of this paper—in particular, for his suggestion that it be reorganized with a focus on "means-end" and "part-whole" relations; a formulation along these lines with special reference to symbolization is presented in a forthcoming volume by H. Werner and B. Kaplan, *Symbol Formation*. I wish to express my appreciation to Dr. D. M. Krus for his constructive criticisms of the manuscript.

[2] Among others, Drs. Donald M. Krus, Joseph H. McFarland, and Peter E. Comalli, Jr.

methodology, and experimental findings so that currently we are concerned not only with perceptual operations, but with cognitive operations more generally; thus, though our focus is on perceptual operations, we also include sensory-motor and conceptual operations within the orbit of our research.

An attempt will be made here to give an overall picture of our work by showing the ties between the character of our theoretical assumptions, our modes of formulating problems, the form of our methodologies, and the nature of our empirical findings.

I plan to do this in three ways: first, by referring to some general aspects of the organismic-developmental approach; second, by referring to a number of comparative studies employing groups ordered developmentally; last, by referring to some of the long-term goals of our research program.

1. SOME GENERAL ASPECTS OF THE ORGANISMIC-DEVELOPMENTAL APPROACH

The "organismic-developmental" approach to the analysis of behavioral events focuses (1) on certain *formal* features of the organism as a living system, and (2) on the nature of the *formal changes* that occur in this living system—the organism—as it grows and develops. Inasmuch as we are concerned with formal, structural, or organizational aspects of behavioral events, both facets of the view, "organismic" and "developmental," feature as a central notion for analysis the relations between *part and whole* on the one hand, and the relations between *means and end* on the other. Therefore, in describing the approach, I will consider, with respect to each of these aspects of analysis (part-whole, means-end), what is meant by "organismic" and then what is meant by "developmental."

Organismic Aspects

PART-WHOLE RELATIONS. The view is essentially a holistic one; that is, the organism is regarded as an entity comprised of interdependent parts which characterize it as a whole. For understanding of the whole system, ideally all parts should be considered. This means that our analysis of behavioral events is in terms of the interrelationship and integration of parts in relation to the whole rather than a treatment of parts in isolation. Thus, for example, in contrast to Gestalt psychology which treats systems (e.g., visual, tactual, motor, etc.) as encapsulated, sensory-tonic theory has focused on the very interrelationship among modalities and on such problems as the contribution of muscular states to perceptual processes.

This emphasis is seen very clearly in the pivotal issue of interaction which was raised as a problem when the sensory-tonic field theory was first formulated. In evaluating motor theories of perception we questioned the appropriateness of the use of interaction of sensory and motor factors as an explanatory concept, and pointed to a paradox, "How is it possible that intrinsically different elements, such as motor and sensory, can affect one another?" (Werner and Wapner, 1949, p. 90.) To our view this paradox of interaction was resolved by postulating the priority of a whole with respect to such factors—namely, sensory-tonic states, i.e., a dynamic process to which both sensory factors and motor factors contribute.

Analysis of perceptual behavior from the sensory-tonic view is not relegated to organismic factors alone; rather, the analysis is made with reference to the relationship between proximal stimuli (sensory input from an object) and states of the organism. Analysis of perceptual processes does not follow the lines of a projective theory which regards perception as the mirror of personality (Werner and Wapner, 1956a); rather perceptual processes are analyzed in terms of a field comprised of two parts, organism and object. Hence, the basic assumption of sensory-tonic field theory is that "perception is a reflection of the relation between proximal stimulation and ongoing organismic states." "Proximal stimulation" is defined as stimulation of sensory surfaces which issues from a physical object; "organismic state" represents the total ongoing state of the organism as it is affected by past history, present internal stimulation, and stimulation from sources other than those of the object attended. Perception is, so to speak, a reflection of a part, "proximal stimulation," in relation to the context of organismic activity, "organismic state" (Werner and Wapner, 1952b, 1956b; Wapner and Werner, 1957).

Given this formulation, it follows that changes in perception can occur as a function of changes in either aspect of the polarity "organism:object," i.e., the organismic context, or the proximal stimulus. We distinguish between two kinds of stimulation related to the two facets of the polarity, viz., object stimulation—from the object attended to—and nonobject stimulation (termed by us "extraneous" stimulation)—stimulation to the organism coming from sources other than the object attended.

This notion of duality of stimulation led to a variety of experimental studies where the state of the organism was manipulated by variation of extraneous stimulation, such as muscular, labyrinthian, auditory, etc., and its consequence on space localization was assessed (Werner and Wapner, 1949, 1952b, 1956b; Wapner, Werner, and Chandler, 1951; Werner, Wapner, and Chandler, 1951; Wapner, Werner, and Morant, 1951; Wapner and Werner, 1952, 1957; Werner, Wapner, and Bruell, 1953; Wapner, Werner, and Comalli, 1956; Comalli, Wapner, and Werner, 1959). Here it was found, e.g., that all forms of extraneous stimulation employed—head tilt, body tilt, direct stimulation of the neck muscle, auditory stimulation, rotary acceleration around the vertical axis of the body—were found to function in an equivalent manner with respect to perception of verticality: the physical position of the apparent vertical, indicated by a rod, shifts opposite the side to which the extraneous stimulation is applied.[3] From these findings and others dealing with effects of cerebellar injury (K. Goldstein, 1939), etc., a hypothetical mechanism concerning the effect of extraneous stimulation on apparent verticality was formulated in terms of "organismic state:proximal stimulus" relationships (symbolized by oRs, where "o" designates "organismic state," "s" designates "proximal stimulus," and "R" designates "relationship"). It would take us far afield to go into

[3] This generalization is restricted to relatively small body tilts in which the E-phenomenon has been generally observed.

this mechanism here. It has been described in the literature (see Werner and Wapner, 1952b, 1955, 1956b; Wapner and Werner, 1957).

Similarly, the notion of duality of stimulation generated another set of studies concerned with the effect of variation of object stimulation on visual localization (Werner and Wapner, 1952a, 1952b, 1954, 1956b; Wapner, Werner, Bruell, and Goldstein, 1953; Bruell and Albee, 1955; Kaden, Wapner, and Werner, 1955; Wapner and Werner, 1955, 1957). Here it was found, e.g., that the position of apparent vertical, the straight-ahead, etc., is relatively close to the position in which the stimulus object was started at the beginning of the trial. The findings on effect of starting position, on effects of asymmetrical extent, and Gibson's observations of figural adaptation (Gibson, 1933; Gibson and Radner, 1937) led to the formulation of a hypothetical mechanism for the operation of static object stimulation.

The mechanism[4] for operation of object stimulation hinges on the assumption that an essential feature of the organism pertains to biological tendencies with respect to relations between impinging proximal stimuli and the existing state of the organism. When stimuli impinge on the organism various relations are possible between the promixal stimuli and the momentary state of the organism. One such relationship is that of stability; i.e., with a particular proximal stimulus there is no tendency for pertinent aspects of organismic state to change. Such a relationship, described as a stable one, reflects itself in a particular percept; that is, a particular percept is a function of an invariant relation between a particular proximal stimulus and a particular organismic state. In contrast, there is also a relationship of instability; this is said to occur when certain stimuli issuing from an object are in disequilibrium with organismic state and there is a tendency for the organismic state to change so that an "organism-object" equilibrium is established. Hence, given a particular proximal stimulus, with a change in organismic state there is a change in perception. To summarize our conceptualization of "organismic state:proximal

---

[4] A fuller description of this mechanism is given in Werner and Wapner (1952b, 1955, 1956b), and Wapner and Werner (1957).

stimulus" relationships, we assume a biological tendency which operates toward maintaining or reestablishing stable relations between "proximal stimulus" and "state of the organism." This idea that there are tendencies to establish "object:organism" equilibria underlies the attempts of sensory-tonic theory (Werner and Wapner, 1955) to account in organismic terms for Ivo Kohler's (1951, 1953) findings on differential figural adaptation. In turn, this theoretical analysis led to experimentation by Giannitrapani (1958) and Ohwaki (1959, 1961), who found evidence for figural adaptation to visual fields distorted by prisms.

In keeping with our holistic view in general, and the studies on figural adaptation in particular, is the more specific implication that the organismic nature of perception is manifested in intermodal effects; that is, the assumption is made that a change in organismic state pertains not to one but rather to many sense modalities. This general assumption of organismic functioning led to experimentation on intermodal effects of various kinds of stimulation and on transmodal effects of figural adaptation. In addition to the various studies which show effect of stimulation in one modality on perception in another (Werner and Wapner, 1949, 1952b; Wapner, Werner, and Chandler, 1951; Wapner, Werner, and Morant, 1951; Werner, Wapner, and Chandler, 1951; Werner, Wapner, and Bruell, 1953; Wapner, Werner, and Comalli, 1956; Wapner and Werner, 1957; Morant, 1959), we may single out the studies by Goldstein (1955) which showed that following adaptation to a tilted visual field there were significant changes in tactual-kinesthetic perception of verticality, the study by Ohwaki (1959, 1961) which showed that figural adaptation to a rotated visual field was not restricted to the eye exposed but was also manifest in the other eye and in another modality (tactual-kinesthetic), and Mayer's (1961) study which demonstrated similar transmodal effects for perception of curvature.

MEANS-END RELATIONS. Another general assumption of importance is that the organism is goal-directed, i.e., it is a system which exhibits directedness. It is in the context of this assumption that we deal with analysis of behavior in terms of means-end relationships. In very general terms we are concerned here with the distinction between process and achievement, which has very broad application (Werner, 1937).[5] This distinction implies that there is no one-to-one relationship between process and achievement or between means and ends but rather that the organism can further its goals or ends by a multiplicity of means.

The notion of functional equivalence introduced in sensory-tonic theory represents a specification of the principle of "means-end" relationships in perception. Functional equivalence states that diverse stimuli ideally lead to identical perceptual end products. The variety of experiments conducted to explore the effect of extraneous stimulation and of object stimulation—referred to earlier—provide evidence for this notion of functional equivalence. For example, the studies dealing with extraneous stimulation show that similar effects on perception of verticality accrue from various forms of stimulation, such as electrical stimulation to the neck muscle, auditory stimulation, body tilt, labyrinthian stimulation; viz., the apparent vertical shifts to the side opposite that to which the stimulus is applied (Werner and Wapner, 1949; Wapner, Werner, and Chandler, 1951; Werner, Wapner, and Chandler, 1951; Wapner, Werner, and Morant, 1951; also cf. Werner, Wapner, and Bruell, 1953).

The principle of multiplicity of means for achieving given ends played a critical role in the extension of our work from dealing exclusively with perceptual processes to dealing with other cognitive operations, viz., sensory-motor and conceptual. That is, the principle was adopted that certain given ends could be achieved through one or the other of the various cognitive operations.[6] H. Werner (1937, 1940) discusses this problem under the general rubric of analogous functions and provides extensive evidence in support of this principle. For example, he shows how perceptual constancy may be achieved by certain physiological, perceptual, and conceptual processes.

---

[5] M. Scheerer (1954) indicates that this distinction is implicitly or explicitly adopted by most cognitive theorists and describes the need for and implications of "process analysis" for the study of personality (See also Scheerer, 1946).

[6] The analysis of cognitive processes in terms of levels of organization presented here complements the views presented in M. Scheerer's (1954) comprehensive analysis and survey of cognitive theory.

For a theory like sensory-tonic theory, which conceives of perception in terms of total organismic activity, this problem of relations among sensory-motor, perceptual, and conceptual operations is of great importance. One methodological approach to this problem has been to inquire whether these operations are related in a *cooperative* or *supportive* fashion, on the one hand, or, on the other, whether they are related in a *vicarious* or *antagonistic* fashion. The problem has been formulated as one of determining experimentally the conditions and factors making for cooperative vs. vicarious relationships between functions. Cooperative relations have been experimentally obtained in studies on lapse of meaning and perceptual recognition of words. Miller (1959) obtained evidence for supportive relationships between different cognitive operations using the lapse of meaning technique. He found that lapse of meaning, which ordinarily occurs with verbal repetition of a word, is delayed significantly when, simultaneous with the *repetition* of a word, there is introduced sensory-motor activity consonant with the *meaning* of the word. The sensory-motor activity operates supportively insofar as it serves to prolong the meaning. An analogous relationship for threshold of perceptual recognition was found by Dowling, Werner, and Wapner in 1960, and by Dowling in 1962; viz., sensory-motor activity consonant with the meaning of a word served to lower recognition threshold. Vicarious relations have been found in tasks dealing with identification of pictures, recognition thresholds for words, and autokinetic motion. With introduction of strong motor involvement, decreases were found in (1) perceptual movement as measured by verbal responses to pictorial material (Krus, Werner, and Wapner, 1953); (2) perceptual sensitivity as measured by recognition threshold (Krus, Wapner, and Werner, 1958); and (3) autokinetic motion (Goldman, 1953).

Developmental Aspects

The developmental point of view[7] represents a way of analyzing change in a living, growing system. Development is not defined in terms of time but rather in terms of a progression of

[7] The point of view described is based upon and represents an elaboration of H. Werner's (1940, 1957) systematic treatment.

stages of a system which is undergoing transition. Thus, it is a manner of ordering data which is not restricted to age changes alone. Changes during the birth-death cycle represent only one specification of behavioral events which can be analyzed by this approach. As we shall see, it makes possible not only study of changes in chronological age, but also study of pathological groups, study of the formation of patterns of behavior, study of the effect of drugs, etc.

Again, just as for the organismic aspect, the developmental aspect is concerned with *formal* analysis of organismic behavior in terms of part-whole and means-end relations; it differs from the organismic aspect, insofar as the latter stresses cross-sectional analysis, whereas the developmental aspect stresses *change* in the living system. The developmental point of view focuses on change in living, growing organisms with reference to two general categories pertinent to analysis of change occurring in part-whole and means-end relations, viz., differentiation and hierarchic integration. The changes in the course of development are characterized as a progression from less differentiation of parts to greater differentiation and hierarchic integration of parts with respect to the whole (cf. Werner, 1940).

PART-WHOLE RELATIONS. An example of the application of the developmental principle pertinent to the analysis of perceptual processes can be seen in the emergence of the sensory modes of experience. With growth of the organism there occurs a differentiation and integration of the sensory modes. This suggests greater effects on one modality of variations occurring in another modality at early developmental stages compared with later developmental stages. This formulation suggests the study of intersensory relations as an important problem, and moreover suggests that there are differences in intersensory effects at different stages of development. Studies based on this notion have been conducted concerning effect of auditory stimulation on such visual perceptual phenomena as critical flicker frequency by Gorrell (1953). He found that auditory stimulation reduced critical flicker frequency to a greater extent in younger than in older children, that low and high tones had no differential effects on critical flicker frequency in 8-year-old children, but became evident in 10-year-old children and increased with age. Thus, there were greater intersensory effects at earlier age levels and there was greater differentiation at later age levels.

The applicability of a developmental analysis in terms of part-whole relations is seen to be specifically pertinent to those perceptual situations where part-whole relations pertain to a feature of the stimulus object. The general expectation is that there is a lack of differentiation of parts early in development, and increasing differentiation and integration of parts later in development. This general expectation may be applied to two illusions, with susceptibility differing depending upon the nature of the illusion and the stage of development. With the Müller-Lyer illusion—illusion based on assimilation of part to whole—greater susceptibility is expected in younger children than in adults; with the Titchener Circles illusion—based on contrast relations of parts—greater susceptibility is expected in adults (who are better able to differentiate parts) than in children. The empirical findings support these hypotheses (Wapner and Werner, 1957; Wapner, Werner, and Comalli, 1960). Supporting evidence also was found by Heiss (1928), who showed that the capacity to isolate a part from a whole increased with age. The situation he developed was used by Podell (1957), Krus (1957), and Krus and Wapner (1959) with adult groups ordered developmentally by criteria other than age; their data were consistent with the developmental ordering of the groups they studied.

MEANS-END RELATIONS. Though our earlier discussion of the importance of means-end relationships for organismic theory considered alternative means (sensory-motor, perceptual, and conceptual operations) in achieving an end, *independent of change,* the developmental view is concerned with the *emergence* of these operations and relations between them. Considering the progression from early to late stages of development, sensory-motor operations emerge first, these are followed by perceptual operations, and finally by conceptual operations (Werner, 1940, 1957).[8]

[8] The importance of the concept of levels of organization for cognitive de-

What is meant by these operations may be clarified by exemplifying them as varying in terms of degree of differentiation and hierarchic integration between self and world. For operations on the sensory-motor level there is lack of differentiation between self and world insofar as these cognitive operations involve direct, motoric, concrete action with the world of objects; for operations characteristic of the perceptual level of organization there is greater differentiation of self and world insofar as the organism is contemplatively directed to properties of objects "out there"; and finally, at the conceptual level of organization, symbols or abstract representations of objects are manipulated by the organism.

These operations are characterized by, emerge, and are related in terms of the general principle of development. Thus, sensory-motor operations are relatively more global or less articulated than perceptual or conceptual operations. An operation that emerges at a later stage in development does not supplant the operation already present, but is hierarchically related to it. When later levels of functioning come into play, earlier levels of functioning act supportively or vicariously, and may be modified during the course of becoming subordinated to later level functioning.

As indicated earlier, the analysis in terms of means-end relations points to the general problem of the relationships among the hierarchically organized operations. As already noted, we have attacked this problem in general terms by inquiring about the conditions under which operations are related in a supportive vs. a vicarious manner. The developmental view, focusing on change at various stages in a developmental series, poses the further problem of relations among operations in individuals differing in developmental status. Some beginning steps have been taken to study this problem (cf. Clarkson, 1961; Dowling, Werner, and Wapner, 1960; Dowling, 1962; Switzer, 1961) and these will be

---

velopment is discussed with regard to J. Piaget's system (1950) and H. Werner's system (1940) by M. Scheerer in his critical review of cognitive theory (1954).

discussed after some further implications of the organismic-developmental approach for experimental inquiry are considered.

A critical feature of the organismic-developmental approach having implications for experimental inquiry is that it can be applied to any series which can be ordered developmentally. The viewpoint is not restricted to a comparison of changes with increase in age; rather, it concerns analysis of the stages of any system which is undergoing transition. This means that a developmental analysis can be applied to a large variety of problems. For example, such general problems as the formation of behavioral acts can be studied by making the assumption that the emergence of behavior is characterized by progressive stages which parallel in structure those stages specified by the developmental principle (Werner, 1957). Hence, the stages of establishment of a sensory-motor pattern, a percept, or a concept are expected to follow the law of development; i.e., there should be differentiation and hierarchic integration of parts in the establishment of the end product, whether it be a sensory-motor pattern of behavior, a percept, or a concept (see, e.g., Clarkson, 1961; Flavell, 1955; Switzer, 1961; Werner, 1956).

Similarly, a variety of groups or individuals under the same or different conditions can be compared if they are orderable in developmental terms. Thus, individuals ordered in terms of age, within the limits of childhood to maturity, can be studied by making the assumption that during growth, certain behavioral changes, when analyzed formally, show a progression which follows the ideal developmental sequence of increase in differentiation and hierarchic integration (Wapner and Werner, 1957; Comalli, Wapner, and Werner, 1959, 1960a, 1960b, 1962; Comalli, Werner, and Wapner, 1959; Wapner, Comalli, and Werner, 1959; Wapner, Werner, and Comalli, 1960).

If one makes the further assumption that through the entire life span there is "developmental progression" followed by "developmental regression," then a working hypothesis is available for study of *aging*. Progression proceeds in terms of an increase in differentiation and hierarchic integration; in the obverse, regression, the shift is reversed, i.e., from more to less differentiation and hierarchic integration. Accordingly, a variety of studies have been conducted, using situations where general mechanisms have been worked out, comparing subjects from 6 to 80 years of age (Comalli, Wapner, and Werner, 1959, 1960a, 1960b, 1962; Wapner, Werner, and Comalli, 1960).

Psychopathology has similarly been approached from this viewpoint on the assumption that psychopathological groups operate formally, in certain areas, at levels comparable to earlier levels of development. Thus, in keeping with this regression hypothesis, schizophrenics were ordered developmentally with respect to normals. Investigations were undertaken on the hypothesis that the schizophrenics relative to normals show formal, structural features of behavior comparable with those found in other groups (relative to normal adults) typically operating at earlier developmental levels, such as children and aged people (Carini, 1955; Liebert, 1956; Wapner and Werner, 1957; Liebert, Wapner, and Werner, 1957; Liebert, Werner, and Wapner, 1958; Wapner and Krus, 1960a, 1960b; Rosenkrantz, 1960).

In a parallel fashion the effects of certain *drugs* can be studied from the organismic-developmental view. Psychopharmacological agents like lysergic acid diethylamide (LSD-25) have been of interest on the grounds that they induce "regressed" states of behavior; accordingly, a number of studies have been conducted which were designed to evaluate whether normal adults under the influence of LSD-25 (relative to placebo conditions) show changes in behavior *structurally* analogous to differences in behavior found when groups of individuals characterized as operating at "earlier" developmental levels, such as children, schizophrenics, and the aged, are compared with normal adults (Liebert, Wapner, and Werner, 1957; Liebert, Werner, and Wapner, 1958; Krus and Wapner, 1959; Wapner and Krus, 1959, 1960a, 1960b; Krus, Wapner, Bergen, and Freeman, 1961).

Other drugs have been of interest on the grounds that they inhibit regression or induce transient "developmental progression." The studies with these drugs utilize aged subjects. Given the assumption that the changes in formal, structural features of behavior during the life cycle consist in a "progression" followed by a "regression," the drugs presumed to induce "developmental progression" are evaluated by determining whether they arrest or inhibit the regressed behavior that ordinarily occurs with this group (Wapner and Krus, 1960a).

Before terminating this description of relations between theory, problems, and empirical methodology, it seems necessary to underline some precautions. In the first place, the similarities hypothesized among groups characterized as having a common relative standing in a developmental series pertain to *formal, structural* features of behavior. Secondly, similarity of behavior does not imply identity. The distinction between process and achievement directs us to examine further the similarities in behavior. That is, there still remains the fundamental problem of identifying possible differences underlying *formally* similar perceptual behavior found to occur in childhood, in old age, in psychopathological states, and under transient conditions, such as drugs. Finally, the developmental hypothesis and its corollary, the regression hypothesis, provide a means for bringing together a large variety of behaviors occurring in different groups under different conditions. Rather than being concerned with a test to determine whether these hypotheses can be generally considered to be verified, we view them at the same time as (1) a means for bringing together under one principle a wide variety of behaviors, and (2) a heuristic device for leading us to new experimental findings. It is a matter of experimental inquiry to determine where these hypotheses are and where they are not verified, and from that pattern of findings to sharpen the organismic-developmental concepts as well as define their realm of applicability.

2. SOME COMPARATIVE STUDIES WITH GROUPS ORDERED DEVELOPMENTALLY

So much for some of our general theoretical assumptions and their relation to experimentation. Now, the approach will be further characterized by describing some comparative studies dealing with a variety of behaviors and problems, viz., localization of objects, relations between localization of one's own body and of other objects, apparent size of body parts, part-whole perception, capacity to maintain directed activity, and relations between cognitive operations. Wherever available, data will be presented on (1) groups ordered developmentally in terms of age; (2) groups ordered developmentally in terms of pathology—schizophrenics vs. normals, etc.; and (3) normal adults under transient, drug-induced conditions, which can be ordered developmentally with respect to placebo conditions.

Object Localization

Following the general principle that developmental studies could profitably be undertaken utilizing situations where general mechanisms had been studied first, a few years ago we conducted a developmental study on perception of verticality (Wapner and Werner, 1957) with subjects between the ages of 6 and 19 years.

AGE CHANGES FROM CHILDHOOD TO MATURITY. Perception of verticality was tested under three body positions, 30° tilted to the left, erect, and 30° tilted to the right. In brief, a striking difference in the effect of body tilt (extraneous stimulation) depending on developmental level was found. For the younger subjects the position of apparent vertical (physical position in which a rod must be placed to be perceived as vertical) was tilted relatively to the same side as body tilt, whereas for the older subjects it was tilted relatively to the side opposite of body tilt. Thus, there was a reversal in effect of body tilt depending upon age level. In these experiments on apparent verticality there were also four starting positions of the rod, representing variation in object stimulation. It was found that irrespective of age level and body tilt the position of the apparent vertical was rotated relatively to the left under left starting position and rotated relatively to the right under right starting position. There was, in addition, a developmental change; i.e., the starting position effect was greatest at the youngest age level and decreased with increase in age.

AGING. More recently, this study was extended to include subjects between 20 and 80 years of age. The whole picture on changes in spatial organization that occur from 6 to 80 years of age is as follows: For young boys from 6 to 15, the apparent vertical is located to the same side as body tilt; between 16 and 50 years, however, the opposite effect occurs, namely, apparent vertical is located opposite the side of body tilt; and finally in older men from 65 to 80 years of age the apparent vertical is again located to the same side as body tilt (Comalli, Wapner, and Werner, 1959). The developmental changes in effect of starting position were found to occur only within the younger age range; namely, starting position effect is greatest at the youngest age level, decreases markedly until the 19-year level, and following this there are no consistent developmental changes throughout the age levels studied, including the 65- to 80-year group.

Both of these effects occurring during the period of growth through adolescence are interpreted by us as an expression of the orthogenetic principle which states that the development proceeds from a state of globality and lack of differentiation—in this case between self (own body) and object—to a state of increased differentiation. We interpret our results in accordance with this principle by assuming that at early stages of development lack of differentiation of self and object manifests itself in two ways: (1) by egocentricity—i.e., the formation of a frame of reference whereby apparent vertical is to the side of body tilt, or proximal stimuli are interpreted in terms of body position; and (2) by stimulus boundedness—which refers to the inordinate impact of object stimuli as evidenced by greater starting position effects. During aging, the reversal in the relation between tilt of body and position of apparent vertical indicates that there is a reversion to a more egocentric organization of space; i.e., in older people once again the object world is determined through self as referent. Thus, in old age, as in childhood, there is decreased differentiation of self and world as manifested by greater egocentricity.

PSYCHOPATHOLOGY. Given the assumption that psychopathological groups operate at levels in certain areas which are formally comparable to earlier levels of development (regression hypothesis), three studies were conducted dealing with perception of verticality in schizophrenics.

In the first study, three groups of subjects were employed which could be ordered developmentally: a group consisting of schizophrenics diagnosed as catatonic-hebephrenics, another group of paranoid schizophrenics, and a control group—normal adults

(Carini, 1955). These subjects were studied in the same situation in which behavior was shown to undergo changes with onto-genetic development; namely, the effect of body tilt and starting position on apparent verticality. A significant relationship was found with respect to the effect of body tilt on the position of the apparent vertical. As found in previous studies, again for the normal adults the position of the apparent vertical was relatively opposite the side of body tilt; in contrast, for the catatonic-hebephrenic group, the position of the apparent vertical was located to the same side as body tilt, and for the paranoids it fell in between these extremes. No significant differences between groups were found in regard to effect of starting position on the apparent vertical. In the second study (Liebert, Wapner, and Werner, 1957) the effect of body tilt was replicated and, more-over, greater starting position effects in schizophrenics compared with normals were found, which approached significance. In a third study (Wapner and Krus, 1960a) the effect of body tilt was replicated a second time and once again there was some limited evidence for greater starting position effects in schizophrenics.

DRUGS. On the assumption that LSD-25 operates as a primitiviz-ing agent, studies were conducted concerning the effect of this drug on apparent verticality. It was found that under LSD, normal adults as well as schizophrenics showed greater starting position effects than under placebo conditions. Though these changes under LSD-25 were not significant in normals, the increase was highly significant in schizophrenics. The results on effect of body tilt on position of apparent vertical under LSD-25 were not in keeping with expectation. The displacement of apparent vertical opposite the side of body tilt was enhanced rather than minimized in normals, and there was no evidence that the drug significantly altered the effect of body tilt on perception of verticality in schizo-phrenics (Liebert, Wapner, and Werner, 1957).[9]

[9] The failure to verify this hypothesis opens an important problem. To the end of clarifying the problem, studies are being formulated to evaluate the effect of body tilt on verticality under LSD-25 in terms of the relations be-tween body position and object position (see McFarland, Clarkson, and Wapner, 1961; McFarland, Clarkson, Wapner, and Werner, 1961. McFarland, Wapner, and Werner, 1962, discussed in the following paragraphs).

Relations Between Position of One's Own Body and That of Other Objects

While our earlier work focused on perceptual properties of concrete, impersonal objects in space, over the past five years we have given considerable attention to perception of one's own body (Werner, Wapner, and Comalli, 1957; Liebert, Werner, and Wapner, 1958; Wapner, Werner, and Comalli, 1958; Wapner, 1959, 1960, 1961a, 1961b). These studies, dealing with apparent size of body parts, emerged from the recognition that the perceptual properties of the body *qua* object could be studied utilizing the same principles employed in study of objects "out there." With respect to space localization, in particular, some large steps have been taken by McFarland and others to deal experimentally with the problem of specifying the nature of the relationship between perceived position of these two classes of objects, one's own body and of other objects (McFarland, Clarkson, Wapner, and Werner, 1961; McFarland, Clarkson, and Wapner, 1961; McFarland, Wapner, and Werner, 1962).

To study this problem, one of the situations employed two tasks. In one task the luminous rod in a dark room is adjusted to apparent vertical (indication of apparent object position); in the other, the rod is adjusted to a position which appears parallel to the longitudinal axis of the body (indication of apparent body position). The two tasks are carried out both when the body is erect and when tilted. By this method, we are currently in the process of accumulating data on the relationship between apparent body and apparent object location. Our data are somewhat limited, but patterns are already emerging which are worthy of mention.

In studies with adults, the apparent body position is overestimated under 30° body tilt; i.e., rotated *beyond* the position of tilt; we also know, from many studies, that apparent vertical is rotated *opposite* the side of body tilt. In keeping with developmental analysis, our assumption has been that the angular separation between apparent vertical and apparent body position can serve as an objective index of the degree of differentiation of body and object position; i.e., we assume that the greater the angular separation between apparent vertical and apparent body position, the greater the degree of differentiation of body and object position. Now, our prediction is undoubtedly obvious. We expect that groups ordered developmentally will differ in terms of the angular separation of apparent body and apparent object position; viz., this angle will be smaller in groups characterized as developmentally "less mature" or "earlier."

AGE CHANGES AND PSYCHOPATHOLOGY.   We are currently testing children from 6 to 14 years, adults, and a few schizophrenics on apparent verticality and apparent body position. Though the data have not been completely analyzed, the preliminary findings are quite promising. Scores on apparent verticality and apparent body position, under 30° left and right body tilt, made by 48 children between 6 and 8 years of age have been compared with those made by 24 normal adults. As predicted, it has been found, under both left and right body tilt, that the angular separation between apparent vertical and apparent body position is markedly less in children than in adults. Thus, our objective indicator provides evidence of less differentiation between body and object position for children than for adults.

To date we have obtained complete, consistent data for only a few schizophrenic subjects. The results for these few cases are also in keeping with prediction. For schizophrenics, the position of apparent vertical under body tilt is in the same direction as that obtained with young children. When body is tilted left, apparent vertical is rotated left of plumb line; and when body is tilted right, apparent vertical is rotated to the right; apparent body position is overestimated, but again, as with the children, the overestimation is not as marked as with normal adults. Thus, the angular separation between apparent verticality and apparent body position, under body tilt, is less for 6–8-year-old children and schizophrenics than for normal adults.

Apparent Size of Body Parts

As noted earlier, some of our recent work has been concerned with apparent size of one's own body. We were interested in studying the body *qua* object, among other reasons, to determine whether the principles uncovered for other objects could be generalized to apply to perceptual properties of one's own body. If the organismic-developmental approach had heuristic value for study of perception of objects other than the body, then we expected that this would also hold for the study of the body-as-object. Since one's body has perceptual properties in common with all other objects, the focus in our initial experimental approach has been on those very properties, such as location, shape, size, etc. The work on relations between body and object already described deals with location. Now let us turn to experiments on apparent size of body parts. The experimental situations are very simple ones.

Consider head size. Here, the task for S, with eyes closed, is to indicate the width of his face or, more precisely, by pointing with index fingers to indicate where the cheekbones of his face would be projected on a meter stick horizontally mounted 18 cm. from his nose. During the test the person's nose touches a rodlike projection mounted perpendicularly to the scale. Using this situation, first of all, it was found that apparent head size is greater than physical head size. On the grounds that overestimation in head size might be interpreted as a function of the relative undifferentiatedness of the experienced boundary of the head in regard to its surroundings, it was expected that articulation of the boundary of the face would make for a decrease in apparent head size. Accordingly, experiments were conducted in which the boundaries of the face were articulated in several ways: under conditions where the cheekbones of the face were touched; under conditions where a block of dry ice was placed six inches from the side of the face; and under conditions where heat from a lamp, placed three feet from S, warmed the sides of his face. Our results were in keeping with expectation; articulation of head boundary through touch, cold, and heat[10] decreases head size (Wapner, Werner, and Comalli, 1957).

---

[10] The results for heat are significant only at the .10 level of confidence. The effect of heat is currently being pursued in a systematic fashion.

A somewhat similar technique is used in studying apparent arm length (Liebert, Werner, and Wapner, 1958; Humphries, 1959). With eyes closed, the subject stretches his arm out in front of him. Over his extended arm a board is placed on which is located a luminous marker that can be moved on a track closer or farther away from the subject. With outstretched arms, the subject tells the experimenter where to move the luminous marker —either closer or farther away—so that the marker appears to be located just over where the subject perceives the fingertip of his outstretched arm to be. This task is carried out both with the fingertips of the outstretched arm touched and also when they are not touched. Similar results were obtained for arm length as were for head size; with articulation of the limb extremity—in this case the fingertip of the outstretched arm—there is a shortening of the apparent arm length (Humphries, 1959).

We learn, then, from the experiments on head width and arm length, that with articulation of a body part, which serves to enhance the boundary between self and world, there is a decrease in the apparent size of that body part.

AGE CHANGES FROM CHILDHOOD TO MATURITY. An ontogenetic study was undertaken based on the assumption that there is less differentiation between self and world in less mature than in more mature individuals and thus that overestimation of head size is relatively greater in children compared with adults.

This developmental study, involving subjects from 4 years of age through 25, was conducted two years ago. Apparent head size was measured, both with and without touch to the cheekbones. Four hundred sixty-three subjects, 248 males and 215 females, were tested. The developmental curves are in keeping with prediction. First, there was a striking overestimation of head size in subjects of all age levels; second, the overestimation was greatest in the youngest children, decreased sharply until age 9, following which the overestimation remained fairly steady through the adult groups; third, at all age levels articulation of the boundary of the head through touch decreased the apparent size of the head; fourth, the efficacy of touch in reducing apparent head size was relatively constant throughout all age levels (Wapner, 1959a, 1961b).

PSYCHOPATHOLOGY. Some further studies with schizophrenics and retarded children complement the results of this ontogenetic study. Preliminary findings suggest that apparent head size is overestimated to a greater degree in schizophrenics than in normals. Further, it is quite clear that a retarded group (13–14 years), IQ's ranging from 62 to 78, overestimate head size to a degree comparable to that of the 6-year-old child.

DRUGS. Studies on the effect of LSD-25 on apparent size of head and arms fit in with the studies concerning ontogenesis and psychopathology. The regression hypothesis suggests that there is an increase in size of body part under LSD-25. In two studies (Liebert, Werner, and Wapner, 1958; Wapner and Krus, 1960a) this expectation was verified; i.e., apparent head size increased under LSD-25. This finding also occurs with arm length; i.e., apparent arm length becomes significantly greater under the influence of LSD-25.

These experiments concerning ontogenesis, psychopathology, and effects of a primitivizing drug should be integrated with the earlier studies on effect of touch, etc. These various experiments—one set where a decrease in apparent size occurs with articulation of the boundary of the body part, and the other set where an increase in apparent size occurs, viz., with younger normal children and older retarded children, schizophrenics, and normal adults under the influence of LSD-25—can be integrated on the grounds that they involve respectively greater and lesser differentiation of body and environment.

Perception of Part-Whole Relations

A systematic series of studies has been conducted from the organismic-developmental view assessing perception of part-whole relations by use of the Heiss-Sander test. The essential feature of the Heiss-Sander test is that S is required to select a part (simple figure such as angular form) from a complex figure made up of that part and other parts. Efficiency in performance of the task is presumed to reflect the degree to which the whole is differentiated into parts and hierarchically integrated in an organization required for successful completion of the task (cf. Heiss, 1928; Werner, 1940; Podell, 1957; Krus, 1957).

AGE CHANGES FROM CHILDHOOD TO MATURITY.   Some years ago, Heiss (1928) obtained data using this test situation with children. His evidence shows that with increase in age there is increase in capacity to isolate the part from the complex figure. This finding is supported by data which we are currently collecting.

AGING.   In the Clark laboratories two studies have been conducted with older people, one with a normal group living in the community, and the other with an older group living in an institution. It was found in general that older people, like the youngest children, are less efficient than normal middle-aged adults (Wapner and Krus, 1960a).

PSYCHOPATHOLOGY.   By means of the regression hypothesis, the performance of schizophrenics was examined on the Heiss-Sander test. In keeping with expectation, schizophrenics were less efficient in performance than normal adults (Wapner and Krus, 1960a).

DRUGS.   Three types of drug studies were conducted using this test situation. The first study employed the "regressive" drug LSD-25. It was found that a group of normal adults and schizophrenics were both less efficient under LSD-25 compared with placebo conditions; the mean differences were significant for normals but not for the schizophrenics (Wapner and Krus, 1960a). The assumption that certain drugs may operate to arrest developmental regression in perception which ordinarily occurs in aging formed the basis for the second study conducted by Krus, which was concerned with the effect of meretran and meprobamate on the perception of part-whole relations in the aged. Some limited evidence is available that efficiency in the Heiss-Sander task tends to increase when older institutionalized people are under the influence of these drugs. A third study uses a different methodology. Here it has been found that the decrease in efficiency ordinarily induced by LSD-25 does not occur when LSD-25 ingestion is preceded by ingestion of a steroid which is counteractive to LSD-25's effects in lower animals and also in other areas of human psychological functioning (Krus, Wapner, Bergen, and Freeman, 1961). These preliminary findings have encouraged us to extend this aspect of our work.

Thus, perceptual situations requiring isolation of a part from a configuration provide findings in a variety of groups which also can be integrated on the basis of organismic-developmental theory.

Capacity to Maintain Directed Activity

Another recent direction of our work is shown in some of our attempts to study the means by which individuals maintain a directed course of activity in the face of intrusive stimuli. We have used the well-known Stroop color-word test to study this problem. The subject's task is to give a sequence of a hundred responses on each of the three cards in a manner specified by the instructions (on Card 1 to read color words; on Card 2 to name the color patches; on Card 3 to name the color of the ink in which the words are printed where the color of the ink and the color referred to by the word are incongruous). For optimal performance each utterance must be insulated (or differentiated) from the ones which surround it, and at the same time combined (or integrated) with the preceding and following responses to form a smooth sequence. Further, on the third, so-called "interference" card, the two functions (word reading and color naming) must be differentiated from each other and hierarchically integrated— word reading subordinated to color naming—so as to maintain separate identity.[11]

Our approach then, grounded in organismic-developmental theory, led to studies with subjects of different ages, comparison of schizophrenics with normals, and study of the effect of LSD-25.

AGE CHANGES FROM CHILDHOOD TO OLD AGE. A study recently published (Comalli, Wapner, and Werner, 1962) utilized 235 subjects from 7 to 80 years of age. Using time scores on the three cards it was found that the degree of "interference" of color words on color naming is greatest with younger children, decreases with increasing age to adulthood, and increases again in older age.

[11] Other investigators have used this test making the assumption that various time measures reflect "cognitive style of control"; cf. Broverman (1960a, 1960b); Broverman and Lazarus (1958); Gardner et al. (1959); Holzman et. al. (1958); Klein (1954); Klein et. al. (1954); Lazarus (1955); Smith and Klein (1953).

PSYCHOPATHOLOGY AND EFFECT OF LSD-25. In another study (Wapner and Krus, 1960b), utilizing the time to respond on each of the three cards, it was found that (1) schizophrenics perform more slowly than normals; (2) schizophrenics are differentially slower on the "interference" card than normals; (3) overall reading time is greater under LSD-25 than placebo for each of the cards; and (4) under LSD-25 time taken on the "interference" task is differentially greater than time taken on the noninterference tasks, and this holds for schizophrenics and normals.

These results, showing formal ties between the behavior of such diverse developmentally ordered groups as children vs. adults, the aged vs. mature adults, schizophrenics vs. normals, LSD-25 vs. placebo, are directly in keeping with the theoretical principles mentioned earlier. Lest the formal similarity between the groups at the "earlier" stage on the developmental continuum be misunderstood, the caution mentioned earlier should be reiterated; i.e., though achievements in terms of time score between, e.g., children, schizophrenics, and the aged are similar relative to the normal adult, it should not be implied that the cognitive operations underlying their achievements are identical.

This assumption is the basis for current studies attempting to differentiate between the similarities in total time score of these groups (Rand, 1961; Rand and Wapner, 1962). The search for different organismic devices, which may be ordered developmentally, that satisfy the same end of maintaining a uniform course of action in the face of intrusions was conducted by making a detailed analysis of behavior on the color-word test. For this purpose tape recordings and some sound movies were made of subjects performing the test.

The first thing one notices in listening to subjects perform this test is that few, if any, attain an ideal performance. Rather, additional words are inserted, the sequence is broken by long time gaps, inappropriate responses are given; i.e., many deviations from an ideal performance occur which are analogous to the imperfections that occur in everyday speech. Our analysis focuses upon these seemingly minor deviations from an ideal performance, which we refer to as "behavioral deviations."

As a first step in describing the behavioral deviations, George Rand listened over and over again to the recordings of nine subjects (3 age 6–7; 3 age 9–10; and 3 age 18–19).[12] Rand's analysis of the tape recordings revealed eight types of behavioral deviation from an ideal performance: (1) *Inarticulate Utterances*—The response corresponds to the item on the card (word, color, ink color) but the subject does not say the word clearly and articulately, e.g., whispering, stuttering, utterance of part of a word, changes in the structure of an utterance (e.g., blauee); (2) *Part-Wrong*—The subject utters part of the wrong word and then gives the appropriate response; (3) *Whole-Wrong, Corrected Responses*—The subject responds with a complete word which is incorrect and then gives the appropriate response before proceeding to the next item; (4) *Whole-Wrong, Uncorrected Response*—The subject utters an incorrect response and proceeds immediately to the next item; (5) *Fusion*—The response is contaminated, i.e., it consists of parts of both appropriate and inappropriate responses (e.g., brue, breen, reg, rue); (6) *Verbal Insertion*—The subject inserts a connective word or phrase between two responses, e.g., "and," "um," "I mean," "this is"; (7) *Temporal Insertion*—The subject hesitates between responses without making any utterance, and thereby interrupts the sequence; (8) *Jumbled Order of Response*—The subject loses his place, omits items, repeats words, responds in a manner which does not correspond to the objective order of the items on the card.

The "overall frequency" of behavioral deviations for each subject's performance on each of the cards provides a set of findings directly analogous to the findings for overall time per card obtained in the developmental study first reported; viz., (1) "overall frequency" is greatest for Card 3, less for Card 2, and least for Card 1, (2) there is a decrease in "overall frequency" with increase in age, and (3) though the "overall frequency" decreases with age on all three cards, this decrement is disproportionately greater for Card 3.

[12] Records are also currently available of some additional 192 subjects. More refined techniques of data reduction and analysis are in progress on the larger sample. However, the latter study is incomplete, and accordingly illustrations will be given on the basis of the first study.

However, most important from the viewpoint of the process analysis, examination of the behavioral deviations taken singly reveals some interesting similarities and departures from the findings for "overall frequency" and time.

Firstly, comparison of the three cards with respect to the individual behavioral deviations shows the same direction of results as "overall frequency and time." Secondly, a comparison of age groups reveals that four of the behavioral deviations (whole-wrong, uncorrected; temporal insertion; fusion; and jumbled order) follow the pattern "high at 6 years, medium at 9 years, and low for adults." In contrast, two behavioral deviations follow different ontogenetic trends. One of these behavioral deviations, "part-wrong," occurs *most* frequently at the 9-year level, *less* so at 6, and *least* at age 18. The second behavioral deviation, "whole-wrong, corrected," occurs with equal frequency in both groups of children, and is very infrequent in the records of adults. Finally, the results for interaction of age x card on the overall measures may be compared with those obtained for the behavioral deviations taken singly. In these overall measures the significant age x card interaction shows a disproportionately high value for the youngest age group on Card 3. A parallel statistically significant relation holds for one behavioral deviation, "whole-wrong, uncorrected," with trends in the same direction for two other measures. The only other statistically significant interaction occurs for "fusion," which in contrast shows the highest frequency on Card 2 for the youngest age group.

These findings, though still tentative, have considerable significance. First, insofar as behavioral deviations occur on all three cards, so-called "interference" is not restricted to the demands provided by the incongruity of word and color on Card 3. Second, in view of the variety of behavioral deviations observed, it is questionable whether it is appropriate to assume that "interference" refers to a unitary phenomenon.

Rather than interpreting the results in terms of "interference," we view the behavioral deviations as reflecting the variety of means by which the individual restores the direction to his activity when intrusive forces, either internal or external in origin, momentarily deflect him from continuing the task in the designated manner. This analysis suggests that the cognitive devices for maintaining a directed course of activity differ, depending upon internal factors which vary with age. Our plan is to characterize different age groups in terms of the particular set of devices which they employ for maintaining a directed activity, and then to continue this type of detailed behavioral analysis with adults, the aged, schizophrenics, and with normal and schizophrenics under LSD-25. Will similarities and differences emerge between groups at the same end of the developmental continuum? What will be the similarities and differences in specific "behavioral deviations" for groups showing similar results in terms of the "overall time" and "overall frequency" achievement measures?

Further, our hope is to extend the analysis to the study of consistent individual differences between adults. We are interested in such questions as: Do some adults use organismic devices characteristic of younger age groups? Do adults differ consistently in the set of cognitive devices they employ? What are the changing patterns in individual differences with increase in age? When the data from a developmental study—now in progress—are analyzed, we hope to have some answers to these questions.

Relations Between Cognitive Operations

As briefly indicated earlier, the problem of relations among processes representing different levels of cognitive organization has been attacked experimentallly in terms of two types of relationships, *vicarious* and *supportive*. A vicarious relationship implies that utilization of one operation mitigates against use of another; e.g., with utilization of sensory-motor activity there is diminution of perceptual and/or conceptual activity. A supportive relationship implies that simultaneously occurring consonant cognitive operations summate to make for greater efficiency in achievement of ends; e.g., simultaneously occurring motor and perceptual activity makes for greater efficiency in perceptual recognition.

Empirical support for the vicariousness relationship in relation to perception is found in studies such as those which have shown that when Ss are immobilized, they perceive more movement on the Rorschach test (cf. Korchin, Meltzoff, and Singer, 1951), or that sensitivity to autokinetic motion is increased (Goldman, 1953). The opposite test concerned with effect of inducing motoric involvement (Krus, Wapner, and Werner, 1958; Krus, Werner, and Wapner, 1953) yielded diminution of perceived movement and decreased perceptual sensitivity.

Another experimental approach to this problem has been to employ subjects clinically characterized as hyperactive and hypo-active. Hurwitz (1954), for example, found that hyperactive boys perceived less movement on the Rorschach test than did hypo-active boys.

General evidence for supportive relationships have already been reported for lapse of meaning and word recognition thresholds. Currently steps are being taken to pursue this problem of relations among operations using these methods for groups differing in terms of age, for psychopathological groups, and for groups under the influence of "regressive" drugs. This will complement the general findings noted by providing further information on the relationships among cognitive operations for groups ordered developmentally.

A Ph.D. thesis completed recently at Clark by Switzer (1961) is worthy of review here because it shows the way in which relations among cognitive operations may be studied in a learning situation.[13] In Switzer's experiments, the performance of subjects ordered developmentally was compared on learning situations presumed to favor use of different cognitive operations. The subjects were ordered developmentally in two ways; viz., chronological age (8- vs. 12-year-old boys) and psychopathology—clinically deviant hyperactive children were contrasted with clinically deviant hypoactive children. One task required learning a sequence of positions through a perceptual-motor organization (place task); and the other, a sequence of color names through a verbal-conceptual organization (name task). In addition, a task

[13] Some relations between stage of development and learning are sketched by Scheerer (1953).

was employed which could be organized in either of these ways (place-name task).

In the latter, place-name task, a higher proportion of the subjects characterized as functioning at an earlier developmental level (relatively younger; hyperactive) organized the task in terms of "place," whereas a higher proportion of subjects functioning at a later developmental level (relatively older; hypoactive) organized the task in terms of "name." Moreover, it was found that during the course of learning more externalized activity was exhibited by the younger than the older children.

In addition, differential performance was found in normals and pathological groups on the place and name tasks. The normal children showed flexibility insofar as they could handle optimally both place and name tasks; the hypoactive children performed relatively poorly on the place task; and the hyperactive children were relatively poorer in performance on the name task.

Thus, the organismic-developmental approach in distinguishing between levels of cognitive operations leads to the finding that the older children spontaneously organize the learning task in conceptual terms, whereas the younger children spontaneously organize the task in sensory-motor or perceptual terms, and further, that the younger children employ more externalized activity during the course of learning than do the older children.

One variation of Switzer's experimental procedure involved forcing the subjects to use externalized sensory-motor operations, "pointing," while learning the task to determine whether these operations could function supportively. Externalized sensory-motor operations under these "forced" conditions functioned to disrupt performance in contrast to such operations when they occur spontaneously. A suggestion from this finding was that for superimposed sensory-motor operations to act supportively in learning a task, the subject must be at a high enough level in development to be able hierarchically to integrate operations of different kinds. In attempting to unravel the complex problem of the relations between various cognitive operations, this possibility seems very fruitful for further inquiry.

The findings obtained for the hyperactive and hypoactive children provide further support for organismic-developmental theory and throw light on psychopathology. The hyperactive group more characteristically functioned at the sensory-motor level, and were incapacitated by their psychopathology to a greater degree than were the hypoactive group.

Another study dealing with this problem of relations among cognitive operations was conducted by Clarkson (1961). He studied maze learning and performance on the embedded-figures task, using 10–12-year-old children and adults from 17 to 30 years of age. Clarkson found that efficiency of performance in both tasks depended on the cognitive processes required by the task and the degree to which they are available in the subject of given developmental status. Further, in keeping with the findings of Switzer, Clarkson found that "forced" sensory-motor activity did not differentially facilitate the performance of children on the embedded-figures task.

The comparative studies reviewed illustrate the ways in which the organismic-developmental view can serve to integrate findings and to direct research on such problems of perception as object localization, perception of location of body, perception of size of body parts, perception of part-whole relations, capacity to maintain directed activity in the context of perceptual intrusions, and relations among cognitive operations for groups ordered developmentally in terms of age, psychopathology, and drugs.

3. LONG-TERM AIMS

To sum up, our research program aims at an understanding of perception, together with related cognitive processes, in terms which are broad enough to encompass their general nature and their specific manifestations in normal individuals as they progress through life, as well as their occurrence in individuals characterized as pathological. In approaching this goal we have restricted ourselves to a behavioral analysis in formal terms from an organismic-developmental viewpoint. In view of this very general nature of our stated goals, it would seem worthwhile to survey briefly some of the problems we hope to attack in the near future.

Though we are concerned with spatiotemporal analysis of behavioral events or achievements defined in terms of temporal changes in the relations between properties of objects, much of our work heretofore has dealt with spatial properties, abstracted from or independent of time. We have made only small beginnings in considering temporal properties of experience, abstracted from or independent of spatial properties of objects (cf. Langer, Wapner, and Werner, 1961; Denner, Wapner, McFarland, and Werner, 1963). We hope to make further inroads on the latter problem, but also to move farther ahead with analysis of problems developmentally prior; viz., event analysis, or changes in the properties of objects with respect to time.

While we have concerned ourselves with perception of objects and of one's own body, we have taken only a few small steps in analyzing problems pertinent to perception of people (Isaac, 1958). We hope to move this area of study ahead, and at the same time give attention to the problem of relations among perceived properties of these three classes of objects.

Moreover, while we have initiated a number of studies on the relations among cognitive operations, this problem and the more complex problem of the interaction of operations, tasks, and groups—all ordered developmentally—require extensive exploration.

To further these specific aims a combined longitudinal, cross-sectional study was launched last year [1961] which includes a variety of situations designed to study these general problems. The study includes experimental situations dealing with "body: object" relationships, part-whole relations, capacity to maintain directed activity, relations between size and value, space-time relations, relations between sensory-motor, perceptual, and conceptual operations, etc. When the findings of this ontogenetic study are integrated with findings on psychopathology, aging, and drugs, we will, we hope, come somewhat closer to the general goals of (1) clarifying the nature of perceptual mechanisms that interrelate sensory and intraorganismic factors; (2) providing links between various levels of cognitive functioning; and (3) bridging the gap between general work in perception and other aspects of cognition with the changes in mechanisms that occur in ontogenesis, psychopathology, and normal personality.

REFERENCES

Broverman, D. M.   Cognitive style and intraindividual variation in abilities. *J. Pers.*, 1960a, *28*, 291–295.

Broverman, D. M.   Dimensions of cognitive style. *J. Pers.*, 1960b, *28*, 169–185.

Broverman, D. M., and Lazarus, R. S.   Individual differences in task performance under conditions of cognitive interference. *J. Pers.*, 1958, *26*, 94–105.

Bruell, J. H., and Albee, G. W.   Effect of asymmetrical retinal stimulation on the perception of the median plane. *Percept. mot. Skills*, 1955, *5*, 133–139.

Carini, L. P.   An experimental investigation of perceptual behavior in schizophrenics. Microfilmed Ph. D. dissertation, Clark Univ., 1955.

Clarkson, F. E.   A developmental analysis of the performance of children and adults on a maze learning and an embedded figures task. Microfilmed Ph.D. dissertation, Clark Univ., 1961.

Comalli, P. E., Jr., Wapner, S., and Werner, H.   Perception of verticality in middle and old age. *J. Psychol.*, 1959, *47*, 259–266.

Comalli, P. E., Jr., Wapner, S., and Werner, H.   Interference effects of Stroop color-word test in children, adults, and aged. EPA meetings, New York, 1960a.

Comalli, P. E., Jr., Wapner, S., and Werner, H.   Interference effects of Stroop color-word test in two groups of aged, one institutionalized and the other living in the community. APA meetings, Chicago, 1960b.

Comalli, P. E., Jr., Wapner, S., and Werner, H.   Interference effects of Stroop color-word test in childhood, adulthood, and aging. *J. genet.* 1962, *100*, 47–53.

Comalli, P. E., Jr., Werner, H., and Wapner, S.   Perception of part-whole relations in middle and old age. APA meetings, Cincinnati, 1959.

Denner, B., Wapner, S., McFarland, J. H., and Werner, H.   Rhythmic activity and the perception of time, *Amer. J. Psychol.*, 1963 (In press).

Dowling, R. M. Effect of sensori-motor and conceptual activity on perceptual functioning. Microfilmed Ph.D. dissertation, Clark Univ., 1962.

Dowling, R. M., Werner, H., and Wapner, S. Effect of motor activity on visual recognition threshold. EPA meetings, New York, 1960.

Flavell, J. Thought, communication, and social integration in schizophrenia: an experimental and theoretical study. Unpublished Ph.D. dissertation, Clark Univ., 1955.

Gardner, R., Holzman, P. S., Klein, G. S., Linton, Harriet, and Spence, D. P. Cognitive control: A study of individual consistencies in cognitive behavior. *Psychol. Issues*, 1959, *1*, No. 4.

Giannitrapani, D. Changes in adaptation to prolonged perceptual distortion: a developmental study. Microfilmed Ph.D. dissertation, Clark Univ., 1958.

Gibson, J. J. Adaptation, after-effect and contrast in the perception of curved lines. *J. exp. Psychol.*, 1933, *16*, 1–31.

Gibson, J. J., and Radner, M. Adaptation, after-effect and contrast in the perception of tilted lines. I. Quantitative studies. *J. exp. Psychol.*, 1937, *20*, 453–467.

Goldman, A. E. Studies in vicariousness: degree of motor activity and the autokinetic phenomenon. *Amer. J. Psychol.*, 1953, *66*, 613–617.

Goldstein, A. G. An experimental study of depth perception from the viewpoint of the sensory-tonic field theory of perception. Microfilmed Ph. D. dissertation, Clark Univ., 1955.

Goldstein, A. G. Linear acceleration and apparent distance. *Percept. mot. Skills*, 1959, *9*, 267–269.

Goldstein, K. *The organism.* New York: American Book, 1939.

Gorrell, R. B. The effect of extraneous auditory stimulation on critical flicker frequency. Microfilmed Ph.D. dissertation, Clark Univ., 1953.

Heiss, A. Zum Probleme der isolierenden Abstraktion. *Neue psychol. Stud.*, 1928, *4*, 285–318.

Holzman, P. S., Gardner, R. W., and Siegel, R. S. The generality of cognitive attitudes and their relation to personality organization. Final Progress Report, NIMH Grant M-1182, 1958.

Humphries, O. Effect of articulation of finger-tip through touch on apparent length of outstretched arm. Unpublished M.A. thesis, Clark Univ., 1959.

Hurwitz, I. A developmental study of the relationships between motor activity and perceptual processes as measured by the Rorschach test. Microfilmed Ph.D. dissertation, Clark Univ., 1954.

Isaac, D. M. The effect of interpersonal feelings on psychological distance. Unpublished M.A. thesis, Clark Univ., 1958.

Kaden, S. E., Wapner, S., and Werner, H. Studies in physiognomic perception: II. Effect of directional dynamics of pictured objects and of words on the position of the apparent horizon. *J. Psychol.*, 1955, *39*, 61–70.

Klein, G. S.   Need and regulation. In M. R. Jones (ed.), *Nebraska symposium on motivation*, Lincoln: Univ. of Nebraska Press, 1954.

Klein, G. S., Holzman, P. S., and Laskin, D.   The perception project: progress report 1953–1954. *Bull. Menninger Clin.*, 1954, *18*, 260–266.

Kohler, I.   Uber Aufbau und Wandlungen der Wahrnehmungswelt. *Oesterr. Akad. d. Wissensch. Philos.-Histor. Kl.;* Sitz.-Ber., 1951, *227*, 1–118.

Kohler, I.   Umgewoehnung im Wahrnehmungsbereich. *Die Pyramide*, 1953, *5*, 92–95; *6*, 109–113.

Korchin, S. J., Meltzoff, J., and Singer, J. L.   Motor inhibition and Rorschach movement responses. *Amer. Psychologist*, 1951, *6*, 344–345.

Krus, D. M.   Consistent individual differences in perception: an analysis from the points of view of developmental and sensory-tonic theory. Microfilmed Ph.D. dissertation, Clark Univ., 1957.

Krus, D. M., and Wapner, S.   Effect of lysergic acid diethylamide (LSD-25) on perception of part-whole relationships. *J. Psychol.*, 1959, *48*, 87–95.

Krus, D. M., Wapner, S., and Werner, H.   Studies in vicariousness: effect of muscular involvement on visual threshold. *Amer. J. Psychol.*, 1958, *71*, 395–398.

Krus, D. M., Wapner, S., Bergen, J., and Freeman, H.   The influence of progesterone on behavioral changes induced by lysergic acid diethylamide (LSD-25) in normal males. *Psychopharmacologia*, 1961, *2*, 177–184.

Krus, D. M., Werner, H., and Wapner, S.   Studies in vicariousness: motor activity and perceived movement. *Amer. J. Psychol.*, 1953, *66*, 603–608.

Langer, J., Wapner, S., and Werner, H.   The effect of danger upon the experience of time. *Amer. J. Psychol.*, 1961, *74*, 94–97.

Lazarus, R. S.   Motivation and personality in psychological stress. Progress Report No. 2, NIMH Grant M-374, Appendix IV, 1955.

Liebert, R. S.   The effects of lysergic acid diethylamide on the perception of verticality in schizophrenic and normal adults. Unpublished M.A. thesis, Clark Univ., 1956.

Liebert, R. S., Wapner, S., and Werner, H.   Studies in the effect of lysergic acid diethylamide (LSD-25): visual perception of verticality in schizophrenic and normal adults. *A.M.A. Arch. Neurol. & Psychiat.*, 1957, *77*, 193–201.

Liebert, R. S., Werner, H., and Wapner, S.   Studies in the effect of lysergic acid diethylamide (LSD-25): self and object size perception in schizophrenic and normal adults. *A.M.A. Arch. Neurol. & Psychiat.*, 1958, 79, 580–584.

Mayer, J.   Influence of inspection of a visually curved field on kinesthetic figural after-effects. *Percept. mot. Skills*, 1961, *13*, 13–14.

McFarland, J. H., Clarkson, F. E., and Wapner, S.   Effect of prolonged body tilt on the relationship between perceived position of one's body and of other objects. APA meetings, New York, 1961.

McFarland, J. H., Clarkson, F. E., Wapner, S., and Werner, H.   Relation between perceptual properties of objects in space and one's own body. EPA meetings, Philadelphia, 1961.

McFarland, J. H., Wapner, S., and Werner H.   The relation between perceived location of objects and perceived location of one's own body. *Percept. mot. Skills*, 1962, *15*, 331–341.

Miller, A.   An experimental study of the role of sensori-motor activity in the maintenance of verbal meaning of action words. Microfilmed Ph.D. dissertation, Clark Univ., 1959.

Morant, R. B.   The visual perception of the median plane as influenced by labyrinthian stimulation. *J. Psychol.*, 1959, *47*, 25–35.

Mulholland, T. B.   The effect of extraneous auditory stimulation on visual perception. Microfilmed Ph.D. dissertation, Clark Univ., 1956.

Mulholland, T. B.   The "swinging disc" illusion. *Amer. J. Psychol.*, 1958, *71*, No. 2, 375–382.

Ohwaki, S.   An investigation of figural adaptation within the framework of sensory-tonic field theory. Microfilmed Ph.D. dissertation, Clark Univ., 1959.

Ohwaki, S.   An investigation of figural adaptation: a study within the framework of sensory-tonic field theory. *Amer. J. Psychol.*, 1961, *74*, No. 1, 3–16.

Piaget, J.   *The psychology of intelligence*. Trans. M. Perry and D. E. Berlyne) London: Routledge, 1950.

Podell, J. E.   Personality and stimulus factors in adult cognition: a development analysis of decontextualization. Microfilmed Ph.D. dissertation, Clark Univ., 1957.

Rand, G.   A developmental study of the Stroop test: a preliminary analysis of behavioral means. M.A. thesis, Clark Univ., 1961.

Rand, G., and Wapner, S.   A behavioral analysis of the color-word test. EPA meetings, Atlantic City, 1962.

Rosenkrantz, P.   Some differences between schizophrenics and normal adults in cognitive functioning. Unpublished M.A. thesis, Clark Univ., 1960.

Scheerer, M.   Problems of performance analysis in the study of personality. *Ann. N.Y. Acad. Sciences*, 1946, *46*, 653–678.

Scheerer, M.   Personality functioning and cognitive psychology. *J. Pers.*, 1953, 22, 1–16.

Scheerer, M.   Cognitive theory. In Gardner Lindzey (ed.), *Handbook of social psychology*. Cambridge, Mass.: Addison-Wesley, 1954. Chap. 3.

Smith, G. J., and Klein, G. S.   Cognitive controls in serial behavior patterns. *J. Pers.*, 1953, 22, 188–213.

Switzer, J.   Developmental differences in place and name sequence learning in normal, hyperactive, and hypoactive eight and twelve year old boys. Microfilmed Ph.D. dissertation, Clark Univ., 1961.

Wapner, S.   Some experiments on body image from the viewpoint of organismic and developmental theory. APA meetings, Cincinnati, 1959.

Wapner, S.   An experimental and theoretical approach to body image. In *Proceed. XVI Int. Cong. Psych.*, 1960, 758–759, *Acta Psychologica*, North-Holland Pub. Co., Amsterdam, Holland, 1961a, Vol. 19.

Wapner, S.   Perceptual properties of one's own body and its relation to that of other objects. Symposium on Body Image and Pathological States, VA Hospital, Houston, 1961b.

Wapner, S., and Krus, D. M.   Behavioral effects of lysergic acid diethylamide (LSD-25). *A.M.A. Arch. gen. Psychiat.*, 1959, 1, 417–419.

Wapner, S., and Krus, D. M.   Behavioral effects of lysergic acid diethylamide (LSD-25). Progress Report, NIMH Grant No. MY-2262, 1960a.

Wapner, S., and Krus, D. M.   Effects of lysergic acid diethylamide, and differences between normals and schizophrenics on the Stroop color-word test. *J. Neuropsychiat.*, 1960b, 2, 76–81.

Wapner, S., and Werner, H.   Experiments on sensory-tonic field theory of perception: V. Effect of body status on the kinaesthetic perception of verticality. *J. exp. Psychol.*, 1952, 44, 126–131.

Wapner, S., and Werner, H.   Gestalt laws of organization and organismic theory of perception: Effect of asymmetry induced by the factor of similarity on the position of the apparent median plane and apparent horizon. *Amer. J. Psychol.*, 1955, 68, 258–265.

Wapner, S., and Werner, H.   *Perceptual development*. Worcester: Clark Univ. Press, 1957.

Wapner, S., Comalli, P. E., Jr., and Werner, H.   Perception of verticality in middle and old age. EPA meetings, Atlantic City, 1959.

Wapner, S., Werner, H., and Chandler, K. A.   Experiments on sensory-tonic field theory of perception: I. Effect of extraneous stimulation on the visual perception of verticality. *J. exp. Psychol.*, 1951, 42, 341–345.

Wapner, S., Werner, H., and Comalli, P. E., Jr. Effect of enhancement of head boundary on head size and shape. *Percept. mot. Skills,* 1958, *8,* 319–325.

Wapner, S., Werner, H., and Comalli, P. E., Jr. Space localization under conditions of danger. *J. Psychol.,* 1956, *41,* 335–346.

Wapner, S., Werner, H., and Comalli, P. E., Jr. Perception of part-whole relationships in middle and old age. *J. Geront.,* 1960, *15,* 412–416.

Wapner, S., Werner, H., and Morant, R. B. Experiments on sensory-tonic field theory of perception: III. Effect of body rotation on the visual perception of verticality. *J. exp. Psychol.,* 1951, *42,* 351–357.

Wapner, S., Werner, H., Bruell, J. H., and Goldstein, A. G. Experiments on sensory-tonic field theory of perception: VII. Effect of asymmetrical extent and starting position of figures on the visual apparent median plane. *J. exp. Psychol.,* 1953, *46,* 300–307.

Werner, H. Process and achievement. *Harvard Educ. Rev.* 1937, *7,* 353–368.

Werner, H. *Comparative psychology of mental development.* New York: Harper, 1940; (2nd ed.) Chicago: Follett, 1948; (3rd ed.) New York: International Universities Press, 1957; (4th ed.) New York: Science Editions, 1961.

Werner, H. Microgenesis and aphasia. *J. abnorm. soc. Psychol.,* 1956, *52,* 347–353.

Werner, H. The concept of development from a comparative and organismic point of view. In D. B. Harris (ed.), *The concept of development: an issue in the study of human behavior.* Minneapolis: Univ. of Minnesota Press, 1957, pp. 125–148.

Werner, H., and Wapner, S. Sensory-tonic field theory of perception. *J. Pers.,* 1949, *18,* 88–107.

Werner, H., and Wapner, S. Experiments on sensory-tonic field theory of perception: IV. Effect of initial position of a rod on apparent verticality. *J. exp. Psychol.,* 1952a, *43,* 68–74.

Werner, H., and Wapner, S. Toward a general theory of perception. *Psychol. Rev.,* 1952b, *59,* 324–338.

Werner, H., and Wapner, S. Studies in physiognomic perception: I. Effect of configurational dynamics and meaning-induced sets on the position of the apparent median plane. *J. Psychol.,* 1954, *38,* 51–65.

Werner, H., and Wapner, S. The Innsbruck studies on distorted visual fields in relation to an organismic theory of perception. *Psychol. Rev.,* 1955, *62,* 130–138.

Werner, H., and Wapner, S. The non-projective aspects of the Rorschach experiment: II. Organismic theory and perceptual response. *J. soc. Psychol.,* 1956a, *44,* 193–198.

Werner, H., and Wapner, S.   Sensory-tonic field theory of perception: basic concepts and experiments. *Revista di psicologia,* 1956b, *50,* 315–337.

Werner, H., Wapner, S., and Bruell, J. H.   Experiments on sensory-tonic field theory of perception: VI. Effect of position of head, eyes, and of object on position of the apparent median plane. *J. exp. Psychol.,* 1953, *46,* 293–299.

Werner, H., Wapner, S., and Chandler, K. A.   Experiments on sensory-tonic field theory of perception: II. Effect of supported and unsupported tilt of the body on the visual perception of verticality. *J. exp. Psychol.,* 1951, *42,* 346–350.

Werner, H., Wapner, S., and Comalli, P. E., Jr.   Effect of boundary on perception of head size. *Percept. mot. Skills,* 1957, *7,* 69–71.

SOME EXPLANATORY HYPOTHESES OF UNDERLYING PROCESSES AND PATHOLOGY IN BRAIN-DAMAGED PATIENTS[1]

C. KERMIT PHELPS

Veterans Administration Hospital,
Kansas City, Missouri

IT HAS BEEN POINTED OUT CRITICALLY of a number of studies conducted using cortically damaged patients that the so-called "organic signs" that are often found may be sometimes also observable in the normal population. It is not their occurrence in the behavior of the brain-damaged patient that is alone important, but rather it is the fact that the "organic signs" occur with significantly greater consistent frequency and with equally measurable qualitative characteristics in the brain-damaged vs. the normal group.

Another question which is often raised is whether the brain-damaged patient shows any difference in test results which would significantly relate to differences in locale or extent of the brain injury. In our research it seems more correct to say that the brain-

[1] This paper is based on the work of Martin Scheerer and the author, which extended over a period of ten years.

damaged patient suffered from different types and differently localized brain pathology, but at the same time failed to show performance losses corresponding to circumscribed damage or a specific syndrome. There was, rather, a performance change characteristic of the group as a whole, namely, a systematic lack of functional integration with a common qualitative direction. On the motor side, we identified this as lack of differentiation and reduced voluntary control; on the cognitive side, we identified this as lack of anticipatory planning and difficulty in simultaneous functioning; in addition, we found a lack of transfer in benefiting from experience with a task, whether this was in terms of learning from errors, from successes, or from incidentally made experiences with features of the task, while focusing on others. The latter findings may suggest further research on incidental learning or the acquisition of learning sets in the brain-damaged which has been less studied than his learning ability under laboratory instruction.

It is, of course, conceivable that questions could still be raised as to the differential effect of the site of possible circumscribed damage as a determiner of the respective performance level in the various patients. The final conclusion would have to be based on the evidence from autopsy. We do, however, believe that our findings do not support the position of adherents to the highly specific localization theory of brain functioning, such as Henschen and Nielsen. In considering such a localizationist theory, we might briefly examine some recent positions on this question.

Halstead (1940) has described the inability of the brain-damaged patient to shift from one thought or act to another with the same ease as the uninjured, to hold thoughts in mind for consecutive patterning, and to group things in a normal manner. He has attempted to relate this behavior to the frontal lobes. Our findings are in accordance with those of Halstead with the Formboard, where normals recalled and located a greater percentage of figures more accurately, and spent less time on the performance on the board, than his experimental Ss, who had sustained frontal lobectomies. They are not in accord, however, with Halstead's other findings that patients with nonfrontal lobectomies and with head injuries perform only slightly below the normal controls on recall of figures and location, whereas only the frontal lobectomy patients performed significantly below normal. The difference in results here may be caused by the fact that Halstead allowed three complete Formboard trials for all his Ss. From this point of view our procedure, using one Formboard trial, seems to be more sensitive than his. By securing more experience-opportunity for his Ss, Halstead may have achieved a masking of the difference between brain-damaged and normal Ss on this test. In obtaining only a difference between normals and frontal lobectomized patients, he could demonstrate the diagnostic value of his method for these patients and support his theory of greater impairment effect of frontal lobectomy vs. other cerebral damage.

Though this possibility may be granted, the noted behavior deviations have also been frequently reported in patients who have suffered injuries in regions of the cortex remote from the frontal lobe. Many writers have advanced various theories to explain this apparent discrepancy. Lashley (1929) holds that "in addition to their specific function, all parts of the cortex exercise a facilitative effect upon the rest." Goldstein (1944) explains the phenomenon as an "impairment of a function due to the damage of a not-directly affected region by irritation emanating from a defect at another place." Recent studies of brain injury, in both adults and children, bring out very general changes in behavior which are found in the great majority of the cases and which bear only a slight relation to the site of the injury.

Furthermore, in considering any specific functional localization in the normal organism, and the assumed functional change in circumscribed damage, due weight must be given to Jackson's profound proposition that "to locate the damage which destroys speech and to locate speech are two different things." This statement should not be misinterpreted as a denial of any localization of function, but rather as presaging the above-cited view of Lashley and also lying at the basis of the thinking of other modern neurologists. Goldstein (1943) has presented an elaboration of their views which can be summed up in the proposition that certain areas of the brain contribute to the total function, particularly of the cortex, more than others for a given function.

This view may be also applied to the relationship between the pyramidal tract and the motor cortex, on the one hand, and the extra-pyramidal and the remaining nervous system on the other hand, in voluntary movement. Pathology of both the pyramidal and the extra-pyramidal systems may contribute to the inadequacy seen in the performance of motor tasks. Lesions of the pyramidal tract result in reduced voluntary movement; and the individual makes awkward, more or less postural, responses to situations that formerly called out quite specific skilled adjustments. Such disturbances are usually greater in the fingers and distal extremities than in the proximal muscles. Thus we see Ss with cortical involvement using the whole arm and shoulder in attempting to execute a task involving the fingers.

The extra-pyramidal system, while chiefly concerned with the postural aspects of behavior, makes an important contribution to voluntary and skilled behavior, for the reason that behind every skilled movement is a requisite postural adjustment. It is therefore necessary for a complete synchronization of the pyramidal and extra-pyramidal systems for precise, skilled, coordinated behavior. The importance of this synchronization is pointed out by Walshe (1948) in his attempt to show that the whole cortex is involved. He states, "By no definition can we easily find a voluntary action that is discrete, for even the apparently very retarded movement employs a large field of musculature phasically. To take a step is an affair, not of this or that limb solely, but of the total neuromuscular activity of the moment—not least of the head and neck."

Regardless of whether the views of Henschen and Nielsen or those of Goldstein are accepted, neither is incompatible with our hypothesis that it is an interruption of the integrative processes of the cortex which results in the difference in the observed behavior between the brain-damaged patient and the normal. Even the localizationist entertains the belief that the different areas of the brain are all connected with association fibers. Hence, it would follow that there is interaction between the different areas. All areas participating are necessary for integration, which is defined here as the co-functioning of all areas, with that area in which the gradient of excitation is highest functioning in a guiding role and all other areas functioning in a supporting role. However, though we must not lose sight of the importance of neurological structures, all the behavior observed in the brain-damaged is not entirely a result of damaged tissues. In part the behavior shows the struggle to meet demands; in part it reveals the S's attempt to avoid situations with which he cannot cope. In various ways he tries to find an environment or make an environment in which demands that are beyond his reduced resources will not occur. The orderliness and often meticulosity which have been observed seem to be merely manifestations of the patient's attempt to establish an environment to which he will always be equal.

The observed behavior seems to be the result of two major factors: first, those attributable directly to the lesion which are considered as primary—leading to the disorder or a disintegration of function in the cortex; second, those which are observable when the brain-damaged tries to regain his mode of functioning and struggles with the inadequacy of his nonintegrated cerebral structure. Always there appears a suggestion of disordered structure underlying the behavior, while the secondary psychological effect follows each aspect of behavior directly traceable to disintegration of brain tissue.

If we take a look at the actual performance of a brain-damaged patient on the Formboard the initial action is one of exploration. The successively-experienced tactual and kinesthetic cues are integrated into a simultaneous form percept and perhaps also translated into a visual conception or image of the figure which cannot be seen. Normally this occurs already when the S investigates the first figure. The various openings in the board are then also explored and from these tactual-kinesthetic impressions the final matching is made and the pieces fitted. What process is occurring here? We may assume that the operation of exploring the figure-object by running the fingers over its surface gives rise to the experience of a boundary that encloses an area and thus leads to the figure-percept of a closed tridimensional shape. The reverse, however, obtains for the exploration of the board-opening. In immediate experience the traced "contour" of this opening does not enclose a figure in the same way as the contour of the figure-piece. The contour of the board-opening as necessarily traced along the inside is an ambiguous clue as to what area it is bounding—an "outside" or an "inside" area. The initial tracing experience must therefore be ambiguous as to which kind of area the contour is bounding. The S follows the direction of that contour in uncertainty until he can experience closure—the returning of that direction to the starting point of his tracing. Until that has happened the traced contour may just as well enclose an area "outside" of the opening, i.e., the ground, as the inside of the opening. In order to be perceptually certain of the enclosed area, however, the contour path traced must be retained in memory as well as the initial starting point; otherwise no adequate closure experience can occur. This requires the corresponding integration of successive tactual, kinesthetic experiences, as in the tracing of the figures, only in this case the contours are perceptually reversed. In the figures they *surround* the solid object, the touch and resistance being felt *inward;* in the openings, they surround the ground, the touch experience of the resistance being felt *outward.*

One of the factors of successful recognition, then, is the readiness to shift from the contour experience of the object-figure to the reversed contour experience of the board-opening—and back again. This would differentiate an adequate performance from an inadequate one. In the normal this shifting takes place very rapidly and often with little hesitation in performance. In the brain-damaged, whenever there is identification of the figure-form through verbal means, there occurs a gap or lag between the recognition of the form, and the fitting of it into the board-opening, which is more often than not recognized neither verbally nor behaviorally.

The S, in the case of cortical pathology, seems to be unable to extract meaning from his tactual kinesthetic percepts and to organize these into whole forms in a manner adequate to the task. This lack of integration may be due to interruption in the interacting brain functions; or it may be hypothesized that the situation is new and the mode of execution strange, in that this is not the accustomed way of performing. In such an unfamiliar situation a patient may react to the most salient and concrete aspects of the object in a piecemeal way, i.e., to the points, corners, curves, and angles of the figures as he attempts to fit them into the openings by searching for their counterpart on the board. Either the absence of integration or such an approach as a coping mechanism leads to a piecemeal mode of solution, i.e., a matching of partial aspects of the figure with partial aspects of the contour opening based on the experience of fitting. Cognitively, therefore, the brain-damaged does not so much display a complete lack of planning, but a very inadequate plan and piecemeal execution. This behavior of a piece-by-piece matching has been described by Scheerer (1946), Werner and Thuma (1942), and Goldstein (1943) as typical of the brain-damaged on tasks which he experiences difficulty in accomplishing—inability to integrate cues into a perceptual or conceptual whole.

It is obvious that the adequate recall of figures depends on two factors: one, the accuracy of the initial form impression allowing for some kind of identification; and second, the availability of any traces based on that impression. We have raised the question whether this identification has to involve certain integration and translation processes. The unaccustomed tactual-kinesthetic impressions are experienced in temporal succession because the figures are too large to be encompassed in *one* touch contact with their contour. Thus we have first a "haptic" form integration in the sense Revesz utilizes. This has to be translated into a visualized form even though its structure may be inconspicuous in awareness and only instrumental in the process of identification. An added difficulty in the translation process should be mentioned; the "haptic" form percepts are often qualitatively different from visually perceived forms. This point has been stressed by Revesz and Berkeley (1950) in their experimental studies which demonstrated, for example, that different types of "haptic" closure laws prevail from those in vision. Any recognition failure or difficulty with the figures could therefore result from defective integration on any of the levels.

All the above factors would also operate in the locations. Here, as was pointed out, recognition based on "reversed" contour experience is more difficult if shifting is impaired. It is therefore possible that a brain-damaged may recall figures better than their locations, which have not become structurally articulated on the board. From a cognitive point of view we also have to consider that registering the formfit as well as its position on the board implies the simultaneous reaction to two different aspects of the action—form and place. It is reasonable to predict that one would have to suffer at the expense of the other, particularly since the locale on the board is in no way intrinsically connected with the task of fitting the figure and board contour. Its location can remain entirely in the background of experience, particularly if the individual is preoccupied with the attainment of the proper fit at the time. This preoccupation with the individual figure-contour fit has, in turn, a cognitive component in itself. Aside from the presumptive difficulty of simultaneous apperception of figure and its spatial locale, we have to postulate an inadequacy on a "higher level" of planning in the brain-damaged. This expresses itself in the previously described lack of a set to learn. We found that in contrast to the normal, the brain-damaged rarely, if ever, utilized any accidental encounter with a Formboard contour, which did not fit the given figure, for connecting it with another figure to be sought out or to be reidentified from previous contact. We may conclude that the cognitive constriction of both the simultaneous function and of the readiness to utilize Formboard information outside of the concrete search for the individual figure-fit plays a role in the inferior memory for the Formboard locations of the figures. Whatever purely retentive impairments enter into this poor showing, we cannot assess.

But it is obvious that adequate trace formation, even of incidental material, would have to suffer if the initial impression was not only of a background character, but of much less articulated clearness than in a normal person not handicapped by the stated cognitive structures. With regard to the number of figures recalled, as well as faithfulness of the drawings, the brain-damaged inferior performance suggests the following: the accuracy of the form identification seems to be restricted inasmuch as not all figures are equally missed in the recall. The analysis of the recall of simple vs. complex figures, in terms of both frequency and order, indicates that the brain-damaged recall proportionally more simple figures of their total recall than the normal. Hence their initial recognition as a base for recall seems to have been differentially favoring the simple figures. In answer to the question whether the recall difference could be explained as a poor retention, one could point to these facts: First, that *poor retention per se should affect all figures equally;* second, that it should also affect figure recall and localization equally, which is not the case. Not only do the brain-damaged have a total figure recall of 34 percent vs. 64 percent in the normals, their location recall is 29 percent of their actual figure recall vs. 51 percent in the normals. Finally, both the normal and brain-damaged do not statistically differentiate on the preferred order in recalling simple figures, but show a common trend herein. They do differentiate, however, in the fact that the normal, over and above this common tendency toward a preferred order for simple figures, recall more complex figures than the brain-damaged—50 percent to 23 percent. One may therefore conclude that there is a lawful tendency shared by both to prefer simpler figures in the recall order. This tendency would not explain why the brain-damaged significantly omitted complex figures in their recall also in rather straight correspondence to their increasing complexity. The assumption that poorer retention for complex figures is the only variable in this case would have to meet the argument that the average recall of three figures by the brain-damaged vs. six for the normal does not even cover the five simple figures for the brain-damaged. In other words there is an overall lower retention in this group, which reproduces less figures than the normal, including the simpler. Therefore, the significant lower recall of complex figures by the brain-damaged speaks not only for a lesser trace availability of these figures, but also for an initially poorer identification of them. The control of finer movements in the distal parts of the limbs has ostensibly suffered, e.g., the primitive form of grasp with the fingers and the tendency to involve the trunk or head in the finger use. There is also a strikingly reduced control in the anticipatory steering of the longer complex movement sequences. This function, necessary for initiating and directing an ordered course of motor acts under condition of speed, is diminished. The reasons for these two changes may be that the integration has leveled off from its normal articulation to a more diffuse spread of excitation, that the integration of the sensory appraisal—the feedback—and of the motor steering is temporally out of step. At the present state of our knowledge, it is futile to speculate on whether this lack of integration is caused by (1) a reduced vigilance in cognitively interpreting the sensory feedback; (2) less distinctness in the feedback itself; (3) reduced articulation on the motor side, i.e., unprecise innervation. Any one of these losses would affect the normal integration of sensory-motor impulses or constituent functions necessary for willed movement. The performance picture of the brain-damaged seems to provide sufficient evidence to conclude that the normal communicative interaction between different brain functions requisite for coordinated motor performance is impaired. This lack of adequate integration has also been described as dedifferentiation of the formal aspects in the organization of brain processes.

In accordance with our hypothesis, any interference with cortical integration will lead to defective sensory-motor performance in both its instrumental and cognitive aspects.

On the first level the defective integration expresses itself in a dedifferentiated motor innervation and coordination of finer movements. The instrumentality of sensory-motor function, be it in terms of sensory-motor feedback, timing, or precision, has become more primitively organized. Behaviorally this leads to clumsiness in execution.

On the second level, that of cognitive planning, the anticipatory as well as simultaneous function has suffered from the lack of integration. This leads to a cognitive restriction. It expresses itself in a difficulty of combining the required, diversified motor acts into a preconceived unitary plan of action and in a difficulty of continuing to hold them in mind while performing.

It is necessary to recognize that anticipation already involves aspects of simultaneous function. This latter is therefore involved in two ways in motor action. There is already simultaneity operative in the plan of action inasmuch as there is now a simultaneous representation—a plot—of the later movement sequence to be carried out. It is true this representation has a more schematic (outline or sketch) character than detailed completeness in all steps. The specific steps are filled in as the concretization of the plan proceeds in response to and supported by the actual demand conditions during the actions. Yet the studies on apraxia, in particular, have convincingly disclosed that normally such an anticipatory simultaneous schema exists as an "idea" or "design" of motor action. Here one has also coined such terms as "ideational plan of movement" or anticipation of "movement-melody."

This simultaneous "ideational plan" represents not only the temporal order of acts in a schema at any time point but it must also encompass the mutual coordination of diverse subacts—different limb and muscle movements. For example, the lighting of a cigarette is preceded by the ideational plan of schematically ordering the temporal sequence: Grasp match packet—pick out match—strike it—bring lighted match to cigarette tip. This plan is executed while holding the cigarette in the mouth—and maybe at the same time conversing, crossing the street, watching the traffic light, etc. At each time point, therefore, different simultaneous postural and muscle coordinations occur, while the movement plot unravels in time. In other words, the ideational plan, the design itself, has to be kept in mind continually at each time point, together with respectively prevailing changes in limb-muscle coordination. This complexity may be boiled down to a simple statement: Every action demands that we continually do different things at the same time while we follow an anticipated direction toward a goal.

From this point of view the sequel to brain pathology as regards cognitive restriction would lead to the following performance deficits: First we would expect a less differentiated ideational plan, so that there is relatively less anticipation of specific motor acts. The action plan may have also shrunken in scope so that a complex sequence of manipulations and the total action goal cannot be sufficiently articulated in the schema. Second, we expect a tendency to become restricted to one partial feature at the expense of other pertinent aspects so that performance is inadequate.

The same impairment may also underlie lack of learning, that is, of not benefiting from the ongoing experience with the task, so as to grasp the principles and incorporate them into an overall plan of attack. Instead a sort of pseudo-learning occurs—a falling into a restricted set, which is carried over from the immediately preceding experience with the task then confronting the S of perseverating or starting over from scratch with each phase of the task.

It is obvious that an understanding of the modification of function has to go beyond the recording of errors or failure scores, particularly since despite much time loss many brain-damaged are able to complete given tasks. Only an analysis of the type of difficulties they encounter can offer clues for the underlying defect. In this respect one has to include in the rationale an explanation of some of the roundabout methods in which the brain-damaged accomplished the task in relation to their difficulty.

REFERENCES

Aita, J. A.   Men with brain damage. *Amer. J. Psychiat.*, 1946–1947, *103*, 205–213.

Allen, R. M.   Test performance of brain-injured. *J. clin. Psychol.*, 1947, *3*, 225–230.

Armitage, S. G.   An analysis of certain psychological tests used for the evaluation of brain injury. *Psychol. Monogr.*, 1946, *60*, No. 1 (Whole No. 277).

Conkey, Ruth C.   Psychological changes associated with head injuries. *Arch. Psychol.*, 1938, 33, 5–62.

Goldstein, K.   Brain concussion: evaluation of the after effects by special tests. *Dis. nerv. System*, 1943, *4*, 325–334.

Goldstein, K.   The significance of mental disturbances in rehabilitation of soldiers with brain injury. *Trans. Amer. neurol. Assn.*, 1944, *70*, 22–24.

Halstead, W. C.   Further analysis of grouping behavior in patients with cerebral injury. *Arch. Neurol. Psychiat.*, 1940, *44*, 1140–1141.

Halstead, W. C., and Settlage, P. H.   Grouping behavior of normal persons and of persons with lesions of the brain. *Arch. Neurol. Psychiat.*, 1940, *49*, 486–506.

Head, H.   *Studies in neurology*, Vol. II. London: Oxford Medical Publications, 1920.

Hebb, D. O.   *The organization of behavior*. New York: Wiley, 1949.

Hunt, H. F.   A practical clinical test for organic brain damage. *J. appl. Psychol.*, 1943, *27*, 375–386.

Klebanoff, S. G.   Psychological changes in brain lesions and ablations. *Psychol. Bull.*, 1945, *42*, 585–617.

Lashley, K. S.   *Brain mechanisms and intelligence*. Chicago: Univ. of Chicago Press, 1929.

Malmo, R. B., *et al.*,   Motor control in psychiatric patients under experimental stress. *J. abnorm. soc. Psychol.*, 1951, *46*, 539–547.

Nielsen, J. M.   *Agnosia, apraxia, aphasia*. New York: Hoeber, 1946.

Revesz, G., and Berkeley, G.   *Psychology and art of the blind*. New York: Longmans, Green, 1950.

Scheerer, M.   Problems of performance analysis in the study of personality. *Ann. N.Y. Acad. Sciences*, 1946, *46*, 653–678.

Scheerer, M.   Measures of impairment of intellectual function: The Goldstein-Scheerer tests. Washington, D.C.: *Military clinical psychology*. Government Printing Office, 1951, 116–152.

Schilder, P.   *Brain and personality*. New York: International Universities Press, 1951.

Slater, P.   Interpreting discrepancies. *Brit. J. med. Psychol.*, 1943, *19*, 415–419.

Walshe, F. M. R.   *Critical studies in neurology*. Baltimore: Williams & Wilkins, 1948.

Werner, H., and Thuma, B. D.   A deficiency in the perception of apparent motion in children with brain injury. *Amer. J. Psychol.*, 1942, *55*, 58–67.

ANXIETY AND COGNITION

SHELDON J. KORCHIN

University of California at Berkeley

Doing Two Things at Once

IT WAS SIR CHARLES SHERRINGTON, I believe, who once observed that one of the remarkable achievements of the human race is that we are capable of doing two things at once. For lower animals, one act, with its attendant perceptual, integrative, and effector processes, occupies the entirety of behavior in the given moment. Man, by contrast, can coordinate without interference appropriate sequences of cognitive and behavioral activities to two or more ends. Attention can be divided and, as required, shift with the demands of each activity. The attentional field at any particular moment consists of focal and peripheral portions; the one accentuated, the other attenuated. However, even when there is only one focal concern, so-called irrelevant or incidental stimuli may be registered, acted upon, and remembered. Thus, incidental learning—an old but still unfairly neglected psychological issue, as Martin Scheerer (1953) once argued persuasively—may be viewed as a special instance of "doing two things at once."

We have just begun to explore some mechanisms which might be involved in the capacity for dual activity, starting with the prototypic problem of incidental cognition. Work presently in progress is concerned mainly with developing some techniques for evaluating the relationship between incidental and focal behavior in laboratory and natural situations and in studying the effects of anxiety on this relationship. However, even cursory consideration suggests the broad range of factors likely to be importantly involved in dual activity: the nature of the coexisting activities and their relative importances to the subject, the skills involved, the degree to which either new or overlearned knowledge is required, the motivational and emotional state of the person, organization of the stimulus field, and the demand qualities of central and peripheral stimuli. Not least, differences in personality organization and cognitive controls are surely relevant—for example, in such factors as proneness to interference (Schlesinger, 1954) and other dimensions of cognitive style described by Klein, Gardner, and their associates (e.g., Klein, 1954; Klein, 1958; Gardner, et al., 1959). Despite our faith in man's potential as a veritable switching yard, certainly some of us do have one-track minds!

The capacities required for dual activity emerge in development and regress in pathology and in states of intense arousal. The relation between stress and what I am here calling dual activity can be illustrated by a commonplace experience. It is perfectly possible to drive a car and simultaneously to carry on an intelligent conversation—at least for those of us skilled in driving. But should there be, for example, a near-accident, it is very likely that one or both of these previously coordinated activities will have to stop. Not unlikely we will be able to continue driving, perhaps more attentively and precisely, but without further conversation. Indeed, comment by a companion may be unheard or misunderstood, or be an intrusive irritant. Should the stress be more extreme, both activities may cease or be reduced to more primitive form. To put it simply, the mature and well-integrated person can do two things simultaneously; with increased anxiety, one thing well (perhaps better); with still greater anxiety, nothing.

Today, I would like to discuss the problem of dual activity, and the special case of incidental learning, in the context of a more general review of the relationship between anxiety and cognition. To understand the effects of anxiety, both the experiential and behavioral aspects of cognition will be considered jointly, since there are important parallels between the changes in phenomenal experience and the sorts of alteration of cognitive functioning which have been studied as indices of behavior under stress. In no sense is this a review of the relevant literature which, even of recent years, is too vast and cumbersome to review intelligently, much less to integrate. (In this sense, if no other, ours is truly an "age of anxiety!") Nor is it meant to cover in any inclusive way the work done by colleagues and myself at Michael Reese Hospital, and more recently at the National Institute of Mental Health, much of it involving studies of patients and normals under experimental and life stress, in order to explore conditions for the arousal and mastery of anxiety and the interrelationships among emotion, psychological, autonomic, and endocrine processes in stress. Some of the findings will be used for illustration, though the original experiments were sometimes done to other ends and in a somewhat different conceptual climate from the one I would like to develop today.

The Problem of Anxiety

After many definitions of anxiety in their *Comprehensive Dictionary* (English and English, 1958, p. 35), the Englishes conclude sagely: "When a term is frequently employed in behavioristic learning theory, in psychoanalysis, and in nearly every field of psychology between them, the variety and shadings of meaning often become very troublesome. *Anxiety* must be read with great vigilance for an author's meaning or, more often than not, his several meanings." Certainly, there is wisdom in this caution. Since anxiety research has arisen in so many theoretical contexts, it is difficult to discuss it within any single conceptual scheme.

 In various usages, anxiety has referred to an unconscious determinant of behavior, a central symptom of psychopathology, a uniquely human phenomenal experience, a drive of prime importance in the study of animal and human learning, discharge of the autonomic nervous system, and an essential condition for the socialization of the child. So, too, it has been indexed by introspective report, psychomotor alterations, observer ratings, inventory self-description, GSR fluctuation, and the analysis of fantasy productions. Obviously, it would be foolhardy and futile even to try to bring together such disparate views in any single conceptual scheme, since each reflects another way of slicing psychological science, and is inextricably tied to its parental theory. But that the problem of anxiety has concerned so many workers of such diverse orientations at least attests to the importance of the problem.

The Phenomenal State of Anxiety

As a conscious affect, anxiety is a state of apprehension, foreboding, or dread, seemingly without appropriate stimulus. Because of the enveloping and apparently objectless quality, many have distinguished states of fear which would be more temporary, more related to external threat, and more likely to be preparatory to adaptive behavior, and have reserved the term *anxiety* for the more intense experience. In such a distinction, true anxiety is experienced as objectless because it derives from internal psychological conflict; fear, from external threat (Freud, 1936). Distinctions between anxiety and fear, or between normal and neurotic anxiety, are difficult to maintain and for heuristic purposes it is perhaps better to visualize a single continuous emotional state which varies in its intensity, duration, and the degree to which it envelops and disables. According to Rollo May (1950), "Anxiety is the apprehension cued off by a threat to some value which the individual holds essential to his existence as a personality." Obviously, the particular threat conditions, the values that are endangered, and the consequent emotional experiences vary greatly along several dimensions, and no simple cataloguing is possible.

Psychoanalysis has called attention to the central function of anxiety in both adaptive and neurotic behavior. As a signal of present or impending danger, protective and adjustive actions are called into play. However, with threats of greater intensity, and when the individual's capacities for integrative and defensive operations are exceeded, anxiety itself is the symptom of disturbance, and the end product of the breakdown of integration. The dual function of anxiety—as signal and as symptom—and the related role of the mechanisms of defense in symptom formation are the major conceptual elements in the psychoanalytic theory of neurosis.

The capacity to know anxiety, certainly in its differentiated signal form, supposes a self-organization which is threatened and is capable of recognizing, remembering, and evaluating threat. Hence, developmentally, for anxiety as signal to exist supposes some prior maturation of cognitive structures, although anxiety as a primitive diffuse discharge phenomenon in response to unmanageable trauma is developmentally earlier. The fact that some degree of cognitive development is required for the transition from one to the other form of anxiety has been used by Goldstein (1951) as the basis for distinguishing between fear and anxiety. For him, fear (i.e., anxiety related to specific threat) is developmentally later since it is differentiated out of the original diffuse emotional experience (anxiety, the prototype of the later catastrophic reaction).

To be anxious requires ego and self organization. But in the anxious state these tend toward dissolution. In Lewinian terms, the boundaries of inner personal regions and of the life space become less articulated. Indeed, the "objectlessness," so often taken as the prime phenomenal quality of anxiety, may as well reflect the individual's inability to distinguish self and object, as the possibility that the threat is unconscious, which has more often been assumed by psychoanalysis. Thus, the anxious person feels enveloped in a dangerous world in which he cannot readily distinguish relevant from irrelevant or safe from dangerous, or, indeed, at greater intensities, real from unreal or self from object. But not only does anxiety lead to reduced capacity for differentiated experience; the reverse is also true. Where the situation prevents knowledge of relevant factors, where accustomed expectations are not met and hence outcomes of action are less predictable, anxiety may be aroused. The unknown is potentially dangerous. In an effort to induce some anxiety for experimental study, a situation was created in which the subject was led to believe that there might be some failure of reality-testing, i.e., that he might be projectively distorting "reality" perhaps because of the intrusion of repressed impulses (Korchin, et al., 1958). This procedure led to greater endocrine response than a failure-stress of the sort more conventionally used in psychological studies (Korchin and Herz, 1960). The reciprocal relation between anxiety and the reduction of cognitive organization also underlies a clinical dilemma. These effects can cycle into each other, creating a kind of positive feedback wherein the anxious person is less able to articulate experience which then is cause for further anxiety, and so on.

A part of the altered state in anxiety are changes in time perspective. The life space shrinks to the immediate present; the future is vague and dangerous, the past irrelevant. As MacKinnon (1944) pointed out in his topological analysis of anxiety, the levels of positive and negative irreality in the future seem to diverge from expected reality, so that there is less assurance that either hopes or fears will be realized. The immediacy in the anxiety state is aptly illustrated by some of David Rioch's (1955) observations on combat troops in Korea. Men cannot exercise complex functions involving the scanning of a large number of factors or long-term foresight because the stress is too massive and time too short for anything but the immediately relevant. Rioch quotes an officer as saying, "Up here, if a man can think five minutes ahead, we make him a squad leader. If he can think half an hour ahead, we make him sergeant. But if he can think all of two days ahead we make him battalion commander" (Rioch, 1955, p. 154). And, sensitive observer that he is, Rioch recalls that he himself was unable to hold in mind the larger research issues of his own work!

Such changes in cognitive organization under conditions of emotional arousal have been commented on in different contexts. Thus, Krech and Crutchfield note: "In states of strong emotion there is a narrowing of the cognitive organization at the moment; the individual loses broader perspective, he is no longer able to 'see' essential aspects of the situation and his behavior becomes, consequently, less adaptive" (Krech and Crutchfield, 1948, p. 252). So, too, Tolman (1948) in his famous discussion of cognitive maps notes that such maps narrow under conditions of emotional arousal.

I would like to suggest that the narrowing of cognitive organization is an essential part of the anxiety process. At more extreme levels, which we have been considering so far, the field is not only narrowed but there is a tendency toward more general cognitive regression. Self and objects fuse, boundaries become indistinct. The distance needed for judgment in terms of qualities external to the self is lost. However, at lower levels of arousal the narrowing of cognitive organization may contribute to more highly articulated (if limited) experience, and thus perhaps increase capacity for effective behavior. This may account for the often-described curvilinear relationship between arousal and the quality of performance, such that the best performance occurs not at the lowest but at an optimum level of arousal, above which there is increasingly greater decrement. A similar view has been proposed by Easterbrook (1959), that arousal reduces the "range of cue utilization" (Bruner, Matter, and Papanek, 1955), and that this reduction can make more understandable apparently diverse findings in studies relating emotion to the organization of behavior. I will return to this hypothesis, but first would like to consider further the relation between anxiety and cognitive functioning in laboratory studies of perception, memory, and thinking.

Cognitive Functioning in Anxiety

At lower levels of arousal, or where simpler tasks are involved, such as simple reaction time or avoidance conditioning, anxiety can facilitate performance. But, if one examines the ways in which people perceive, learn, solve problems, and carry out other cognitive functions at higher levels of anxiety or when under considerable stress, the generalization made by Barker, Dembo, and Lewin (1941) over twenty years ago still holds—the resulting behavior is generally more primitive. Psychomotor integration breaks down, as Luria (1932) and later Magda Arnold (1942) showed. In perceptual experiments, Postman and Bruner (1948) found that psychologically stressed subjects compared to non-stressed had greater difficulty in recognizing three-word sentences presented tachistoscopically, and were more likely to volunteer reckless hypotheses. Similarly, Korchin, Singer, and Ballard (1951) found that stressed subjects who had to reproduce the geometric figures of the Bender-Gestalt test, viewed tachistoscopically, produced more primitive drawings, that is, drawings more like those of children or brain-damaged adults. It was not simply that the reproductions were less correct—this could have been achieved by errors of a complicating sort—but they were simpler and sometimes better organized, yet at a lower level. In that study, we argued that anxiety might operate to lower the level of vigilance (in Henry Head's sense, 1926) necessary for precise reproduction and thus to allow the freer operation of autochthonous field-organization factors, against which the subject must strive in order to reproduce the figure as it is. To pursue these findings, Basowitz and I (Korchin and Basowitz, 1954; Basowitz, Persky, Korchin, and Grinker, 1955) used a series of circles, some of which had a segment of arc missing, others of which did not. These were presented tachistoscopically, and subjects had to identify the open circles. The technique was used under the life stress of parachute jumping, to test whether anxiety would decrease the ability to resist closure. It was found that men performed less well when anticipating jumping than when tested outside of the threatening situation. Moreover, those who were more stress-resistant—judged in terms of a biochemical index—performed better under stress. Moffitt and Stagner (1956) have similarly shown an increased tendency toward closure under experimentally induced stress. A considerable number of studies have found that problem solving becomes more rigid (e.g., Beier, 1951; Cowen, 1952; Pally, 1955), that learning of complex material is less efficient (e.g., Malmo and Amsel, 1948; Montague, 1953; Lucas, 1952), and that people perform less well in a variety of vigilance, sorting, and coding tasks (e.g., Davidson, Andrews, and Ross, 1956; Katchmar, Ross, and Andrews, 1958). Psychometric and clinical studies converge with experimental research to show evidence of lessened attention and concentration in anxiety; for example, deficit in digit-span performance has been commonly reported (e.g., Rapaport, Gill, and Schafer, 1945; Moldawsky and Moldawsky, 1952; Lewinski, 1945; Diethelm and Jones, 1947).

In general, deficit is greater insofar as the task at hand is novel, complex, requires maximal effort or skill, or allows for the interference of old habits. Thus, difficulty in mirror tracing is described as pathognomic of clinical anxiety by Wechsler and Hartogs (1945). Largely under the impetus of the learning theory of Spence, Taylor, and their associates, a considerable body of work has accumulated indicating that the anxious person has greater difficulty in learning if the material to be learned contains competing response tendencies (e.g., Taylor, 1956; Spence, 1956).

As another example of the effects of anxiety on learning, Korchin and Levine (1957) administered two types of paired associates to more and less anxious subjects. The first of these lists consisted of familiar and logically related words, such as man—boy; the second list was a series of false equations, of the sort $3 \times 5 = 6$. There were no important differences in the rate of learning the word-associates, but the groups differed distinctly in their learning of the false equations. More anxious subjects had greater difficulty in learning incorrect arithmetical statements. Moreover, closer analyses of the type of error made during learning yielded an even more sensitive index of anxiety effects. The more anxious the subject the more likely was he simply not to respond during the time the stimulus remained in view. By contrast, for the less anxious subjects a greater proportion of their errors in the false-equation task consisted of volunteering some response, most usually a number which was correct elsewhere in the series, although not for the particular stimulus item. Perhaps the more anxious person is simply more cautious, or requires more time than was available to produce any response, but we speculated that there might be evidence here of some difference in the learning process itself. Prior to the learning of discrete stimulus-response pairings, there is ordinarily an earlier phase in which people learn the range of responses which are correct *somewhere* in the series. When anxious, however, this earlier phase may be bypassed, and learning consists principally of the formation of the particular stimulus-response pairings. This tendency to isolate the stimulus-response units was interpreted as a possible particular manifestation of the cognitive constriction found in anxiety and in other states of limited ego functioning. In an earlier study the same phenomenon was found to be more characteristic of the learning of older compared to younger persons (Korchin and Basowitz, 1957).

There is not sufficient time to review with any thoroughness the enormous literature which has grown in recent years, describing various aspects of cognitive functioning in anxiety. In general, it is found that the effects of anxiety depend on the intensity and extent of arousal, the nature of the activity, and of course qualities of the person, in regard to stress tolerance, the type and effectiveness of defenses, and other personality qualities beyond our present concern.

Arousal, Vigilance, and the Effects of Anxiety

Overall, the relationship between anxiety (or arousal generally) and performance can be conceptualized in terms of a curvilinear relationship, so that at lower levels increment of anxiety leads to more efficient function and at higher to more disorganized. After surveying our own and the work of other investigators, Basowitz, Persky, Grinker, and I suggested the following formulation:

At low levels of anxiety there is a general alerting of the organism, an increase in vigilance (Liddell, 1950). In this state there is an increased sensitization to outside events and increased ability to cope with danger. The organism is in the state of preparedness early described by Cannon (1932). The threshold for potentially noxious stimuli particularly is lowered as the alert and apprehensive organism seeks the sources of danger in its world. This sensitivity continues at higher levels of anxiety, but the ability to differentiate the dangerous from the trivial becomes reduced. However, at lower levels of anxiety there is generally an integrating of behavior and an increase in the ability for productive performance. Thus, it is reported that low levels of distraction-stress can lead to improved performance.

As stress increases, however, or anxiety mounts, the organism becomes less capable of mastery. Behavior loses its spontaneity and flexibility. There is a general rigidification and individuals respond in terms of the more habitual and hence safer response tendencies. Anything novel is threatening and the ability to improvise (Ausubel, et al., 1953) is reduced. Increased effort has to be expended in order to maintain adequate behavior.

At higher levels of free anxiety there is no longer the ability for effective action. The organization of behavior breaks down. Regression to simpler and more primitive modes of response occurs. All aspects of psychological functioning are affected; coordination and integration are greatly reduced. In this state the organism can no longer adequately differentiate between dangerous and harmless stimuli, nor respond in

a differentiated way. Clinically, this is manifest in the great distracti-
bility, generalized irritability, and random-appearing behavior of the
anxiety patient. It is as if the central control mechanisms were disordered (Basowitz, Persky, Korchin, and Grinker, 1955, pp. 12–13).

The concept of an intensive dimension of activation or arousal
underlying motivational and emotional phenomena has been proposed in many theoretical contexts. Elizabeth Duffy (1941, 1951)
early suggested the importance of such a dimension to integrate
diverse phenomena of motivated and emotional behavior. Similarly, Freeman (1948) and more recently Malmo (1959), both
concerned with the role of the autonomic nervous system, have
proposed such an arousal continuum as reflecting the energization
of behavior, indexed in their work by measures of muscle tension
and other autonomic functions. Lindsley (1952, 1960) evolved an
activation concept and its relation to emotional behavior from the
EEG correlates of the sleep-wakefulness continuum. Similarly,
Hebb (1955) utilized such a continuum as a central concept in the
functioning of his "conceptual nervous system." With the cumulat-
ing evidence of neuropsychological research, it is clear that mid-
brain structures, particularly in the reticular system, are importantly involved in the alteration and maintenance of activation.

In all of these views, the relationship between activation and
performance is described in terms of an inverted U, so that maxi-
mally effective behavior occurs at an optimum rather than minimum or maximum level of arousal. This new concept thus resur-
rects and gives new stature to the old Yerkes-Dodson law (1908).
For present purposes, there is no need to review the details and
differences of various activation theories, except to note the con-
vergence from diverse quarters of emphasis on an intensive
dimension correlated with behavior alteration ranging continu-
ously from states of complete inactivity, hyporesponsivity, and *un*-
organized behavior, at the one extreme, to states of maximal activation, hyperresponsitivity, and *dis*organized behavior, at the
other.

Obviously, anxiety, arousal, and activation are not simply cog-
nate concepts, and my usage thus far has been too loose. It is
helpful, I believe, to view the phenomena of anxiety as part of

the more general organismic state connoted by such terms as arousal or activation. But anxiety, defined in terms of characteristic painful affect, is only one among many conditions of activation. It is obvious that one can be aroused without being anxious, though the reverse is not true. Moreover, the term anxiety might best be reserved for the mid to high portion of the activation continuum, rather than be used to cover the entire spectrum, as in the passage quoted above. But at this stage I would rather not dwell on definitional issues or consider what is unique to anxiety and the ways in which other states of activation (intense need or other affects) might differ, but simply to view anxiety as a particular manifestation of activation. In any case, I should like to call attention today to the relation between increased activation—experienced as a continuity from sleep, apathy, boredom to alertness, vigilance, excitement, apprehension, and at more intense levels anxiety and panic—and corresponding changes in capacity for integrative action.

Despite general agreement that increased activation and performance are related in an inverted-U function, there are relatively few studies which bear directly on this assumption, at least under experimental conditions. In one of these, Stennett (1957) found that when groups tested under increasing stress were compared, performance improved at lower stress levels though it deteriorated at higher levels. In one of our studies, anxiety-prone patients were subjected to stress interviews on three consecutive days, and before and after each such interview were given a simple area judgment test (Korchin, et al., 1957). When the occasions when each subject was at his lowest anxiety level were combined for all subjects, a positive correlation was found between anxiety and the accuracy of judgment; i.e., when all were relatively least anxious, the more anxious persons performed better. But on the occasions of greatest anxiety, the correlation was negative; i.e., the more anxious subjects judged less accurately.

The Organization of Attention in Anxiety

I should like now to consider the problem of attention in relation to activation, and to the changes in cognitive functioning earlier discussed, and then finally to return to the question of dual activity and incidental cognition raised at the outset.

It is worth an aside to note that while attention was once a central issue of psychology, over the years the term and many of the issues with which it dwelt fell into disuse and disrepute. Today, however, both the term and the problems once discussed have returned with renewed strength and in very diverse quarters, among behavioristic psychologists concerned with vigilance problems in human engineering settings (e.g., Broadbent, 1958), among neuropsychologists concerned with the study of brain function and central integrative processes (e.g., Lindsley, 1960), and among psychoanalytic ego psychologists concerned with the "autonomous functions of the ego" as well as the drives, affects, and defenses (e.g., Rapaport, 1960). Not only can the fact be recognized (and mentioned without embarrassment) that behavior is selective, and that items of experience do not have equal representation, but more importantly that man searches out and organizes stimuli, as well as responding to the most oft-repeated or reinforced or to those which have the greatest demand-quality or figurality in the Gestalter's sense. The person as active perceiver and cognizer has come into his own.

The optimally functioning person mobilizes and directs attention as required by the task in hand. This may involve focusing down to a narrow band with complete exclusion of the irrelevant. This is essentially the situation in many so-called vigilance tasks. Other times, a broader band is needed, and wider-ranging, scanning type of attention is more functional. Moreover, attentional fields can be maintained over time, and changed as task requirements change.

The processes involved in the self-initiated search for the relevant and inhibition of the irrelevant are reduced in anxiety. Rapaport (1958) and Schachtel (1954) have each pointed out that autonomous ego functioning (focal attention, in Schachtel's term) depends on relative freedom from imperative need or anxiety.

A continuum can be visualized from lower to higher orders of attention organization. At the lowest level, no voluntary focusing is possible and response occurs to the most immediate and demanding stimulus. Somewhat higher is the capacity to focus and hold fast, so to speak, in the given situation, but a relative inability to shift to new foci. At the highest level, there is ability to shift from broad to narrow and to exclude appropriately. At this level, we might note, there are also the capacity and interest to scan freely and take note of the environment, quite aside from the person's immediate purposes. Such incidental cognition is, I believe, importantly related to the highest order of intellectual accomplishment in problem solving and creative thinking.

Under stress, functioning is reduced from higher to lower order along such a continuum. At the extreme, as part of the general breakdown of organized behavior, attention becomes diffuse. The anxious patient is unable to concentrate, hyperresponsive, and hyperdistractible. However, at lower levels, the attentional field becomes more limited and focused. Whether such constriction disturbs or facilitates performance in a particular test situation depends in large measure on the demands of that task, whether it requires that a broader or narrower range of cues be utilized. This is the essential thesis of a paper by Easterbrook (1959), who argues that the effect of arousal is to reduce the "range of cue utilization." The narrowing of attention in emotional states has been proposed in other contexts as well (e.g., Callaway and Dembo, 1958).

An alternate, but not contradictory, theory emphasizes the reduced capacity to inhibit under arousal conditions (e.g., Malmo, 1957). Many of the phenomena of anxiety, and its effects on performance, can be interpreted in terms of the weakened inhibition of response to irrelevant stimuli. At one level of understanding, performance decrement interpreted in terms of weakened inhibition or in terms of lessened capacity to focus might amount to the same thing, but emphasis on the inhibitory processes might under other circumstances bring different problems into view. One might recall, for example, McGranahan's (1940) finding that more anxious subjects were less able *not* to give associates of a prohibited class.

Attention Alteration and Incidental Cognition

From this analysis, one should expect evidences of a narrowed attentional field under conditions of heightened arousal. Such effects should be particularly evident if the subject is "doing two things at once," if the task at hand entails both focal and incidental aspects, and one assesses performance in the two parts separately. Easterbrook (1959) garners ample experimental evidence for this proposition.

If the experimental procedure requires close attention to a central task, and occasional response to a peripheral one, anxious or stressed subjects show decrements in the peripheral task though able to maintain or improve central performance. Thus, Bursill (1958), testing under different conditions of heat and humidity, found that, with increased heat stress, correct responses to signals at distances from the center of the visual field decreased significantly, while central pursuitmeter performance was unimpaired. Under stress, he notes, "there is a tendency for the field of awareness to be funneled toward the centre." Bahrick, Fitts, and Rankin (1952), using a somewhat similar test procedure, found that increasing incentive facilitated performance of the central task, but interfered with performance of the peripheral. Studies of incidental learning are conceptually analogous to such experiments, in that they assay the spread of attention from a central focus (defined by the examiner's instructions and subject's intention) to more peripheral (incidental) activities. In a number of experiments, more anxious or stressed subjects showed considerable reduction in incidental learning going along with slight change in intentional learning (Aborn, 1953; Kohn, 1954; Silverman, 1954; and Silverman and Blitz, 1956).[1]

In our present work, we are attempting to pursue these findings further and to explore in greater depth the relation between central and incidental activity as an index of cognitive functioning in anxiety. This has necessarily involved us in questions of the organization of attention generally and in the problem of inter-

[1] Within the context of this presentation, I have focused on cognitive changes related to anxiety, but it should be noted that many of these can also be seen in other conditions of pathology and reduced ego functioning. Thus, for example, Mayman and Gardner (1960) have described narrowed attention in brain damage, and Wimer (1960) has found that older persons compared to younger perform relatively less well in incidental than in intentional learning.

personal differences in the capacity to segregate and respond differentially to the relevant (central) and irrelevant (incidental) portions of the field. In one study, Joseph Tecce and I have developed relatively complex visual displays which are presented in rapid sequence. The central task consists of searching out a particular item, which may or may not be present; following this, incidental learning of the other material is tested. So far, our concern has been largely with the development of procedures, the study of the effects of varying task parameters such as presentation time, and the relation of central-incidental behavior to other measures of cognitive functioning which involve central and incidental elements. In another study, we are more directly involved with the effects of arousal on incidental learning in a natural situation. The setting of this study is the waiting room of the obstetric department of a nearby hospital; the subjects are "expectant" fathers awaiting the birth of their babies. After a period in the room, the man is invited into an adjoining room and questioned in detail about the waiting room. Here is a situation in which there is predictably emotional arousal, and we are interested in discovering the amount and kind of "incidental learning" which goes on, and the way it varies as a function of the level of arousal.[2] Quite aside from the explicit purpose of the study, it may also serve to illustrate the kind of thing Martin Scheerer (1953) had in mind when he stressed the need for more research on incidental cognition and particularly in ecologically natural settings.

SUMMARY

Examination of various aspects of both phenomenal experience and cognitive functioning suggests some generalizations about the relation of anxiety and cognition. Under conditions of extreme arousal, integrative functioning is greatly reduced and ego organization tends toward dissolution. At lower levels, however, increased arousal may lead to a narrowing of attention which facili-

[2] We are grateful to Dr. Thomas Lebherz of the National Naval Medical Center for making this study possible.

tates adaptive behavior, though perhaps still reducing the capacity for complex behavior. Such alteration of attention has been discussed as a possible mechanism in the often-described curvilinear relationship between arousal and performance. An expected consequence of the reduced attentional field is the relatively greater restriction of incidental than focal cognitive activity. Some research exploring the relationship between focal and incidental cognition is discussed. The term "dual activity" is used, somewhat loosely, to include incidental cognition and other instances of the co-functioning of multiple psychological activities. The capacity for such "dual activity," an important quality of the optimally functioning person, is reduced in anxiety.

REFERENCES

Aborn, M.   The influence of experimentally induced failure on the retention of material acquired through set and incidental learning. *J. exp. Psychol.*, 1953, *45*, 225–231.

Arnold, Magda B.   A study of tension in relation to breakdown. *J. gen. Psychol.*, 1942, *26*, 315–346.

Ausubel, D. P., Schiff, H. M., and Goldman, M.   Qualitative characteristics in the learning process associated with anxiety. *J. abnorm. soc. Psychol.*, 1953, *48*, 537–547.

Bahrick, H. P., Fitts, P. M., and Rankin, R. E.   Effect of incentives upon reactions to peripheral stimuli. *J. exp. Psychol.*, 1952, *44*, 400–406.

Barker, R., Dembo, Tamara, and Lewin, K.   Frustration and regression. *Univ. Iowa Stud. Child Welf.*, 1941, *18*, No. 1.

Basowitz, H., Persky, H., Korchin, S. J., and Grinker, R. R.   *Anxiety and stress*. New York: McGraw-Hill, 1955.

Beier, E. G.   The effect of induced anxiety on the flexibility of intellectual functioning. *Psychol. Monogr.*, 1951, *65*, No. 9.

Broadbent, D. E.   *Perception and communication*. London: Pergamon Press, 1958.

Bruner, J. S., Matter, Jean, and Papanek, Miriam L. Breadth of learning as a function of drive level and mechanization. *Psychol. Rev.*, 1955, *62*, 1–10.

Bursill, A. E.   The restriction of peripheral vision during exposure to hot and humid conditions. *Quart. J. exp. Psychol.*, 1958, *10*, 114–129.

Callaway, E., III, and Dembo, D. Narrowed attention. *Arch. Neurol. Psychiat.*, 1958, 79, 74–90.

Cannon, W. B. *The wisdom of the body*. New York: Norton, 1932.

Cowen, E. L. The influence of varying degrees of psychological stress on problem-solving rigidity. *J. abnorm. soc. Psychol.*, 1952, *47*, 512–519.

Davidson, W. Z., Andrews, T. G., and Ross, S. Effects of stress and anxiety on continuous high-speed color naming. *J. exp. Psychol.*, 1956, *52*, 13–17.

Diethelm, O., and Jones, M. R. Influence of anxiety on attention, learning, retention and thinking. *Arch. Neurol. Psychiat.*, 1947, *58*, 325–336.

Duffy, Elizabeth. The conceptual categories of psychology: A suggestion for revision. *Psychol. Rev.*, 1941, *48*, 177–203.

Duffy, Elizabeth. The concept of energy mobilization. *Psychol Rev.*, 1951, *58*, 30–40.

Easterbrook, J. A. The effect of emotion on cue utilization and the organization of behavior. *Psychol. Rev.*, 1959, *66*, 183–201.

English, H. B., and English, Ava C. *A comprehensive dictionary of psychological and psychoanalytical terms*. New York: Longmans, Green, 1958.

Freeman, G. L. *The energetics of human behavior*. Ithaca: Cornell Univ. Press, 1948.

Freud, S. *The problem of anxiety*. New York: Norton, 1936.

Gardner, R. W., Holzman, P. S., Klein, G. S., Linton, Harriet B., and Spence, D. P. Cognitive control. *Psychol. Issues*, 1959, *1*, No. 4.

Goldstein, K. On emotions: Considerations from the organismic point of view. *J. Psychol.*, 1951, *31*, 37–49.

Head, H. *Aphasia and kindred disorders of speech*. London: Cambridge Univ. Press, 1926.

Hebb, D. O. Drives and the C.N.S. (conceptual nervous system). *Psychol. Rev.*, 1955, *62*, 243–254.

Katchmar, L. T., Ross, S., and Andrews, T. G. Effects of stress and anxiety on performance of a complex verbal-coding task. *J. exp. Psychol.*, 1958, *55*, 559–564.

Klein, G. S. Need and regulation. In M. R. Jones (ed.), *Nebraska symposium on motivation: 1954*. Lincoln: Univ. of Nebraska Press, 1954. Pp. 224–274.

Klein, G. S. Cognitive control and motivation. In G. Lindzey (ed.), *Assessment of Human Motives*. New York: Rinehart, 1958. Pp. 87–118.

Kohn, H.   The effect of variations of intensity of experimentally induced stress situations upon certain aspects of perception and performance. *J. genet. Psychol.*, 1954, *85*, 289–304.

Korchin, S. J., and Basowitz, H.   Perceptual adequacy in a life stress.
J. Psychol., 1954, *38*, 495–502.

Korchin, S. J., and Basowitz, H.   Age differences in verbal learning.
J. abnorm. soc. Psychol., 1957, *54*, 64–69.

Korchin, S. J., and Herz, M.   Differential effects of "shame" and "dis-
integrative" threats on emotional and adrenocortical functioning.
Arch. gen. Psychiat., 1960, *2*, 640–651.

Korchin, S. J., and Levine, S.   Anxiety and verbal learning. *J. abnorm.
soc. Psychol.*, 1957, *54*, 234–240.

Korchin, S. J., Basowitz, H., Chevalier, J. A., Grinker, R. R., Hamburg,
D. A., Sabshin, M., and Persky, H.   Visual discrimination and the
decision process in anxiety. *Arch. Neurol. Psychiat.*, 1957, *78*, 425–
438.

Korchin, S. J., Basowitz, H., Grinker, R. R., Hamburg, D. A., Persky,
H., Sabshin, M., Heath, Helen, and Board, F. A.   Experience of
perceptual distortion as a source of anxiety. *Arch. Neurol. Psychiat.*,
1958, *80*, 98–113.

Korchin, S. J., Singer, J. L., and Ballard, R. G.   The influence of
frustration on the reproduction of visually-perceived forms. *Personality*, 1951, *1*, 54–66.

Krech, D., and Crutchfield, R.   *Theory and problems of social psychology.* New York: McGraw-Hill, 1948.

Lewinski, R. J.   The psychometric pattern: 1. Anxiety neurosis. *J.
clin. Psychol.*, 1945, *1*, 214–221.

Liddell, H. S.   The role of vigilance in the development of animal
neurosis. In P. H. Hoch and J. Zubin (eds.), *Anxiety.* New York:
Grune & Stratton, 1950. Pp. 183–196.

Lindsley, D. B.   Psychological phenomena and the electroencephalo-
gram. *EEG clin. Neurophysiol.*, 1952, *4*, 443–456.

Lindsley, D. B.   Attention, consciousness, sleep and wakefulness. In
J. Field (ed.), *Handbook of physiology.* Vol. 3. *Neurophysiology.*
Washington, D.C.: American Physiological Society, 1960. Pp. 1553–
1593.

Lucas, J. D.   The interactive effects of anxiety, failure, and intra-serial
duplication. *Amer. J. Psychol.*, 1952, *65*, 59–66.

Luria, A. R.   *The nature of human conflicts.* (Trans. by W. Horsley
Gantt.) New York: Liveright, 1932.

MacKinnon, D. W.   A topological analysis of anxiety. *Charact. &
Pers.*, 1944, *12*, 163–176.

Malmo, R. B.   Anxiety and behavioral arousal. *Psychol. Rev.*, 1957,
64, 276–287.

Malmo, R. B. Activation: A neuropyschological dimension. *Psychol. Rev.*, 1959, *66*, 367–386.

Malmo, R. B., and Amsel, A. Anxiety-produced interference in serial rote learning with observations on rote learning after partial frontal lobectomy. *J. exp. Psychol.*, 1948, *38*, 440–454.

May, R. *The meaning of anxiety.* New York: Ronald, 1950.

Mayman, M., and Gardner, R. W. The characteristic psychological disturbance in some cases of brain damage with mild deficit. *Bull. Menninger Clin.*, 1960, *24*, 26–36.

McGranahan, D. V. A critical and experimental study of repression. *J. abnorm. soc. Psychol.*, 1940, *35*, 212–225.

Moffitt, J. W., and Stagner, R. Perceptual rigidity and closure as functions of anxiety. *J. abnorm. soc. Psychol.*, 1956, *52*, 354–357.

Moldawsky, S., and Moldawsky, Patricia C. Digit span as an anxiety indicator. *J. consult. Psychol.*, 1952, *16*, 115–118.

Montague, E. K. The role of anxiety in serial rote learning. *J. exp. Psychol.*, 1953, *45*, 91–96.

Pally, S. Cognitive rigidity as a function of threat. *J. Pers.*, 1955, *23*, 346–355.

Postman, L., and Bruner, J. S. Perception under stress. *Psychol. Rev.*, 1948, *55*, 314–323.

Rapaport, D. The theory of ego autonomy: A generalization. *Bull. Menninger Clin.*, 1958, *22*, 13–35.

Rapaport, D. On the psychoanalytic theory of motivation. In M. R. Jones (ed.), *Nebraska Symposium on Motivation, 1960.* Lincoln: Univ. of Nebraska Press, 1960. Pp. 173–247.

Rapaport, D., Gill, M. M., and Schafer, R. *Diagnostic psychological testing.* Chicago: Year Book Publishers, 1945–1946. 2 vols.

Rioch, D. McK. Problems of preventive psychiatry in war. In P. H. Hoch and J. Zubin (eds.), *Psychopathology of childhood.* New York: Grune & Stratton, 1955. Pp. 146–165.

Schachtel, E. G. The development of focal attention and the emergence of reality. *Psychiatry*, 1954, *17*, 309–324.

Scheerer, M. Personality functioning and cognitive psychology. *J. Pers.*, 1953, *22*, 1–16.

Schlesinger, H. J. Cognitive attitudes in relation to susceptibility to interference. *J. Pers.*, 1954, *22*, 354–374.

Silverman, R. E. Anxiety and the mode of response. *J. abnorm. soc. Psychol.*, 1954, *49*, 538–542.

Silverman, R. E., and Blitz, B. Learning and two kinds of anxiety. *J. abnorm. soc. Psychol.*, 1956, *52*, 301–303.

Spence, K. W. *Behavior theory and conditioning.* New Haven: Yale Univ. Press, 1956.

Stennett, R. G.   The relationship of performance level to level of arousal. *J. exp. Psychol.*, 1957, *54*, 54–61.

Taylor, Janet A.   Drive theory and manifest anxiety. *Psychol. Bull.*, 1956, *53*, 303–320.

Tolman, E. C.   Cognitive maps in rats and men. *Psychol. Rev.*, 1948, *55*, 189–208.

Wechsler, D., and Hartogs, R.   The clinical measurement of anxiety. *Psychiat. Quart.*, 1945, *19*, 618–635.

Wimer, R. E.   Age differences in incidental and intentional learning. *J. Geront.*, 1960, *15*, 79–82.

Yerkes, R. M., and Dodson, J. D.   The relation of strength of stimulus to rapidity of habit formation. *J. comp. neurol. Psychol.*, 1908, *18*, 459–482.

THE PROCESS OF
FREE RECALL[1]

SOLOMON E. ASCH

Swarthmore College

FREE RECALL IS A PROCESS OF SINGULAR IMPORTANCE. It makes an indispensable contribution to intellectual functioning, bringing the materials of past experience to the activities of thinking and of imaginative construction. It has of course a secure place in the psychology of memory; it also poses a challenge to the theory of recall. Recently I have been studying, with the help of colleagues and students, the properties of free recall. The investigations are still continuing, but a sufficiently clear direction has emerged that warrants description.

The phenomenon of free recall is well known and is easy to identify descriptively. It refers to the reproduction of past experiences in an order that is regulated from within the person. Two phases of free recall may be distinguished. There is, first, the occasion that initiates it; the latter may be some feature of the environment that communicates with the materials of the past, or it may be an internal event that performs the same function. There is, second, the continuation of recall once it is initiated. The distinctive feature of free recall, and the reason for the designation "free," is that the course of recall is not under external control. In this respect it differs from another well-known avenue to past experience, namely, aided recall.

[1] This discussion is based on investigations supported by grants of the Ford Foundation and the National Science Foundation.

In recall traces of past events are contacted and aroused. The functional problem of free recall, as of recall generally, is that of trace action. Concerning the two steps of free recall mentioned above one may ask: (1) How does the present occasion—external or internal—initiate communication with traces of past events? (2) Once initiated, what conditions determine the course of subsequent recall, or the occurrence of subsequent trace contacts? The following remarks will be confined to the second of these questions.

The Associative Theory of Recall

To come closer to the functional problems, it is helpful to relate them first to existing concepts in the psychology of memory. The dominant theory of recall today, as in the past, is that of association. The fundamental principle of this theory is that each instance of recall is initiated by an event with which it was previously associated. Although the process of free recall has hardly been studied, the application of this principle to it is clear in general, if not in detail.

Current associationism is a form of stimulus-response theory. The basic idea of this position is that each step of recall is a response elicited by a stimulus with which it is associated. To illustrate, when one has formed an association, say by the method of anticipation in a paired-associate experiment, the first member of the pair has, according to this account, the property of a stimulus, the second that of a response. The clearest instance of this formulation is provided by the method of aided recall, which consists of the presentation of the first member under instructions to recall the second. The learner's ability to supply the missing term is taken as evidence that the association is functioning, or that the stimulus has successfully elicited the response. Failure to produce the second term serves as an index of the failure of the association, or of the failure of the stimulus to perform its eliciting function.

The preceding formulation provides also the outline of a stimulus-response interpretation of free recall. The event which initiates recall is assumed to do so associatively; it is further assumed that the subsequent flow of recall is prescribed by associative connections. A noteworthy feature of this analysis is that it treats free recall as an instance of the apparently more general case of aided recall. To be sure, there are also differences. In aided recall one can easily specify the stimulus at each point; this identification is more difficult in free recall. Such differences are real, but they do not affect the main point, namely, that free recall is a function of stimulus-response connections.

The associative position sketched above finds no fundamentally new problems in the phenomena of free recall. The observations we have made have forced upon us the conclusion that free recall has properties not derivable from association. Further, we have found that the determinants of free recall are a necessary condition of associative recall itself. These conclusions contradict the associative theory of recall, and form the basis of an alternative theory. The abandonment of the associative theory of recall raises new questions about the properties of recall and association, and requires a reexamination of current concepts in the area of human learning and memory.

A Nonassociative Property of Free Recall

Once initiated, free recall occurs in a particular order, for which there are no external guides or constraints. We saw that the tacit assumption of psychology has been that such order is prescribed by associative connections. This assumption, namely, that the order of associations determines the order of free recall, has been the ruling idea of all doctrines of association.

Let me now describe an investigation by Ebenholtz and myself (Asch and Ebenholtz, 1962b) that addresses itself to the determinants of the order of free recall. The learner was shown in the memory drum a set of eight nonsense syllables which he pronounced under instructions to commit them to memory. There followed immediately a test of free recall, during which he called out all the syllables he could, in the order in which they came to his mind. The syllables were now shown again, but in a different order, to be again followed by a test of free recall. The alternating learning and test trials continued until the subject could recall all eight syllables in one trial.

Learning under these conditions was quite rapid. This result is hardly surprising, but one aspect of it deserves attention. The sequence in which the items were seen (and read) varied on successive trials, the purpose being to prevent the formation of associations between them. If the procedure achieved its aim, we would have succeeded in demonstrating consecutive recall in the absence of interitem associations. Our analysis focused on this issue. We studied the order of each subject's recall on each test, comparing it with the order in which items appeared on the immediately preceding learning trial. A number of such analyses were performed; we asked whether items adjacent in recall were adjacent in earlier experience, whether they occurred in the same relative order, and a number of related questions. There was very low correspondence between order of recall and order of original experience. Thus the recall obtained could not be accounted for on the basis of these correspondences, except to a minor degree. It appears that order of recall is not governed by sequences of associations.

We were also able to identify some of the determinants of sequential recall. Among them were the properties the items had as members of their series: items that appeared last and first on the immediately preceding learning trial were recalled earliest. For the reason mentioned above, these effects of recency and primacy cannot be referred to interitem associations. Evidence from other studies shows that frequency of prior anticipation is also a condition of order of recall. There are doubtless other conditions of sequential recall.

So far we have spoken of the determinants of order of recall, not of the occurrence of recall. Whether an item was recalled or not was a function of the same conditions as those governing order of recall. We also found evidence in delayed recall of a strong relation between recall of an item and the frequency with which it was anticipated during learning. The conclusion follows that the occurrence as well as the order of free recall is not a function of interitem associations.

Free Recall and Associative Recall

One might claim that the preceding result holds for a particular condition, one that prevents associative connections between data. Is there any reason to doubt, though, that when associative connections are present, they do determine the occurrence of recall? The investigation to be now described provides a definite answer to this question.

The specific question that we (Asch and Ebenholtz, 1962a) studied in this connection may seem far removed from the issue under discussion, but the relation will become quickly clear. It centered around an old problem concerning associations—the relation between forward and backward association. The weight of empirical evidence appeared to support the conclusion that backward associations are weaker than forward associations. Indeed, many students have, on the basis of theoretical considerations, doubted the authenticity of backward association altogether. For reasons that will be explained, we became doubtful of the one-sidedness of associations. Our investigation showed that the supposed asymmetry is an artifact, the consequence of an error of theory that was responsible for a defect in experimentation. The evidence we obtained provided support for a principle of associative symmetry, or of the equality of forward and backward association.

It is necessary to describe the procedure that is generally followed in the study of this problem. As a rule, the learning is of the paired-associate form. Usually the learner sees or reads the first member of each pair, and anticipates the second member until he has reached a set criterion. The test of forward association employs the method of aided recall; one shows the first member and asks for the second. For the test of backward association one reverses the procedure by showing the second member and asking for the first. This procedure has provided consistent evidence of a difference between forward and backward performances.

There is nothing wrong with this finding; we were able easily to duplicate it. As the following analysis shows, a difficulty does, however, arise when one infers associative asymmetry from the inequality of forward and backward performances. The forward test just described asks the learner to recall terms (i.e., the second members) that he has been anticipating throughout the period of learning, but the backward test requires him to recall terms that he has not been anticipating. The two tests differ in ease of recall of the required terms; does it follow that the associations in question differ? To decide this point, it might be advisable to equalize recall in both directions. When Ebenholtz and I did this, by familiarizing the learner with all the items before paired-associate learning, the difference between forward and backward performances either disappeared or decreased to a comparatively low level. A further investigation with M. Lindner (Asch and Lindner, 1963) confirmed and extended this result.

These findings introduce a distinction between association and recall. Two conditions must be fulfilled in associative recall: the presence of the association and the ability to recall the required datum. Associative recall can fail although the association is present. This conclusion contradicts the stimulus-response definition of an association. The latter defines an association operationally in terms of the probability of obtaining a response to a stimulus with which it was previously connected. It takes the occurrence of a response as evidence that the association has persisted, and failure of the response as evidence of failure of the association. If the preceding findings are correct, the response-definition of an association must be incorrect. The error of an unqualified response-definition of association consists in absorbing the contribution of recall proper into the functioning of associations. In confirmation of this analysis one may also cite the superiority of the method of matching to that of aided recall.

The Availability Hypothesis

If associative recall can fail when association is intact, it follows that a recall process is a necessary condition of associative recall. What is the character of this recall? The answer we propose is that there are memory traces for data, that these possess a property of availability which determines the occurrence of recall. Memory traces differ in availability as a function of specific conditions of past experience; some of these have been described in connection with the study of free recall (e.g., serial recency and primacy, frequency). According to this account, the property of availability pertains to traces of data, and is not a function of their associative connections. Recall is, we propose, a function of availability, not of association.

We will now examine a few consequences of this hypothesis.

1. LOSS OF ASSOCIATION VS. LOSS OF AVAILABILITY. It has been unquestioningly assumed that loss of associative recall is due solely to loss of associations. The availability hypothesis raises the alternative possibility that decrement of retention is a consequence, at least in part, of loss of availability. Investigations we have been conducting show that this is indeed the case. The following may serve as a simplified illustration. We test for the recall of paired associates by the method of aided recall after substantial decrement has occurred. Immediately prior to the test of aided recall the subjects receive "rehearsal practice." The latter consists of showing the subjects the second members of the pairs, under instructions to give them back in free recall. There are several alternating learning and test trials; the order of the items is varied from trial to trial. In short, these subjects receive practice in recalling the "response" terms. A comparable control group receives no such rehearsal practice. We have repeated this experiment several times, and have found regularly that practice of this kind has a pronounced effect in raising the level of aided recall. It can be shown that the procedure of rehearsal does not involve practice of the associations. We interpret this result to mean that rehearsal practice raises item availability, thus raising aided recall, and that decrement of associative recall is, at least to a significant degree, a consequence of loss of item availability.

2. AVAILABILITY AND STRENGTH OF ASSOCIATION. One must raise a corresponding question concerning the concept of associative strength. It has been a postulate of the psychology of human learning that associative practice increases strength of associations. Since associative practice also increases item availability, it is necessary to ask whether any of the effects attributed to associative strength are a function of availability. Recently M. Lindner and I (Asch and Lindner, 1963) have discussed this problem in relation to the issue of associative symmetry. The interpretation of the empirically obtained differences between forward and backward associative recall has been that forward and back-

ward associations differ in strength. The findings we have reported earlier establish that the difference in question is a function of availability. The availability hypothesis requires us to ask further whether *all* effects hitherto attributed to associative strength are effects of availability, or whether associations increase at all in strength once they have formed. Investigations of this question are now in progress.

3. THE ELICITOR FUNCTION OF ASSOCIATIONS.   The demonstration of the role of item availability in associative recall prompts a further question: What is the role of association in aided recall? According to the stimulus-response account, the "stimulus" elicits or instigates the associated response; that is, it increases the likelihood of its recall. The evidence described earlier limits this proposition decidedly. The studies of associative symmetry have shown that aided recall will fail if recall of the items is low, or that a process of recall makes an independent contribution to associative recall. To be sure, this result does not exclude the possibility that associative recall depends upon both item availability and stimulus instigation. However, the availability hypothesis, which asserts that recall is a function solely of availability, raises the radical possibility that associations do not at all determine the level of recall.

We have studied this question in several ways, one of which will be briefly described. A group learns a set of paired associates, consisting of syllables and words, under instructions to associate them. The test that follows is one of free recall; the subjects are instructed to recall all the pairs they can; they are also directed to reproduce all the single or unassociated items. A second group learns the identical set of pairs under the same objective conditions, but they are instructed to disregard the pairings and to concentrate on the items. The test is identical with that of the first group; departing from the original instructions we direct the subjects in this group to reproduce the associations they have formed as well as the unassociated items. This procedure provides information concerning the recall of content and of associations in each group. We find first that the groups differ consistently in level of association, in accordance with the learning instructions they received. At the same time they differ only negligibly in recall of content. Further, this is the result at different levels of practice (Asch, Ebenholtz, Lindner, and Rescorla, to be published).

The equivalence of content recall at different levels of association removes the ground for the assumption of associative instigation. The recall of a datum does not become more likely when an item with which it is associated is recalled. Although we have not explored the limiting conditions, the effect is beyond question over a wide range of learning. The conclusion follows that an association is not an elicitor; whether a datum will be recalled or not is a function solely of its availability, not of its associative connections. What, one may ask, is the function of association in associative recall? The answer we propose is that an association has a selector function: it selects the associatively belonging item from among those that are available. Item availability determines the occurrence of recall, association decides the selection of recall.

The latter finding may be considered from a somewhat different point of view. When materials have been associated, they are said to be contacted by means of aided recall. When they are not associated with each other, or are poorly associated, they are reached by means of free recall. The preceding result tells us that free and aided recall produce the same levels of recall. This is in accordance with the availability hypothesis, but it creates a grave problem for the theory of association.

4. ASSOCIATIONS AS STIMULUS-RESPONSE CONNECTIONS. For technical reasons psychologists have favored the methods of anticipation and of aided recall in the study of associations. Given these procedures, and the associative starting point, it appeared reasonable to formulate that associations are instances of stimulus-response connections. The evidence against associative instigation cannot be reconciled with this view. There is also another reason for rejecting it. We learn from the principle of associative symmetry that "stimulus" and "response" do not differ in associative functioning, that the differences between them are solely those of availability. We conclude that the stimulus-response analogy is not relevant to the phenomena of association and recall.

CONCLUSION

This partial account of recent investigation may nevertheless suffice to illustrate the import of free recall, and its relevance to a general theory of recall. The major conclusion we have reached is that recall and association are different processes, that there are laws of recall distinct from laws of association. There is, we saw, recall of data in the absence of associations between them, and there is association without recall. We have attempted to derive some phenomena of recall from the theoretical construct of availability, the latter denoting a property of traces for data that is independent of their associative connections. The theoretical distinction between acquisition and recall alters our conception of the properties of association and recall, and of the relations between them. It sets before us the task of reexamining the ideas in the psychology of learning and memory that have been erected on the foundation of the associative axiom.

REFERENCES

Asch, S. E., and Ebenholtz, S. M.   The principle of associative symmetry. *Proc. Amer. Phil. Soc.*, 1962a, *106*, 135–163.

Asch, S. E., and Ebenholtz, S. M.   The process of free recall: evidence for non-associative factors in acquisition and retention. *J. Psychol.*, 1962b, *54*, 3–31.

Asch, S. E., and Lindner, M.   A note on "Strength of Association." *J. Psychol.*, 1963, *55*, 199–209.

Asch, S. E., Ebenholtz, S. M., Lindner, M., and Rescorla, R.   The role of association in recall. To be published.

ON THE PSYCHOLOGY OF THE
PSYCHOLOGICAL EXPERIMENT

JOSEPH LYONS

Veterans Administration Hospital,
Lexington, Ky.

ALTHOUGH MARTIN SCHEERER DID NOT WRITE a theoretical text in
English, perhaps because he was too busy, and did not under-
take to propound a systematic position, probably because he was
too wise, he did leave us a more enduring contribution in his
expression of a coherent and consistent attitude toward psychological problems. To him this attitude, under the name of *cognitive theory*, was distinguishable from S-R theories of all sorts
because it called for the organism, as holistically conceived, to deal
meaningfully and even creatively with its total situation (Scheerer,
1954). That phenomenon which the S-R theorist now treats under
the barren rubric of "behavior" is, instead, viewed as a performance—that is, as a patterning which is structured by the organism
(Prentice, 1961), which is made functionally relevant to a total situation through the medium of selective representation
(Scheerer, 1953), and which is an adjustive, spontaneous, and
creative "action process." How our science would be altered if
this view were taken by all of us as the starting point for its
fundamental concerns!

In this light, cognitive theory has to be viewed not simply as a
theory about cognition—as Brunswik (1957), for example, would
have it—but as a way of thinking about cognition, and about other
issues as well; just as psychoanalytic theory does not refer so

much to a set of ideas about psychoanalysis as to a movement in psychology, a position which confronts all the rest of the discipline. Indeed, Donald Campbell (1963), in attempting recently to assimilate the soft underbelly of psychology into its more hard-headed counterpart (if you will permit me a dreadfully confused organismic metaphor), chooses to oppose "cognitive theories" in general to all of the "behavioristic" approach. This is a distinction which Fritz Heider (1957) has also emphasized, in remarking that cognitive theory is an aspect of psychology as a whole, that it was suppressed by the behavioristic revolution, and that it has only lately begun to reappear in the guise of new studies of perception and communication.

As Martin Scheerer's writings have amply demonstrated, it is possible to subject any of psychology's problems, wherever they are encountered, to that special "test of significance" which stems from cognitive theory—whether the problem is the development of stages of meaning (Scheerer, 1959), or problem solving (Scheerer and Huling, 1960), or the observed behavior of the brain-damaged patient (Goldstein and Scheerer, 1941). Therefore I feel quite comfortable today in adopting this stance, so to speak, in order to examine some aspects of the interpersonal ritual which determines the activities of so many of us—I mean the psychological experiment itself.

The period immediately following World War II gave psychology, rather unexpectedly, the full flowering of a clinical profession within a profession. For good reason George Kelly has called this period the Golden Decade of clinical psychology. Experimentalists too have some reason to be grateful for the rise and spread of the clinical influence, for out of its concern for observing every ingredient of the clinical situation came the first studies of the clinician himself—preparing us, in theory at least, for that current venture which is known as the social psychology of the experiment. The idea of subjecting the clinician himself to examination is, of course, implicit in clinical theory. In psychoanalytic practice he belongs inescapably at one end of the transference dynamic; and his centrality as an object of interest in nondirective theory too may be seen in Rogers' insistence on writing almost as much about himself as about his clients. To the true clinician, his own world is as fascinating a topic as it is that of any of his patients. His theory is therefore devoted as much to examining his own motives as those of his opposite number; and the similarity of their roles is clearly stated in the psychoanalytic directive that the one role is a necessary preliminary to the other.

From the lesson that psychotherapy could not be studied by itself—if only because there can be no treatment unless both patient and therapist are caught up in their common situation—it was soon realized that the same would hold true for testing. A whole series of studies some ten years ago, under the general direction of Max Hutt (Gibby, 1952; Gibby, Miller, and Walker, 1953; Sanders and Cleveland, 1953), examined the proposition that characteristics of the Rorschach examiner, from simple ones such as sex to elaborate ones such as degree of covert hostility, affected the subject's protocol. The results of these and other studies (Lord, 1950; Holtzman, 1952; Alden and Benton, 1951) were by no means in agreement in their results, but they did support the premise that the clinician is amenable to study by means of his own instruments. The nonclinical school of testing made the same point, though equally indirectly, in Cronbach's (1946, 1950) contribution of the notion of *set*. For it can be argued that this conception is interpersonally neutral, even though Cronbach originally termed it "response set" and defined it simply as a tendency on the part of the subject alone (1946, p. 476). I suspect that if we but had the wit to do it, we might apply it to tester as well as to testee.

Clinical theory battens on all the evidence that the clinician is part and parcel of the clinical situation; and this is all to the good. However, the logic is never extended to include the researcher, whether in clinical or experimental areas. In every instance in which the tester is tested, as in the studies just cited, the design of the experiment excludes the researcher himself, even though he may then use the results of his study to proclaim the universal applicability of the test instrument. One recent exception to this generalization gives us a hint of the chaos that might ensue if a critical eye were to be cast at clinical researchers themselves. I refer to the ingenious study by Levy and Orr (1959) in which, as you will recall, they compared the work of academic and nonacademic experimenters in terms of two criteria: whether their validity studies of the Rorschach emphasized construct validity (that is, a theoretical construct) or criterion validity (that is, the use of a practical criterion), and whether they found for or against the validity of the Rorschach. As we might have expected, Levy and Orr found significant relations between where a study was done and the kind of validity that it tested, as well as between the setting of a study and its outcome. Their conclusion, that "there *does* appear to exist a social psychology of research" (p. 82), may not surprise us, but perhaps it should begin to arouse our curiosity about the experimenter himself. Is he also amenable to study by means of experimental research?

Oddly enough, this question is never raised in textbooks on the experimental method in psychology. I do not mean that the experimental situation has never been logically explored, but rather that it does not seem to have been considered a psychological as well as a methodological problem. Osgood (1953), for example, has surprisingly little to say about the very method which is supposed to generate all the data that he discusses so well. Similarly, a recent important text by Sidman (1960), although it is entitled *Tactics of scientific research*, and although it deals with a number of "guideposts," as he calls them, for evaluating data, simply takes for granted the most obvious of the matters within its scope—the situation in which an experimenter gathers data from a human subject. Spence's (1960) recent collection of papers does not mention the topic, in spite of the fact that methodology is admittedly one of his major concerns. I know of nothing, in all the current literature on the experimental method, which offers anything more than does this cursory dismissal by Townsend (1953): "The main effect of a human being studying another human being is to introduce the probability for more errors to creep into the investigation" (p. 14).

We have come a long way from the *Handbook* of Murchison in 1934 to that of Stevens in 1951, but apparently not in respect to our understanding of the experimental situation. Our findings multiply alarmingly; our experimental designs become increasingly more sophisticated and complex; but beyond the purely methodological contributions of Brunswik and his pupils (Hammond, 1948; Brunswik, 1956, p. 131), and some cogent discussion of related issues by Coleman Griffith (1943, pp. 452–470), the experimenter himself, like the fabled legs of the Queen of Spain, remains a topic almost beyond the pale of informed discourse.

Some experimentalists, however, have by this time become concerned about the problem, especially in the light of a few scattered findings (Newman, Katz, and Rubenstein, 1960; Matarazzo, Saslow, and Pareis, 1960) which appear to cast doubt on even the most respectable of laboratory studies. F. J. McGuigan, in particular, both in a text on experimental psychology (1960) and in an APA symposium (1961), undertakes to analyze some of the issues. He notes that we have rarely tried to study the experimenter as an independent variable. Rather, we have looked on him as an "undesirable but necessary" influence on our dependent variables and have attempted to exorcise his influence by ever more stringent controls. McGuigan, on the other hand, begins by recognizing that the experimenter may well affect the results by virtue of his variability—that is, either because he demonstrates some relevant characteristic which is unique to him as one experimenter, or because of differences among experimenters on one or more relevant characteristics. In short, here is a totally unsuspected source of variance. McGuigan now proposes that this source be controlled by employing an even more elaborate factorial design "that allows us to vary Es—we should randomly sample from a population of Es and replicate the experiment for each E used" (1961). The immense complexity of such a program does not escape him, of course, and therefore he concludes by raising the question of whether there is not "a more efficient approach." His answer is worth pondering: "The only other possibility that occurs at present is to eliminate the E from the experiment. . . . For instance, a number of completely automated devices have been developed and successfully used in running rats—the Ss are never exposed to a human E. . . . At the human level , , , it seems reasonable to have S enter the experimental room and be directed completely by taped instructions, thus removing all visual cues, olfactory stimuli, etc., emitted by the E" (1961).

On logical grounds alone, one is tempted at first to agree with him. Given the choice between eliminating the experimenter and eliminating the subject, particularly in the face of such unsuspected issues as, in his delicate phrasing, olfactory stimuli emitted by E, the solution certainly seems obvious. But before taking this plunge into technological unemployment, may we not first consider the implications of our desperate situation as experimenters? For one thing, there is an appalling discrepancy here between an increasingly more sophisticated statistical methodology and a steadily more barren theoretical formulation. This widening gap, it is now proposed, is to be covered over by ever more complex arrangements of variables, factors, and levels. And indeed, it turns out to be precisely this contrived "complexity" which it now becomes the task of electronic computers to untangle for us. Thus do technological complications feed on methodological complexity, in an ever dizzier spiral. Undeniably, human performance *is* complex, but I would offer that its complexity may be of a special sort—not like that of a big clock as compared with a little clock, but perhaps rather like that of an organ as compared with a cell. It was out of recognition of just this kind of complexity that Martin Scheerer pleaded so often that we attend to the *how* and *why* of human performances, to the psychological conditions of failure and success on a task, and to an analysis of the task rather than to a mere tabulating of its end products (1946).

Consider, too, the fact that the dedicated experimentalist such as McGuigan has been brought to this extremity by the very logic of his own approach. It would perhaps be comforting to be able to argue that the fatal flaw in his procedure was discovered by an intuitive theorist who was bent on destroying a carefully built edifice of scientific accomplishment. But this is not so. Stated in its most general terms, the discovery is this: that some characteristic of E_1 which is determinable by E_2 is bound to affect the experimental results. Now, you will recognize E_2, I trust, even under this impersonal pseudonym. It is McGuigan himself. His new role, as E_2, is to carry out an experiment which is sufficiently complex in its design to include the variance produced by the behavior, as experimenters, of a representative sample of other Es. However, when the issue is stated in this way, an even more frightening possibility begins to emerge. As the study by Levy and Orr seems to show, do not the various E_2s themselves fall into discriminable categories? Just as there are academic Es who do construct validity studies of the Rorschach, as distinct from nonacademic Es who obtain better results with studies of criterion validity, may there not also be groups of E_2s whose complex factorial designs are in turn a function of their own work settings and predispositions? In principle there is no reason why this should not be so, for nothing at all has been changed in the logic of this kind of experiment except to make it more complex. Whatever flaw it contained originally, which led inevitably to the present unhappy situation in which McGuigan finds himself, is still there, hidden under bigger piles of IBM Accounting Punch paper but eventually to be revealed nonetheless. All that has been accomplished is to make each E into an experimentally manipulatable object who is in no essential way different from the Ss already familiar to us.

The question I now raise is whether this helps us in any way toward our goal of understanding the behavior of S as a meaningful performance; and as a corollary, whether there might be another way of looking at the matter which avoids the endless regress at the heart of the experimentalist's method. What is suggested immediately, when we pose the question in this way, is the method of choice of the clinician—for here, if anywhere, the clinician's approach differs from that of the experimentalist. Therapist and clinical examiner are alike in this respect, that they maintain their role integrity, as it were; although they are always bound up in a common situation with their clients or test subjects, they claim never to be reducible to the positions occupied by the latter. The examiner who administers a Rorschach is not himself being tested by this instrument; and there is no possibility of an even more complex kind of Rorschach which will test his testing—as, for example, a more complex factorial design might be devised as an experiment on experimenters. Of course, a tester might himself become a test subject at another time, or a therapist in training may himself be in treatment or might act in a quasi-patient role during a therapeutically-oriented supervisory session; but this says no more than that persons may play different roles at different times. The distinction has still to be made between the dedicated experimentalist, who appears to be reducible finally to just another subject—and whose experimenter is now reducible in exactly the same way, and so on and on—between this E of the experimental situation and the E of the clinical testing situation, who cannot ever resolve his difficulties by abdicating from his role.

This point has to be emphasized, I believe, because of the implications of a recent turn of events in experiments on the psychology of the experimental situation. A few years ago Binder and his colleagues (Binder, McConnell, and Sjoholm, 1957) studied the problem of the verbal conditioning of verbs of hostile meaning by using two "experimenters," one a small and very feminine girl and the other a large and very masculine man. The results showed a much faster rate of conditioning for the female E when the reinforcer was the word "good" each time that the S uttered a hostile verb, and the authors take this to be evidence that she provided a "less threatening environment" which made the subjects less inhibited. (Quite incidentally, I am bothered here by the suspicion that if the results had turned out the other way around—that is, if the female examiner had conditioned hostile verbs at a slower rate—an equally plausible explanation could have been offered, to the effect that subjects chose to act more gentlemanly in her presence. But these are the dangers that one runs when doing experiments in the total absence of theory.) In any case, it is significant, I believe, that these authors are by no means unaware of the implications of their work for other areas of psychological research. They discuss its relevance in regard to the problems faced by public opinion pollsters as well as by social scientists who do large-scale interviewing, and they refer to the parallels between their findings and those obtained in the clinical setting. Awareness of the "clinical" implications would indeed seem to be demanded by their results, for we can see that these are much like those obtained in experiments on the use of different examiners in a clinical testing situation (Lord, 1950; Gibby, 1952). In the latter type of study it was shown that the number of responses of a certain kind, such as hostile, also varied as a function of certain characteristics of the examiner. But I would remind you that in his study of verbal conditioning, Binder obtained these findings without the necessity of administering a projective test. Instead, the instrument that he used to elicit these diagnostically significant responses from his subjects was the least clinical, the most unambiguous phenomenon in all of psychology. It was that supposedly impregnable stronghold of the impersonal—the operant conditioning experiment.

Even more striking are the results obtained by Spires (1960), who studied the relation between subjects' MMPI scores and their reactions to an induced set toward the experimenter in a verbal conditioning experiment. As might be expected, subjects who score high on the Hy scale, and are given a positive set for the experimenter, condition significantly better than those who score high on the PT scale. A vast amount of clinical data supports this finding in indicating that the hysteroid dimension of personality functioning represents a particular susceptibility to positive support from figures of authority and power. Thus, the verbal conditioning experiment may turn out to be just the clinical instrument for which all of us have been searching: one which is sensitive yet powerful for diagnostic purposes, highly reliable and also capable of being subjected to quantitative treatment. I think you will agree that we have one of the most delicious of historical ironies—that in our current battle of the *Zeitgeist*, the operant conditioning enthusiasts should have gained victory in the clinical area by this totally unexpected flanking attack.

But this is only one reason that we should emphasize the relation between experimental and clinical findings on these problems. A more cogent reason may be found in the series of ingenious studies that have been carried out by Rosenthal (1959b, 1961; Rosenthal, Fode, Friedman and Vikan, 1960) on what he terms "experimenter bias." By this he means the tendency of a specific experimenter to elicit predictable kinds of responses from his subjects. His procedure—which is ideal for this purpose—is to have each of a number of students who are enrolled in a graduate course replicate an experiment with undergraduates as subjects. What these "experimenters" do not know, however, is that they are themselves serving as subjects in Rosenthal's experiment—or meta-experiment, as we might call it—by virtue of acting under a specific set induced by him: for example, that they will receive extra pay if their subjects make high "scores" on the test device used, or that their rats are especially bred for brightness or dullness, or that they will probably obtain a certain average score from their subjects. The results of Rosenthal's program of studies are uniformly striking. Experimenters tend to obtain significantly different sets of data from comparable groups of subjects; and this general result has been shown to be a function of, among other things, E's expectancy, his motivation, his knowledge of the results he is obtaining, the source of his hypothesis, the kinds of data he tends to give when he himself is a subject, and the way in which he is perceived by his subjects. Our first suspicion, of course, is simply that the student experimenters were dishonest; but Rosenthal assures us that this possibility may be ruled out. A second alternative is not so easily taken care of and may, in fact, account for the findings in many of the experiments with animals—that the experimental procedure was such that some leeway was allowed the person who gathered the data, for example, in how he handled the animals. It is extremely difficult to set up a procedure, especially one in which inexperienced students act as experimenters, in which complete control in these respects can be guaranteed.

However, neither of these alternatives, I would guess, will account fully for the impressive results obtained by Rosenthal in a wide range of studies, with experimenters and subjects of all kinds, and under a variety of experimental conditions and settings. The phenomenon of experimenter outcome-bias is, as he puts it, a general as well as a robust phenomenon. To understand it, I think we have to turn to the source of his original data on human subjects, in the task which was presented to them. Here is his description of the task: "Each E presented his individually run Ss with a standardized series of 10 photographs of faces and asked them to rate the degree of success or failure that the person pictured had been experiencing. Ratings of each photo were made orally by Ss on a rating scale that ran from −10 (extreme failure) to +10 (extreme success) and recorded by E. The mean rating of the set of photographs yielded by the standardization sample of 104 Ss was exactly zero" (Rosenthal, Fode, Friedman, and Vikan, 1960, pp. 325–326). Notice that the stimulus photographs have been deliberately chosen, first, so as to be "objectively" neither successful nor failing in their appearance, and second, so that in spite of this a subject will still be able to make a sensible judgment. Have we met this unique kind of stimulus material before? I think we have, for it has an honorable history in recent experimental psychology. Rosenthal's photographs conform completely to the requirements of the ambiguous stimulus in a projective test. Like the Rorschach blot or the TAT picture, or like the ambiguous profile used by Schafer and Murphy (1943) in their classic study of the influence of needs on perception, these photographs are objectively undefined yet may plausibly appear to the subject as definable. Indeed, their character as ambiguous stimuli —usable for familiar purposes of diagnosis when they are presented as a clinical test—was demonstrated by Rosenthal himself (1959a) in his initial use of the procedure successfully to distinguish paranoid schizophrenics from normals.

In direct contrast with this type of stimulus material, a true experimental situation requires that the subject be presented with something which is unequivocal. Bruner has stated the basic requirement very well: "It is of the essence in any given experiment that we define in advance what we as experimenters mean by relevant information and do not depend upon the subject's response to do it for us; otherwise we would be in a complete circle" (1951, p. 131). We have all seen the kind of stimulus situation which we cannot thus define in advance. Its use has given us an armamentarium of diagnostic instruments, and it has even enabled us to explore some of the varieties of preconscious and unconscious perception which seem to be active in the subject during the taking of a projective test. But I would question seriously whether it can properly be used to furnish the experimental data that we need for a social psychology of the laboratory experiment. In fact, Rosenthal seems to have less than perfect faith in his own approach, for he concludes one presentation (1961), just as did McGuigan, by suggesting a "major implication" of his findings: that "whenever possible, E eliminate himself and his surrogates from the experimental situation."

Here, perhaps, is our clue to a further understanding of the problems in this area. Implicit in the orientation of the writers that we have reviewed thus far is the premise that every confrontation of E and S somehow constitutes a methodological crisis. Should the crisis become acute, as it clearly does when E is shown to be a major source of variance, the only solution that can be conceived is to eliminate the experimenter and thus keep the subject chaste and uncontaminated. Such an extreme of interpersonal chastity may remind us of more familiar instances in which purity is rigidly preserved by an elaborate code; and like them, this instance merits our grudging respect even if not our wholehearted approval. But in any case it should serve to remind us that no other solution to the problem is available to psychologists who insist that there is nothing basically wrong with the laboratory experiment—or at least nothing wrong with it that a little more of the same thing won't cure. In part, their difficulties surely reside in the circumstance that they have been trying to arrive at some understanding of the experimental situation in the face of the fact that this situation is itself the source of whatever understanding they might gain in psychology. The difficulty, therefore, that experimentalists face is that on principle they are unable to subject the experiment to analysis. They have no way to test out their ideas except to construct another situation whose structure is just like the first. Thus, rather than develop a social psychology which will help them to understand the psychological experiment, they maintain that a social psychology still embedded in the psychological experiment will finally lead to a better psychology in general; and their position begins to be untenable as soon as they suspect the experiment itself as a source of data. They are in the unhappy position of having no cure but the hair of the dog that bit them.

While I would hardly deny the efficacy of this approach to cure in all areas of civilized activity, I would insist that a way out of our present dilemma in psychology is to be found only by stepping completely out of the experimental situation, so to speak. One should start by suspecting the orientation toward the psychologist's work which is embalmed in our current experimental methodology. But a suspiciousness which cuts this deep has not, so far as I am aware, appeared in a respectable psychological journal for at least thirty years (Rosenzweig, 1933). The followers of Titchener, who were, as the great man put it, interested in describing the world "with man left in," once waged a bitter-end fight against a behavioristic psychology which has since nearly overwhelmed us all. Bentley (1929), for example, insisted on a sharp distinction between the psychological *observer* and the experimentalist's *subject;* the observer's "functions of observation and report [were] complementary to those of the experimenter" (p. 683), whereas the subject was simply "put through [according to] the paradigm of the rat's maze or the freshman waiting line" (p. 682). Indeed, the quarrel over introspection as a method touched on precisely the issues that I have been discussing in this paper, and it might be most rewarding and enlightening to review the topic in this light today.

It would appear that an approach in psychology which never steps outside the constraining limits of the narrowly conceived experimental situation confronts only a dilemma in analyzing the psychological experiment. Perhaps, then, a cognitive theory, when it is defined as I have done at the opening of this paper, will give us the promise of some gain in understanding. Its own "test of significance," which always has reference to the meaningful act of the whole person, may have something to teach us about the experiment as a way in which two persons meet and play out the complex roles in their mutually rewarding drama. I should like to devote the time remaining to me today to a preliminary statement of this analysis, as it might take shape within cognitive theory. The faults you recognize, I can assure you, will be mine rather than those of my inspiration.

It is in the nature of an experiment that the felt purposes of its two participants, experimenter and subject, not be identical. An experiment occurs when the experimenter frames his idea in the form of a question, states it as a hypothesis, and then proceeds to test it out. There is certain information which he now requires in order to decide whether Nature is ordered in such a way as to support or refute his hypothesis. He does not have the information at his command, for if he did he would simply present an argument supported by evidence; nor is it a matter of public knowledge, for he would then only have to appeal to generally known facts. Not having the information, then, he proceeds to obtain it. In psychology—or at least in the brand of psychology I am considering here—one obtains information from people rather than from cloud chambers or chemical mixtures. But the way in which an experimenter gets his information from people is a little unusual. He does not, for example, go to them as though they were colleagues and ask factual questions; this is not the kind of information he is after.

Suppose that I find myself in a railroad station waiting for a train but I do not know the track on which it will arrive. I might now seek out certain persons in order to get the information I need. This, like the example of going to one's colleagues with a question of fact, also involves obtaining information from people —but clearly the situation of the passenger in the railroad station is not the same as that of the psychologist in his laboratory. Just how do they differ? I suggest that the difference must lie in the relation between questioner and questioned; and this in turn is tied to, and expressed through, the distinction between their purposes. When I ask a redcap in a railroad station for some train information, my purpose at this moment is to be sure of catching my train. If he is disposed to answer my question correctly, then to this extent his purpose is the same as mine: he too would like to make sure that I catch my train. Therefore he takes the trouble to answer as accurately as he knows how. If he did not have the same purpose as I do—if, for example, his purpose were actually to get rid of me as quickly as possible, or perhaps to make sure that I missed my train—then he might refuse to answer, or he might give me the wrong answer. Our relationship at this point, we now see, refers to a dual aspect of a single action, my portion of it requiring his resources in order to reach a goal of which both of us are aware. The two of us may be likened to the drivers of a pair of automobiles, the first with a stalled motor, the second one behind and pushing in the direction in which the first one chooses to go. Only if their directions of movement are the same, and only if both are aware of this, can the push be effective.

Compare this, now, with the situation which must exist in the case of an experiment. The experimenter, too, needs to go to appropriate sources for his information, for the validity of his findings will depend in large part on the size, the nature, and the representativeness of his sample. In this respect at least he is like the questioner in the railroad station—but here the similarity ends. The experimenter's purpose is to find out whether certain things are true about the very people whom he asks for information. His interest is in them; and the way he phrases his question is meant to help him achieve this goal. By contrast, the questioner in the railroad station has a primary interest in the answer he will receive and only a secondary interest in the person whom he questions. The experimenter needs a question in order to arrive at some goal in regard to his informants, whereas the traveler needs an informant in order to arrive at some goal in regard to his question.

Because of this fundamental difference, the experimenter can never express in his question the full truth concerning his purposes. There are two reasons for this. The first is that his goal does not reside in the question itself but is to be achieved on the basis of answers given only after his question is asked. The second reason is that the experimenter himself cannot know the full truth until he is in a position to say something about his subjects, and this he can do only on the basis of information gained by questioning them. The subtle but basic principle involved here is that the person who serves as a subject by supplying information in an experiment simultaneously fulfills two roles. One of these corresponds to his own deliberate and often explicit awareness of his purposes—that he is someone who has certain information which on request he will convey to another; and in this respect he resembles the redcap in the railroad station. But his other role is one which corresponds, to some degree, to the purposes of the experimenter—and in this role, which as subject he more or less unwittingly plays, he is not a possessor of information but rather someone who *represents* a kind of truth or *expresses* a kind of phenomenon. For this reason he need not play the latter role uniquely or individually, but as a representative who is in some measure interchangeable with any other subject in his group. When he plays this role in an experiment, he differs from the test subject, who is always questioned for himself alone; but he differs even more from the respondent who is asked a straightforward question in order to elicit some information.

There are two roles, then, which may be distinguished—the one in which the subject takes his stand as an informant, his behavior corresponding to that of the redcap; and the second in which he goes along with the experimenter's purposes. The success of any experiment will depend on the extent to which the experimenter is able to arrange that the subject's first role supports rather than impedes his second. For example, if the subject's awareness of his own purposes, in his "redcap" role, comes to include something of his second role—that is, if he becomes aware of the experimenter's purposes—he may be unable to support the latter but will interfere with him. Psychologists who use other psychologists as subjects usually discover that this sort of sophistication ruins their chances of obtaining valid results. In general, the subject who is more concerned with how he is doing than with the doing of it, or who attends more to the experimenter's aims than to his own task, will be a poor subject in spite of the most exemplary of motives to cooperate. His performance will tend to be contaminated by just the role factors which the structure of an experiment is aimed at suppressing.

An approach to understanding the psychological experiment as a "very special form of social interaction," which is close to what I am suggesting here, has recently been offered by Orne (1961). He too argues that "the experimental situation is one which takes place within the context of an explicit agreement of the subject to participate," and that "as far as the subject is able, he will behave in an experimental context in a manner designed to play the role of a good subject." Orne suggests that "the totality of cues which convey an experimental hypothesis to the subject" be called "the demand characteristics of an experimental situation," and he notes in particular that the most potent demand characteristics are those which "convey the purpose of the experiment effectively but not obviously"—or, as I have just put it, those which implement the subject's "redcap" role without making too explicit his role as codeterminer of the experimenter's purposes. While Orne has clearly recognized that the subject's total pattern of action should be understood as a self-chosen role, I would offer that the role he describes so well may be too simple. True, the experimental subject *is* engaged in cooperating with the experimenter, at times to a remarkable degree; yet his engagement, since it is a meaningful act, has been prompted by a kind of decision; and thus it is not pure but a compromise and a choice, as all meaningful decisions must be.

If we were to express the experimenter's aim in one sentence, it would be this: to get the subject to act as an agent in carrying out the purposes of the experiment. Now, it happens that there is one kind of person, familiar to all of us, whose role it is to carry out the aims of another person, deliberately subordinating his personal wishes yet without surrendering his initiative or freedom of action. This person is, of course, the servant. The experimenter keeps looking for the perfect servant—who will carry out the master's wishes with understanding and intelligence yet will not go beyond them; who will accede without obsequiousness and cooperate without being servile; who will be independent and unrestricted, yet neither negativistic nor resistive; and who will never cut through the entire master-servant relation, and thereby destroy it, by seeking to put himself in the master's place, for example, by trying to know as much about the experiment as does the experimenter himself.

You will recognize what I am proposing here—that in order to understand the situation that we know as the psychological experiment, we can do no better than to begin by analyzing the universally familiar relationship between master and servant.

There is its historical aspect, for example, and our study might note that the motor for this relation, what keeps it happening, is always some influence exerted on the servant by someone who has power over him, either through sheer force as in the case of the slave, or duty and obligation in the case of the medieval vassal, or tradition in the case of the old-fashioned servant, or finally money in modern times. By contrast, a person's own work is done out of a motive which has its psychological origin within him. Thus, influence is to serving as motivation is to acting—and on this thesis we might construct an authentic social psychology.

But we should also note that even in the extreme case in which one person accedes completely to the bidding of another and we then refer to him as abject or fawning, or in a word, "servile," the term describes his act rather than himself. When we say that a person is angry or selfish we mean that this word describes him totally—at least for the moment—and that this is what he *is;* but when we say that he is servile we imply just as strongly that this is what he *does* rather than what he is. Intrinsic to the meaning of the root *sirvo,* and to the conception itself, is the distinction between what a person is and what he does, between himself and his act. It is for just this reason that the role of the servant can be applied to the subject in an experimental situation, for as we noted above, the experimental situation is unique in that it requires that the person simultaneously adopt two roles—the one referring to what he *is* by virtue of his own motivation, and the other referring to what he *does* under the influence of another person.

The relation between experimenter and subject is as complex as that between master and servant—and occasionally also as productive of good works. It is a matter of delicate balance between influence and independence, and it is always in danger of being disrupted when one of the two finds himself too much aware of the motives or wishes of the other. Herein, I suspect, lies the root of so much of our difficulty in performing controlled experiments in social and clinical areas. Here, too, may be the reason that experiments with human subjects, if they produce truly meaningful performances, are so impossibly difficult to arrange; why the experimenter often learns as much from the doing of his experiment as from its results; and why the most useful addition to our armamentarium might be not a new procedure, but a social psychologist as observer of our actual experimenting. And here, finally, may be the reason that the true test case for the psychological experiment is the problem of malingering—that is, if we begin by defining the malingerer as the kind of subject who refuses to play the role of the servant and insists on parading in the master's clothes. It is a problem that welcomes analysis; but that is another topic, for another time.

REFERENCES

Alden, P., and Benton, A. L.   Relationship of sex of examiner to incidence of Rorschach responses with sexual content. *J. proj. Tech.*, 1951, *15*, 231–234.

Bentley, M.   "Observer" and "subject." *Amer. J. Psychol.*, 1929, *41*, 682–683.

Binder, A., McConnell, D., and Sjoholm, N. A.   Verbal conditioning as a function of experimenter characteristics. *J. abnorm. soc. Psychol.*, 1957, *55*, 309–314.

Bruner, J. S.   Personality dynamics and the process of perceiving. In R. R. Blake and G. Ramsey (eds.), *Perception, an approach to personality*. New York: Ronald, 1951. Pp. 121–147.

Brunswik, E.   *Perception and the representative design of psychological experiments*. Berkeley: Univ. of Calif. Press, 1956.

Brunswik, E.   Scope and aspects of the cognitive problem. In Colorado Univ., Psychology Dept. *Contemporary approaches to cognition*. Cambridge: Harvard Univ. Press, 1957. Pp. 5–31.

Campbell, D. T.   Social attitudes and other acquired behavioral dispositions. In Koch, S. (ed.) *Psychology: A study of a science*. Vol. 6. *Investigations of man as socius: their place in psychology and the social sciences*. New York: McGraw-Hill (1963).

Cronbach, L. J.   Response sets and test validity. *Educ. psychol. Measmt.*, 1946, *6*, 475–494.

Cronbach, L. J.   Further evidence on response sets and test design. *Educ. psychol. Measmt.*, 1950, *10*, 3–31.

Gibby, R. G.   Examiner influence on the Rorschach inquiry. *J. consult. Psychol.*, 1952, *16*, 449–455.

Gibby, R. G., Miller, D. R., and Walker, E. L. The examiner's influence on the Rorschach protocol. *J. consult. Psychol.*, 1953, *17*, 425–428.

Goldstein, K., and Scheerer, M. Abstract and concrete behavior: An experimental study with special tests. *Psychol. Monogr.*, 1941, *53* (Whole No. 239). Pp. 1–151.

Griffith, C. R. *Principles of systematic psychology*. Urbana: Univ. of Illinois Press, 1943.

Hammond, K. R. Subject and object sampling—a note. *Psychol. Bull.*, 1948, *45*, 530–533.

Heider, F. Trends in cognitive theory. In Colorado Univ., Dept. of Psychology, *Contemporary approaches to cognition*. Cambridge: Harvard Univ. Press, 1957. Pp. 201–210.

Holtzman, W. H. The examiner as a variable in the Draw-a-Person Test. *J. consult. Psychol.*, 1952, *16*, 145–148.

Levy, L. H., and Orr, T. B. The social psychology of Rorschach validity research. *J. abnorm. soc. Psychol.*, 1959, *58*, 79–83.

Lord, E. Experimentally induced variations in the Rorschach performance. *Psychol. Monogr.*, 1950, *64* (Whole No. 316).

Matarazzo, J. D., Saslow, G., and Pareis, E. N. Verbal conditioning of two response classes: Some methodological considerations. *J. abnorm. soc. Psychol.*, 1960, *61*, 190–206.

McGuigan, F. J. *Experimental psychology: A methodological approach*. Englewood Cliffs, N.J.: Prentice-Hall, 1960.

McGuigan, F. J. The experimenter—A neglected stimulus object. Paper presented at APA symposium, New York, Sept., 1961.

Murchison, C. (ed.). *Handbook of general experimental psychology*. Worcester: Clark Univ. Press, 1934.

Newman, R., Katz, J., and Rubenstein, R. The experimental situation as a determinant of hypnotic dreams. *Psychiatry*, 1960, *23*, 63–73.

Orne, M. T. On the social psychology of the psychological experiment. Paper presented at APA symposium, New York, Sept., 1961.

Osgood, C. E. *Method and theory in experimental psychology*. New York: Oxford Univ. Press, 1953.

Prentice, W. C. H. Some cognitive aspects of motivation. *Amer. Psychol.*, 1961, *16*, 503–511.

Rosenthal, R. Perception of success or failure in pictures of others. *J. clin. Psychol.*, 1959a, *15*, 216–217.

Rosenthal, R. Research in experimenter bias. Paper presented at APA symposium, 1959b.

Rosenthal, R. On the social psychology of the psychological experiment: with particular reference to experimenter bias. Paper presented at APA symposium, New York, 1961.

Rosenthal, R., Fode, K. L., Friedman, C. J., and Vikan, L. L. Subjects' perception of their experimenter under conditions of experimenter bias. *Percept. mot. Skills*, 1960, *11*, 325–331.

Rosenzweig, S. The experimental situation as a psychological problem. *Psychol. Rev.*, 1933, *40*, 337–354.

Sanders, R., and Cleveland, S. E. The relationship between certain examiner personality variables and subject's Rorschach scores. *J. proj. Tech.*, 1953, *17*, 34–50.

Schafer, R., and Murphy, G. The role of autism in visual figure-ground relationship. *J. exp. Psychol.*, 1943, *32*, 335–343.

Scheerer, M. Problems of performance analysis in the study of personality. *Ann. N.Y. Acad. Sciences*, 1946, *46*, 653–678.

Scheerer, M. Personality functioning and cognitive psychology. *J. Pers.*, 1953, *22*, 1–16.

Scheerer, M. Cognitive theory. In Lindzey, G. (ed.), *Handbook of social psychology*. Cambridge, Mass.: Addison-Wesley, 1954. Pp. 91–142.

Scheerer, M. Spheres of meaning: An analysis of stages from perception to abstract thinking. *J. indiv. Psychol.*, 1959, *15*, 50–61.

Scheerer, M., and Huling, M. D. Cognitive embeddedness in problem solving: A theoretical and experimental analysis. In *Perspectives in psychological theory*. New York: International Universities Press, 1960. Pp. 256–302.

Sidman, M. *Tactics of scientific research*. New York: Basic Books, 1960.

Spence, K. W. *Behavior theory and learning*. Englewood Cliffs, N.J.: Prentice-Hall, 1960.

Spires, A. M. Subject-experimenter interaction in verbal conditioning. Unpublished Ph.D. dissertation, New York University, 1960.

Stevens, S. S. (ed.) *Handbook of experimental psychology*. New York: Wiley, 1951.

Townsend, J. C. *Introduction to experimental method*. New York: McGraw-Hill, 1953.

TOWARD A COGNITIVE
THEORY OF ASSOCIATIVE
LEARNING

IRVIN ROCK and JOHN CERASO[1]

Yeshiva University

THE TOPIC OF HUMAN ASSOCIATIVE LEARNING, since the 1930's, has typically been treated within the context of S-R theory. Earlier workers in this area were associationists, but association theory ceased to exist as a point of view as various of its tenets were incorporated into behavior theory. Gestalt psychologists, although in possession of theoretical alternatives to S-R theory, were more concerned with perception on the one hand and higher mental processes on the other. In fact, Wertheimer viewed rote learning with a certain disdain in contrast to the more productive and creative processes involved in thinking. He did not want thinking to be reduced to the mere utilization of prior habits. In any case, although there was some work by the Gestaltists on associative learning, such as that of von Restorff and of Köhler, on the whole they neglected this territory. Those American psychologists who

[1] This paper is largely the result of collaboration of the two authors over several years of jointly teaching a course in memory and thinking at Yeshiva University. Although John Ceraso did not personally know Martin Scheerer, he was influenced by his thinking, largely through contact with colleagues and former students of Scheerer's.

This paper was supported by Research Grant M-3435, National Institute of Mental Health, Public Health Service, and Research Grant G-19538, National Science Foundation.

110

were influenced by Gestalt thinking, as for example Tolman, preferred to work on animal learning.

In this paper, we will direct our attention to the area of human associative learning and memory. We will try to make explicit the premises which we believe underlie a cognitive theory, at the same time examining the assumptions underlying S-R theory. In recent years there has been a growing interest in this area by cognitively oriented psychologists, but a succinct statement of various shared assumptions seems to be lacking.[2]

We will deliberately avoid discussion of the higher mental processes—i.e. understanding, concept formation, thinking, and problem solving—because, unlike Wertheimer, we believe these processes can only be understood in the long run when we have a better understanding of certain more fundamental processes. This is not to say that the laws of thinking will prove to be derivable from the laws of associative learning and memory. But it seems advisable to start with processes which appear to be simpler and more readily isolable. To some extent at least, thinking involves the utilization of previously established associations. Of course, the converse is sometimes true; namely, higher mental processes are involved in associative learning. For example, a subject may employ deliberate strategies in learning a list or he may creatively invent mnemonic devices. Hence there is the danger of believing we have isolated a simple process when, in reality, we have not.

The cognitive position we will outline is *not* meant to be an extension of Gestalt theory although it derives some of its fundamental notions from this school of thought. Rather, our point of departure is the simple fact that there are *mental* events whose relationship to one another can be studied. The mental events with which cognitive theory is concerned are perceptual, ideational, or memorial. The task of a theory of human learning and memory is to explain how experienced contents became associated and how they are recalled or, if not, why they are forgotten. A

[2] We have in mind thinkers such as Köhler, Koffka, Scheerer, Asch, Wallach, and Henle, all of whom have very much influenced our own ideas as expressed in this paper. During 1961–1962 we have been meeting regularly with Solomon E. Asch and Sheldon Ebenholtz. At these meetings many of the ideas presented here were discussed.

central feature of cognitive theory is the construct of a representational memory trace. This memory trace is conceived of as the
product of learning, and serves as the basis of memory. The
memory trace is taken to be representational in the sense that
activation of a trace corresponding to a prior experience will give
rise to a new experience similar to that prior experience. The
reason why any adjective is needed in front of the word "theory"
in the title of this paper can only be understood by contrast with
what S-R theory tries to do in the area of verbal learning. S-R
theory follows the conditioning paradigm of stimulus-response
connections. Learning an association therefore means learning a
response to a stimulus. Forgetting means failure to make the response, given the stimulus. Innocent as this may sound, it is really
quite loaded with implications as to how various facts are treated,
and even what kinds of facts can be treated. For example, such a
theory does not account for the *experience* of familiarity which
underlies recognition, unless *experience* is considered a response.
S-R theorists do speak of the recognition response, but this is a
liberty they are taking. It sounds as if they are then treating the
facts concerning recognition. However, the crucial fact is not that
a subject *says* "I recognize this" but that he says this because he
experiences the object as familiar. It is the issue of whether we are
interested in the experience per se or the verbal report. We do not
think this issue can or should be avoided here any more than
elsewhere. (S-R theory has difficulty with recognition for reasons
other than the one mentioned and we will return to this point
later.)

Another fact that is not adequately treated by S-R theory is
memory in the sense of recall of prior experience, which is probably the way the term is most often used in everyday discourse.
Reiff and Scheerer (1959) have called this type of recall *remembrance*. After an evening at the theater watching an absorbing
play, one often finds that incidents from the play keep coming to
mind. To say that such recall is the making of the same responses
as one made while watching the play is a violation of language;
a response is an event of a different category than an experience.
On the other hand, if an experience is assumed to depend upon

some cortical event, then the remembrance of that experience should also depend upon some cortical event, such as the activation of a memory trace. Another example of remembrance would be the recall of a face. Even if we translate our example into the experimental task of requiring the subject to draw the face (response) upon hearing the associated name (stimulus), would we equate the drawing with the memory? The point is that the memory is of a prior *perception*. It therefore shares some of the characteristics of the perception—for example, it has spatial character—we may see the face in imagination. But if the prior perception is called a response, the very nature of the phenomenon we should be dealing with is distorted from the outset. It is of course true that focusing on the perceptual side of memory leaves unexplained the mechanism by which the correct response can be emitted. Nevertheless it seems to us that the response question is a separate one which need not be tackled simultaneously with perceptual or associative questions. Besides, S-R theory, paradoxically enough, does not explain the response. Rather it assumes response as what is learned and tells us no more about it.

Our intent in using the word "cognitive" is to do justice to the experiential aspects of learning and recall. If we do not give it any other surplus meaning (as, for example, notions about parts and wholes, emergentism, or the like) our meaning is approximately the same as that of classical association theory. Thinkers such as Locke, Hume, Titchener, and James were concerned with the association and recall of ideas. It is only the displacement of association theory by behavior theory that makes it necessary at this time to point up certain of its features that have been prematurely cast aside.

There are, however, certain differences in approach from classical association theory we would advocate. Many thinkers in the associationist tradition were concerned with the problem of connecting up two distinct units through experience (the successive association) and also with the fusing of certain elements into units through experience (the so-called compound or simultaneous association). We are not concerned with this second problem here for several reasons. For one thing, Gestalt psychology has taught us that many perceptual units do not have to be built up through prior experience, but are given on the basis of autochthonous organizing principles. For another, even if such units do have to be achieved, problems of associative *learning* begin only after the person perceives an organized world of segregated figures. In this sense it is irrelevant whether the units are given at birth or only through learning. A second difference from classical association theory is that more weight should be given to explanatory constructs than to purely descriptive laws. It is fundamental to the approach taken here that the construct of the memory trace be developed so that it does justice to the experience and behavior that accompany learning and memory.

ITEM LEARNING

The minimum assumption is that each perceived unit leaves behind a unit trace. Perceiving even a single unit, therefore, is a form of learning—in fact, a very typical form of learning. It entails no associative process—merely perception. As long as a trace is preserved, the possibility exists for the item to be recognized or recalled.

Recognition of a single item that has previously been perceived is obviously some function of that item as a stimulus making contact with its trace. Basically, recognition involves an experience of familiarity accompanying the perceived stimulus and this experience may or may not be communicated by an appropriate response. Since this can easily be achieved despite changed location or other transposition of the proximal stimulus, and therefore of its projection in the nervous system, the basis of contact with the trace would seem to be similarity—i.e., the similarity of the stimulus to the trace of the earlier stimulus. This point has been discussed by Köhler and others in various places and need not be amplified further here. (See a recent discussion of this problem by Rock, 1962). Suffice it to say that recognition generally occurs effortlessly and successfully. One prior exposure—even incidental

—will generally lead to correct recognition unless the recognition task deliberately requires a fine discrimination. But even in the latter case recognition may be excellent. Recognition can be used as an index of the presence of and condition of a trace at any interval following initial exposure.[3] In a study by Rock and Engelstein (1959) subjects were briefly shown a nonsense shape under instructions which precluded any attempt to try to memorize it. When (unexpectedly) tested even after a one-month interval, they demonstrated that they could successfully discriminate that shape from other quite similar shapes. From this we can conclude that (1) learning of a single unitary item occurs from mere perception, (2) a trace veridical to the percept is left behind, (3) it endures with little or no change over a long time period (thus incidentally throwing more cold water on the early Gestalt idea of autonomously changing memory traces), and (4) the trace can be activated in some way when the stimulus is re-presented and in this way can mediate recognition and correct discrimination.

How does S-R theory deal with single-item learning? In recent years more and more attention has been paid to item learning. That is, it has been recognized that there are two aspects to the learning of lists: the learning of the items per se and the formation of associations between them. But not much attention has been paid to the theoretical difficulties involved in the postulation of item learning by S-R theory. In some way it must be reduced to the learning of stimulus-response connections. Where the item is a nonsense syllable composed of letters, it can be argued that such connections must be formed. However, suppose the items are nonsense figures rather than syllables. Few today would argue that any associative process is entailed in perceiving a figure as a single unit, at least for adult subjects. Hence it would seem inescapable that, with some material, item learning consists of

[3] It is true that the difficulty of the recognition test can be affected by certain factors, such as the similarity of the critical figure to the noncritical figures at the time of test. We do not regard this as invalidating recognition as an index of the state of the trace. If recognition scores decrease when a fine discrimination is required we would take this as indicating that those aspects of the stimulus necessary to make the fine discrimination are not preserved in the trace.

nothing more than perception plus preservation of what is perceived in the form of a trace.

Quite apart from the question of the *learning* of single items, S-R theorists apparently accept the recognition test as a measure of the prior learning and retention of items. When a subject selects the correct item, it is said he is making a "recognition response." It is not clear what "recognition response" implies in S-R theory. Is it a response associated with the item? This would imply that, in learning, the subject associates each item with the response "I recognize this." Otherwise how can we explain his making a response he never associated with that item? It may be argued that the recognition response refers to some implicit response which the subject makes to any member of the class of familiar objects. What, however, is the internal stimulus which enables S to know this is a familiar object? This internal stimulus would be very similar to what we call the experience of familiarity.

For both S-R and cognitive theory there is a problem in explaining free recall where learning did not consist of forming specific associations and where, therefore, the responses are not triggered by a specific stimulus. For cognitive theory the question of how the trace of a single item would be activated or aroused in the case of recall is a problem, where learning did not consist of forming specific associations. In free recall the subject remembers various items in seemingly random fashion and the evidence is against the idea that the order of recall in free recall is based on specific associations among the learned items. (This is the problem Asch discusses in his article in this volume.)

This would have been all we would have had to say about single-item learning, were it not for the fact that Asch has recently raised a question that apparently no one ever thought about before (Asch, Ceraso, and Heimer, 1960). Suppose there are distinguishable aspects of a single unit—as for example its shape and its color or its shape and the nature of the contour line. Can one talk about associating these aspects or is this item learning by mere perception? In one of Asch's experiments, subjects were asked to associate color with shape when the shape was shown *in* a given color; and, by way of contrast, other subjects had to learn when these were presented as perceptually distinct—for example, the colorless shape on the left and a patch of color on the right.

Asch's results showed that the connection in memory between the shape and color was far easier to make when the stimuli were presented as part of a unit than when presented as distinct units. Also, errors of confusion were rare when the former unitary presentation was used. These results were also true for other types of material. Differences in association between items which are parts of units and items which are separate units are so large that the question arises as to whether a different process may not be involved in each case. It is quite possible that the learning that goes on in the case of a unit such as a nonsense syllable is a case of the first type.[4] The ultimate clarification of item learning may, therefore, depend upon the further exploration of this question.[5]

ASSOCIATIVE LEARNING

So much for item learning or single-trace formation. Where associative learning is involved we may assume there are two (or of course more than two) units perceived, both of which leave traces, and, in addition, some kind of unification of the two items is achieved. The unification would have to be preserved in memory, so that we would have to speak of a trace connection. The unification that occurs is *not* one in which a new whole dissolves the identity of the parts. It must be a unification in which

[4] Whether a nonsense syllable is such a unit is open to question because it consists of separate letters. It is only a unit because it is pronounceable as one syllable and because we have learned to regard an array of letters placed together and pronounceable as a single word. Although nonsense *figures* might be preferable as units, theoretically speaking, they require drawings as responses. For reasons of convenience, therefore, the use of nonsense syllables can be justified, but we should be mindful of what we are doing and its possible theoretical implications.

[5] The problem Asch raises may be interpreted as bearing on the question of the compound or simultaneous association. However, it refers to cases where there are clearly distinguishable subparts or aspects of the unit.

the parts preserve their identity. Otherwise it would not be possible to recognize either item alone later and, in addition, to respond with the other item.

However, the question of an association is complicated. Suppose a person encounters only two items, as when he is introduced to someone. Let us consider one item the first name and the other the second name. The next day he is asked to recall the person's second name when given the first. Success in this task does not conclusively establish that a unification of the items was necessary during the initial encounter and hence that a trace connection was established. It is possible to argue that two distinct items were learned, having been perceived, and that each can be recalled separately (in the sense of free recall as discussed by Asch). Of course it is true that each item would have to be considered to be associated with the same situation, or else why would the correct second name be emitted at all? (Traces of many other names exist in our subject's nervous system.) But "association with the situation" is a general and somewhat vague notion and is different from a specific association between two items.

Contrast this situation with one in which the subject must learn a list of paired associates. Here all items may be associated with the situation, but that will not suffice for successful performance. If pairs A-B, C-D, E-F, etc., are learned, the subject must connect A with B and *not* D or F, etc. There is thus no question in this case that specific trace connections must be established. Perhaps, therefore, it is desirable to speak of a simple association in the first case and a discriminative association in the second case. The discriminative association is conceptually clearer, but it does not follow that our selection of the multiple-pair paradigm for all laboratory experimentation is most representative of the typical case in daily life. The simple association may be the more representative and may entail entirely different processes or mechanisms.

As far as simple association is concerned, a recent experiment suggests that it is established effortlessly, on one exposure as a matter of fact, even under conditions of incidental learning (Deich, 1961). Virtually all subjects can respond with a second nonsense syllable when presented with the first, 10 minutes after being exposed to the two together. Eighty percent can do so even after an interval of one week. Beyond contiguity, it is difficult to see what other principle of learning is necessary in such a case. Perception of two units seems to lead easily to traces of each being established and each connected with some trace representation of the situation-as-a-whole.

Discriminative associations are obviously not established easily, judging by the fact that many trials are required to master a list of pairs and also by the fact that intentional learning is virtually required if the entire list is ever to be learned. Unlike the case of a simple association, contiguity is no longer a sufficient condition although of course it remains a necessary one. The insufficiency of the principle of contiguity represents another difference between classical association theory and contemporary cognitive theory. The early experiments by Woodworth, Thorndike, and others show very clearly that although C may follow B at about the same interval that B follows A, it will rarely be associated with B if the subject understands his task as one of learning pairs. C *belongs* with D, not with B. Similarly the classical work of Müller and Schumann shows the importance of rhythmical grouping. In other words, with multiple items the subject tries to form particular units, to get straight what goes with what. Something like collective attention to the items to be associated with one another seems to be required. This step is not required in the case of simple associations. The subject probably soon learns all the items and identifies them with the particular learning task. He probably also quickly learns which are "stimulus" and which are "response" terms, but the connecting up of each stimulus term with only one response term is the difficulty. Miniature illustrations of this phenomenon are the cases in daily life where one learns several items in the same context as, for example, the two terms abscissa-ordinate and the two directions of the intersecting lines. One easily learns the amalgam of four components, i.e., the two words and the two directions, but one has incessant trouble with which word goes with which direction. Stalagmite and stalactite are generally confused with one another as to which hangs down and which rests on the ground. It would be easy to give many other examples of this type.

An interesting illustration of easily achieved discriminative association based on easily achieved belongingness is the case of pairs of meaningful words. Even though the pairs are selected so that the items are as unrelated as possible—for example, shoe-lake —it is particularly easy to learn such a list. We would agree with Köhler's hypothesis (1947) that pairings of this kind readily lend themselves to unitary groupings because the two items can be combined in imagination into a single conceptual unit, so to speak. Thus, for example, one can imagine a shoe floating in a lake. The learning of such a list is particularly easy because shoe is now specifically linked to lake rather than to any other item in the list. Recent experiments have supported this interpretation (Epstein, Rock, and Zuckerman, 1960). Pairs of nouns were shown to be easier to learn than pairs of conjunctions or prepositions. Although the latter are equally familiar, they do not possess the kind of representational meaning that would allow for combination into conceptual units. Noun pairs were also easier to associate than pairs composed of items which would have been often experienced contiguously in the learner's past—for example, pairs such as are-not or that-this. Hence transfer theories cannot account for the superiority of noun pairs (see Epstein, Rock, Zuckerman for a discussion of possible alternative explanations of these findings). Other evidence supporting Köhler's hypothesis was obtained which space limitations prevent us from discussing at this time.

It seems to us that intentional learning is required in learning lists not because the items would not be learned without it but *discriminative* associations would not easily be formed. The intention probably gives rise to specific groupings, sometimes via mnemonic devices, and it is the groupings that are crucial. Certain strategies may be employed in trying to achieve these groupings and they differ from subject to subject. There has been much confusion over the intentional-incidental distinction in verbal learning. Intention has generally been made synonymous with reinforcement, and the lack of it with nonreinforcement. Actually reinforcement is not the issue at all in the typical paradigm. In the method of anticipation it is true that when the subject anticipates the correct response for the first time, its appearance a moment later is probably gratifying (and certainly informative), but his ability to anticipate it suggests it may have been learned on the prior trial when the response was wrong. This is all the more plausible because individual associations often remain correct once they are anticipated correctly on a given trial. In other words, they may be learned already on the trial prior to the first reinforcement and thus could not be said to build up gradually via reinforcement. The same point is even clearer using a method of trial and test, i.e., all pairs exposed for learning on one trial and all pairs tested on a subsequent trial by showing only the left-hand member of each. In this method it is clear there is no reinforcement at all during the learning trial; the subject is merely exposed to each pair and he tries to learn it. He will not test himself out until the test trial and if he gets a pair right on the test it is because he learned it on the learning trial. In short, verbal learning generally requires intention, not reinforcement. Intention may be a type of motivation, but motivation is not synonymous with reinforcement. The intention seems to be important for achieving the necessary grouping.[6]

[6] In addition to the difficulty mentioned above, there are further problems in even defining the reinforcer in most verbal learning experiments. If the subject learns paired associates by the anticipation method, it seems absurd to say that, e.g., GAX is a reinforcer. As Meehl (1950) has argued, the circularity of effect can be broken by showing that the stimulus is a trans-situational reinforcer. GAX, however, can only reinforce one response, and that is "GAX." One could argue that GAX is not by itself the reinforcer; it only becomes a reinforcer when it is preceded by the subject uttering "GAX." The subject experiences a sense of gratification when he realizes the response he uttered is the correct one. This interpretation of reinforcement would, of course, depart very far from the usual notion of a reinforcer as a stimulus which the experimenter can manipulate, and whose effect is "automatic," i.e., not dependent on how the subject interprets his task or what he is doing.

In passing, it might be well to mention that although we believe grouping, organization, or something like belongingness to be important in forming discriminative associations, this does not imply acceptance of Köhler's recent attempt (1941) to explain such grouping on the basis of the Gestalt prin-

Perhaps this is the time to take up the even more fundamental question about what is being associated in the typical experiment. The S-R theorists speak of the left-hand member of a pair as the stimulus and the right-hand one as the response, in the case of paired associates. These are convenient names, but more than convenience is involved. Only if this designation is correct can S-R theory hope to apply principles of conditioning to verbal learning. The designation is rather seductive because in the method of anticipation, for example, the left-hand member appears as a stimulus and the subject must produce the right-hand member as a response. Yet before he can make the correct response, his learning hinges on associating the two items, both of which are *stimuli*. This point is even clearer in the case of the method of trial and test described above. No response at all need be made during the learning presentation. One might argue that the subject makes an implicit response to each item in the case of verbal material, but suppose the items are both nonsense figures? How could either be called a response? The most unbiased description of the verbal learning procedure, it seems to us, is that one is presenting the learner with *stimuli*. That the learner generally communicates or indicates his learning by responding with the right-hand item, given the left-hand item, is merely a function of the task we impose. It is a fact of performance, not of learning per se.

The existence of backward associations shows that to a considerable extent the so-called stimulus item can be given as a response and the so-called response item can serve as a stimulus. If stimulus and response were rigorously defined here, such backward associations would be logically impossible. In conditioning, it would make no sense to ask whether leg withdrawal would lead to the response of buzzer, once the former had been condi-

---

ciples of perceptual organization. We agree with Postman and Riley (1957) that the similarity between nonsense syllables (in contrast to nonsense syllables vs. numbers or nonsense figures) is not perceptual but categorical. Hence it is difficult to see how perceptual similarity can be invoked as a factor in the learning of verbal material. Other principles of perceptual grouping are even less readily applied to the typical instances of verbal associative learning in daily life or in experiments.

tioned to the latter. By definition, buzzer cannot be a response. Even if we transform it into "hearing" an auditory image, this is an experience, not a response. Also, leg withdrawal cannot be a stimulus. If we transform leg withdrawal into kinesthetic feedback of the withdrawal response this involves changing the original meaning of what was learned. Yet in verbal learning it *does* make sense to ask about backward association because the items are really both stimuli. All "backward association" means in this case is responding with what was the left-hand stimulus when presented with what was the right-hand stimulus. The only question remaining is why this is not as successful as is the forward type of response. Recent findings of Asch and Ebenholtz (1962) suggest that it may be an artifact of the manner in which paired associates are learned. During learning, the subject must be able to produce the right-hand member, whereas the left-hand member is always given. Hence the left-hand member need not be learned as well. That is why so-called backward associations seem to be weaker.

Relevant to this issue is the use of matching as a test of association. There are various ways of conducting such a test; but to illustrate, suppose the subject is given all the left-hand items in a column in random order and all the right-hand items in a second column, also in random order. The subject has to match up the items in the two columns. Many school tests employ this technique, but its theoretical significance has been overlooked. It obviously makes little sense to speak of stimulus and response in such a test since all that these terms could refer to now is left and right position. Success on this test is generally greater than in the case of aided recall. Often a subject will succeed in matching where he would have drawn a blank in aided recall. Everyone has had similar experiences in daily life, where, unable to recall, he can pick out the answer if supplied with a few alternatives. Matching seems to test recognition of an association, and correct performance would seem to rest on the existence of the correct trace connection in the nervous system. Since success on a matching test establishes the existence of an association, it argues against the frequently heard operational definition of an association based on response with the second item when the first is presented.

The view that the association is between stimulus and response has led to a particular way of interpreting transfer of training. It would follow that if a stimulus-response connection is formed, and a subject is then required to learn a new response to the earlier stimulus, there will be difficulty or negative transfer in the new learning, since new and old responses will compete. If, on the other hand, the new task involves giving the old response to a new stimulus, then no competition will occur since the stimulus does not bring forth a competing response; or if the new stimulus resembles the old, then there will be facilitation in learning the new association since the new stimulus already has some capacity to produce the response. It, therefore, would follow from the S-R approach that learning an old response to a new stimulus would be easier than learning a new response to an old stimulus. In point of fact, results of many transfer experiments do seem to support these predictions (summarized in the Osgood surface, 1949).

If, however, one views the association as entailing a connection between two *stimuli*, the transfer phenomena may be viewed somewhat differently. Since two stimuli are of equal status, it might be expected that the utilization of *either* of these items in a new association would lead to difficulty in learning that association. This expectation, known as the Müller-Schumann law (1894), is now generally believed to be invalid because of the asymmetry of the transfer outcome depending on whether the stimulus or response is the new term, as mentioned above. This asymmetry, however, may not be related to the different functions of stimulus and response terms, as S-R theory would hold, but to another fact. An unpublished experiment by Sheffield (1946) indicates that prior familiarization with response members helps more than prior familiarization with stimulus members in the later learning of paired associates.[7] These findings could explain the asymmetry of the transfer data in keeping with the Müller-Schumann hypothesis. Learning an old response to a new stimulus may be

[7] A possible explanation of why this is the case is offered later in the paper.

easier than learning a new response to an old stimulus because in the former case the *response* item remains in and is familiar, whereas in the latter case the *stimulus* item remains in and is familiar. Furthermore, the response member is probably all the more familiar because, as we pointed out in discussing backward associations, it is better learned than the stimulus member. In other words, we propose two principles to explain the findings summarized in the Osgood surface: (1) All transfer involving the need to learn an association where one of its members was previously associated with a different item is negative (Müller-Schumann law) and equally so, regardless of which member. (2) Familiarization with either item in the transfer test based on prior learning may be helpful, but much more so for the response item. There is some evidence to support this interpretation and studies are now under way at Yeshiva University in which the two transfer paradigms will be compared when item familiarization is controlled. Under these conditions we would expect the Müller-Schumann law to hold; i.e., we would no longer expect the asymmetry but rather equal interference in both cases.[8]

To return to the question of the difficulty of learning a list of paired associates, we have offered one explanation relating to the presence of the several items which logically requires discriminative associations and which otherwise would not be necessary. There are, however, other possible factors at work. The material which is exposed subsequent to any given pair prior to the end of the list may act as an anticonsolidation or antirehearsal factor. Peterson and Peterson (1959), and more recently Murdock

[8] After this discussion we can now view the question of reinforcement in verbal learning in a new light. If the task consists of associating two stimuli (or, better, two perceived units) does it make sense to speak of reinforcement? Behavior or response can be reinforced, but it is dubious if it is plausible in this context to speak of reinforcing the experiencing of two contiguous stimuli. Hence if learning can be distinguished from performance in verbal learning, as many feel it can be in animal learning, and if such learning involves the establishing of traces and connections among traces, then it is not plausible to expect reinforcement to be a factor. Certainly in the case of single-item learning, where there is no question at all of forming associations, nothing more is involved than perception plus preservation of the perception by a trace.

(1961), have shown that merely requiring a subject to count backwards during the few seconds between exposure of an item and test for that item will produce substantial forgetting. We have recently performed this experiment using pairs of nonsense syllables and obtained a similar effect. A third possible factor is that the many pairs could also have a detrimental effect on the availability of the items for recall. That is to say, the subject may be unable to bring to mind a particular response item when needed. He could recognize it as correct in a matching test but fail to produce it in the usual aided recall test. Why the presence of the multiple pairs should have such an effect is not clear. It is different from the deleterious effect of crowding thought to exist by von Restorff, because the integrity or individuality of the trace is not lost; the item would be recognized and discriminated from other items. It merely cannot be evoked at a certain time. Trace *a* fails to redintegrate *b* for some reason.

These speculations concerning the causes of intraserial interference can be contrasted with the prevailing S-R theory originally suggested by Eleanor Gibson. According to this hypothesis, the difficulty is caused by stimulus generalization. The stimuli of all pairs are said to be similar to one another, presumably because they are all nonsense syllables. As a result there will be a tendency to respond not only to A with B but also to C or E with B. With practice the stimuli are said to become differentiated so that C or E will no longer elicit B. This theory is saying something quite different than the point we have made about the need to form discriminative associations. In the S-R hypothesis the correct specific associations (presumably still subthreshold) are formed between all pairs but are generalizing between pairs. Our contention, on the other hand, is that discriminate or specific associations are not formed at all at the beginning except perhaps for one or two pairs. (This point will be clarified shortly when we come to the question of all-or-none vs. incremental learning.) Also we do not hold that the stimulus items are necessarily undifferentiated. Nonsense syllables are generally not chosen to be very similar to one another.

What S-R theorists mean by stimulus differentiation is not clear.

If they mean merely that subjects no longer give the wrong responses to stimuli, this is not an explanation but a statement of fact. To use it as explanation of the fact would be completely circular. Learning, according to this meaning of stimulus differentiation, implies the attaining of sufficient strength of the correct over and against the incorrect association, but has no implications about differentiation of the stimulus as such. If they mean that the *stimuli* become differentiated over time—where initially they were not—this presumably refers to a perceptual change. We would have to hear more about the mechanism for such a change (if it exists). But in any case the empirical evidence seems to go against this hypothesis. In the unpublished study by Sheffield mentioned earlier, the subjects learned paired associates when either the stimulus items had previously been familiarized or the response items had previously been familiarized. Prefamiliarization of items certainly serves to differentiate them from one another. Yet Sheffield found there was no gain from stimulus familiarization as compared to no such familiarization. Paradoxically, there was a gain from response differentiation.[9] The latter could be understood as improving the availability of the response items; i.e., being very familiar they are more easily evoked, they are less vulnerable to the depressing effect that multiple pairs have on availability of a response.

The attempt to derive verbal learning from a conditioning paradigm presupposes the gradual strengthening of an association by repeated reinforcement. We have questioned the assumption that what is learned is the connecting of a response to a stimulus. We have questioned the applicability of reinforcement to verbal learning. It remains to point out that the *gradual* nature of the acquisition of an association (as presumed in conditioning) has recently been called into question. Evidence has been presented which suggests that associations are formed on a single trial (Rock, 1957; Rock and Heimer, 1959). To be sure, these findings have been challenged and the final verdict on this question is

[9] We would hold that even following stimulus and response differentiation the difficulty based on the need to form discriminative associations would still be present.

not yet in. That is to say, the claim that there is no incremental build-up at all in the formation of an association could prove to be incorrect. Nevertheless, the work in this area does make amply clear that to a very considerable extent associations even between nonsense syllables are formed on one trial, and this fact was not clearly understood in the past. It cannot be a point of dispute that subjects given no opportunity to see pairs more than once (by using the substitution procedure) will nevertheless learn an entire list in a reasonably small number of trials. Gibson's notion of stimulus generalization is predicated on the assumption that on every trial associations between all stimulus-response pairs are formed—or else how could they generalize? Since, however, only few pairs are gotten right at the outset, the remaining associations must be subthreshold according to this view. It is difficult to see how such a theory could accommodate itself to the finding that associations are formed on a given trial, i.e., without prior incremental growth. If no subthreshold connection is established between A and B, certainly no subthreshold generalized association can be formed between A and any other response item. Although already-formed, above-threshold associations could generalize, at the beginning, when none or few associations are formed, generalization should be at a minimum. Yet this is precisely the time when generalization is thought to be most disturbing.

On the other hand, although a cognitive theory does not necessarily require association on a single trial, it is certainly highly compatible with it. The unification of two perceived units on the basis of some form of grouping might well be expected to be achieved at a given time on an all-or-none basis, rather than gradually. The failure to achieve such a unification for *all* pairs on a given trial would account for the need for many trials to master the entire list. The difficulty in achieving unification of all pairs on one trial would then have to be understood in terms of factors such as those mentioned above, namely, the need for discriminative association of all pairs, anticonsolidation or restricted rehearsal which prevents retention of much of the material, and impaired availability of items for recall. One final thought on this topic: If associations are formed on a single trial, the negatively accelerated curve of acquisition cannot be explained in terms of the diminishing incremental growth of habit strength as Hull has suggested. The rate of all-or-none association formation may decline over trials for any number of reasons as, for example, the fact that the more difficult pairs are left on the later trials.

SERIAL LEARNING

In all our examples thus far we have referred to the paired-associates paradigm. What can be said about the serial-learning paradigm with which Ebbinghaus launched experimental work on human learning? S-R theorists have assumed that serial learning is based upon a chain of stimulus-responses units in which all items but the first and last are at once responses to the previous item and stimuli for the next item. Major interest has centered around the ease of learning items in the different positions in the list. Plotting errors against serial position yields a bow-shaped curve, reflecting the earlier learning of the beginning and end of the list. The bow-shaped curve has been interpreted in terms of the presence of remote associations and inhibitory tendencies directed against the remote associations being elicited prematurely. Remote association refers to a connection between items which are separated by other items. Ebbinghaus discovered this phenomenon when he showed there was a savings in learning derived lists, lists made up by some systematic transformation of the original list—for example, arranging the new list by selecting every third item in order from the original list. Learning this derived list showed a savings in comparison to a new list and it was easier to learn it than one derived by skipping every four or every five items.

Lepley (1934) later suggested that remote associations could be explained in terms of trace conditioning. Pavlov had found that conditioned responses could be established which would occur only after some interval had elapsed following a stimulus. Presumably some inhibitory factor is at work during the interval that prevents the response from occurring prematurely; Pavlov called it inhibition of delay. If such an inhibitory factor were operating during serial learning it would be present throughout the series because at each point some remote association would be under inhibition. However, Hull *et al.* (1940) pointed out there would be more such inhibition in the center of the list. At that position each of the prior items has remote associations with each of the subsequent items and there are many such combinations. The inhibition presumably summates and opposes the excitatory strength of the immediate association which is the correct response at a given point. Hence learning the middle of the list is poorest because it has to work against maximum inhibition.

There are many difficulties with this interpretation. In the first place, remote associations may not even exist. The savings in Ebbinghaus' derived lists may be based in part on familiarity with the items and in part on the subject's realizing during relearning that he was confronted with a list systematically altered from the original in a specific way (Ebbinghaus as his own subject knew how the derived list was created). The subject could then use the original list to mediate correct performance on the derived list. There are certain other facts often taken as evidence for remote associations, but they are equally open to question. There are ways of checking on the reality of remote associations and this should be done. But even if remote associations do exist, there is no evidence that inhibition of delay would be present when other stimuli are present in the interval. In fact, according to Pavlov the intervening stimuli should disinhibit the inhibition. Another point is that each item is supposedly the remote association to certain earlier stimuli. The excitatory tendency should summate with that of the immediate association of which that same item is the response. The items at the end of the list would be the remote associations to the greatest number of prior stimuli. Hence the end of the list should be learned sooner than any other part, and the right half of the list sooner than the left half. This is contrary to fact.

The cognitive theory of the bow-shaped curve is rather simple. The subject becomes aware of the temporal positions of the various items, and the beginning and the end of the list are distinctive positions. Hence associations are formed more readily in these distinctive positions. A somewhat more radical interpretation is that serial learning is to a considerable extent based on the associating of each item with a position. Learning an item's precise position in the middle would be far more difficult. There is considerable evidence for the "distinctive position" hypothesis. Schulz (1955) showed that recall for position parallels learning of the list and yields a bow-shaped curve. Ebenholtz (1961) recently confirmed this finding. Eysenck (1959) arranged the time intervals in such a way that the first item immediately followed the last. From the standpoint of the Hull-Lepley interpretation, all positions are now equalized because there will now be remote associations between the end of the list and other positions. (It is curious that Hull and others never considered the beginning of the list as following the end. Perhaps this is due to *cognizing* the end as end and the beginning as beginning.) From the standpoint of cognitive theory the Eysenck design does not entail much change because the subject would still be aware of which was the first and which the last item. The result was that the typical bow-shaped curve was obtained. Along the same line is an experiment by Wishner, Shipley, and Hurvich (1957) in which a long list was divided into two or three parts by using different colors and type for the items of each part. The subject was told that he was to try to learn two (or three) lists simultaneously and that the lists were distinguished by different colors and type. The result was that double (or triple) bow-shaped curves were obtained. The end of a list and the beginning of the next were distinctive positions psychologically speaking, although temporally speaking these items were embedded in the center of the total list.

So much for the bow-shaped curve. Recently Ebenholtz has obtained impressive evidence for the position-learning interpretation of serial learning (1961). He devised a method whereby the subject was forced to learn a list by position. The items were arranged one under the other, printed on the right side of wooden slats. Any slat could be selected by pushing it to the left so that the red spot on it appeared in an aperture. When the red spot on the slat appeared in the aperture the subject had to guess what the syllable was. The slat was then pushed farther to the left so that the syllable printed on the far right side appeared in the aperture. The slats were selected by the experimenter in random order, but they always maintained their spatial position in the series. No slat ever followed the one before it. Hence the subject could *not* learn by forming sequential connections. He could learn only by associating a syllable with a spatial position. The result was that learning proceeded satisfactorily and a bow-shaped curve was obtained. Furthermore, when the same list was now presented in the traditional fashion in a memory drum, transfer was excellent. It required little more than one trial. Apparently the spatial order easily transferred to a temporal one. The implication is that typical serial learning could easily be achieved by position learning only. The assumption that serial learning consists of forming a chain of associations may be false.

In a companion experiment Ebenholtz forced his subjects to learn by sequence only, depriving them of the advantage of fixed position. He did this by rotating the series from trial to trial so that the same item was never in the same position. However, the sequential order remained constant. This task proved extraordinarily difficult and most subjects imposed a fixed position by selecting a particular item and regarding it as first, wherever it appeared from trial to trial. In fact, plotting errors against the subject's report of subjective position yielded the first half of a bow-shaped curve. Ebenholtz has other evidence in support of position learning as the fundamental (if not exclusive) basis of serial learning.[10]

FORGETTING

Finally we should like to discuss the differences between trace and S-R theories of forgetting. We will first discuss current S-R conceptions about forgetting, and then go on to suggest certain directions for trace theory. S-R theories of human forgetting are

[10] It is probable that serial learning involves locating each item in a spatio-temporal schema, rather than merely associating each item with a discrete numerical position.

more or less derived from theories developed to explain extinction on the animal level. Cognitive theorists have always found these explanations forced in the sense that the phenomenon to be explained is not properly described. Forgetting seems to be an event quite different from extinction. The person who now chews gum instead of smoking may remember very well what it was like to smoke. However, in spite of what seems a "forced fit" to cognitive theorists, it can be argued that extinction explanations work very well in treating the experimental data. We therefore propose to take a critical look at two of these explanations.

The most important of the S-R explanations goes by the name of competition of response. The heart of the competition of response notion is the radical idea that there is no such thing as a forgetting process—decrement in recall or performance can be dealt with by learning constructs. If two responses are learned to the same stimulus, then at the point of recall the dominant (stronger) one will occur, even though nothing has happened to the weaker response; or if two responses are of equal strength, they may each block the other's occurrence. Sometimes the notion of confusion has been used; the subject after learning the two responses often confuses them and offers the incorrect response. (Actually, insofar as confusion purports to be an explanation and not merely a description of what happens, we fail to see how it can be claimed by S-R theory. It has a cognitive ring to it.)

There seems to us to be something missing from the competition of response notion. Why should the occurrence of one of the two responses to a stimulus preclude the occurrence of the other? It seems to be assumed that only one response to a stimulus can be given. Perhaps what competition of response theorists have in mind is that within the short time period (two seconds) used in most experiments the subject has time to give only one response. If the wrong response occurs, then the subject does not have time to give the correct response even if he recalls it; or if both responses occur to the subject simultaneously, by the time he decides which to say his chance will be gone. Barnes and Underwood (1959) seem to accept this interpretation since in their retroactive inhibition experiment, where the subject is given extended time to respond, they argue that failure to respond due to response dominance or to blocking should not occur. The implication of this very simple point would seem to be that competition of response, at least in its present form, is limited to cases where the time of recall is quite short. The Barnes and Underwood study also establishes that confusion (whether S-R or not) is simply not a factor leading to forgetting when the subject is not pressed for time. Competition of response would be important, then, in explaining events such as an airplane pilot, unfamiliar with the controls of his aircraft, making a wrong move in a moment of crisis, but would not be applicable to the majority of events which we call forgetting.

Many interference theorists would probably accept the conclusion that competition of response is not of great importance in retroactive inhibition (RI), where the unlearning hypothesis (to be discussed below) can be used to explain most of the forgetting which occurs. The main contribution of competition of response is thought to occur in proactive inhibition (PI), where, by definition, unlearning is not involved. This limitation of competition of response to PI does not relegate it to a minor position for S-R theories, since Underwood (1957) has argued that most of the forgetting with which we are ordinarily concerned is due to proactive interference. However, if competition of response can only explain the forgetting which occurs when recall time is short, then one of two things follows. Either PI occurs only when recall time is short (making it of minor importance in ordinary forgetting), and therefore competition of response can explain it; or it occurs when longer recall times are used, and therefore a different explanation is required. Two recent experiments at Yeshiva University seem to indicate that the second alternative is the correct one. In both experiments subjects were given as much time as they wanted to respond at the point of recall, and in both experiments PI was produced. In summary, it seems to us that competition of response cannot serve as the major explanation for either RI or PI, and at most can be used for those instances of forgetting which occur when brief recall times are used.

The second major notion used by S-R theorists to explain forgetting is the unlearning hypothesis. In contrast to the competition of response theory, the unlearning theory holds that during the interpolated learning the original response is inhibited and therefore does not occur at the point of recall. The chief virtue of the unlearning hypothesis lies in the fact that it predicts that the forgotten response will be unavailable at the point of recall, and not merely that it is displaced by another response. There is, however, little more to the unlearning hypothesis than the statement that during the learning of the second response the first response is inhibited. It is true that there is a tentative suggestion that the inhibition of the first response is due to its nonreinforcement during second-list learning. This suggestion derives by analogy from animal extinction, one theory of which states that inhibition occurs to a nonreinforced response. The force of this suggestion of course depends on how seriously one takes the analogy between a human being learning a second list of paired associates and a rat suddenly finding the food box empty after running down the alley way. Our earlier discussion of the difficulties with reinforcement as a factor in human associative learning is relevant here.

A major limitation of unlearning is the fact that, by definition, it cannot explain PI. The findings discussed previously which show that PI is obtained with extended recall time indicate that PI also involves unavailability. Now since the major evidence for unlearning is unavailability in RI, and since unlearning cannot handle unavailability in PI, this leads to the interesting speculation that the unavailability which occurs in RI and PI is caused by a common factor which of course could not be unlearning. At any rate we feel that the unlearning hypothesis has made an important contribution by drawing attention to unavailability as a characteristic of forgetting. But we have also tried to indicate some of its shortcomings as an explanation of forgetting.

S-R theories of forgetting rely on extinction as the basic model, because in extinction it is clear that learned responses stop occurring. The reasoning is that if learning is the making of a response, then forgetting is the ceasing of a response. Theories of extinction and forgetting are thus constructed to deal with response processes and the reasons for their nonoccurrence. Competition of response boils down to saying that you cannot utter two words at the same time (or that forgetting occurs in the throat). To postulate an extinction theory of unlearning is to maintain that if a person says something and no good comes of it, then he will no longer be able to say that something. The analogy here is with something like fatigue. The person is no longer able to say something, because saying it is fatiguing. This, of course, works only if forgetting is really like not saying something because you are too tired to do so, especially when you get nothing for your pains.

If cognitive theorists are right, however, and learning and recall are only indirectly related to responding, then response-type processes will not explain learning or recall. If, on the other hand, memory is taken to be dependent upon the activation of memory traces, then forgetting would have to involve failure in the activation of memory traces. From this point of view we will try to sketch the outlines of a trace theory of forgetting by suggesting certain things that might happen to the trace.[11] A crucial part of this analysis involves various methods of testing for recall which may reveal what particular process or processes are responsible for a given instance of forgetting.

If we start with the assumption that associative learning consists of the formation of memory traces and the formation of some kind of connection between them, two basic reasons for forgetting would seem to be (1) difficulties involved with the trace itself and (2) difficulties involved with the trace connections.[12]

Difficulties in recall associated with the trace itself can be placed in at least two categories which we will call trace destruc-

[11] It is unfortunate that the cognitive theory of forgetting has been so completely identified with the notion of qualitative change of the memory trace based on *prägnanz*. Trace theory has always been broader than this particular hypothesis which not only is somewhat vague but has not been supported by experimental results.

[12] The reader may note similarities to some of the factors we believe cause interference in learning discussed earlier. However, the short-term memory involved in learning may be affected by different factors than the kind of memory we are discussing at this point, namely, memory for material which has been previously learned.

tion and trace unavailability. Whether traces are ever actually destroyed is, of course, an open question. If, however, the recognition technique, which is probably the most sensitive measure of recall available, is used, and there is failure of recognition, then, for all intents and purposes, we can talk of trace destruction. But the recognition test is important in trace theory, more for the role it plays in determining whether a trace is present than whether it is absent. If a subject succeeds in recognition and fails in a matching test or aided recall, then it is clear that trace destruction is not the cause of forgetting. As pointed out earlier, however, it is difficult to produce nonrecognition with the experimental techniques now available. Hence we would suspect that trace destruction is rarely a cause for forgetting.[13]

Trace unavailability *does* seem to be a very frequent cause of forgetting. Trace unavailability on the phenomenal level can be seen in those cases where an item to be recalled is said to be on the tip of the tongue. Here failure of recall cannot be said to be due to a loss of association, since the associated item is almost brought forth (in many cases there is even an awareness of the nature of the item to be recalled) and if the sought-for item is given to the subject he immediately knows it to be the correct one. Experimentally one can get at trace unavailability by comparing results obtained using the matching technique (discussed earlier) with those obtained by aided recall. Aided recall confounds the effects of item unavailability and of associative disturbance. The response term may not be recalled because either something has happened to the connection between it and the stimulus term or this connection may be preserved, but the stimulus may not be able to bring the response to mind. The matching test relieves the stimulus of the burden of evoking the response member; instead the response trace is directly evoked by the response member which is given to the subject. In matching, then, one is testing only for the recall of the connection be-

---

[13] We should be cautious about this point, however, since laboratory procedures never reproduce the conditions of everyday life, and there may be factors—for example, long time intervals—which could lead to deterioration or destruction of traces.

tween the items. The fact that matching scores are higher than aided recall scores would indicate that a good bit of forgetting is due to item unavailability. Asch discusses additional evidence for unavailability in his paper in this volume.

So much for difficulties involving the individual trace itself. Is there evidence that forgetting ever consists of a loss of trace connections? There are few RI or PI studies using the matching technique, which should indicate forgetting due purely to associative disturbance. Jacobson (1961), in an unpublished paper, demonstrated RI using matching when the interpolated list consisted of a new stimulus and new response (K–K). In an unpublished study performed at Yeshiva, PI could not be demonstrated when a matching test was used at the point of recall, yet when an aided recall test was employed a large amount of PI was obtained. This might indicate that associative interference is only produced in RI experiments, while the effect of PI is limited to item availability.

In some recent experiments at Yeshiva we have been exploring further the nature of associative interference. We have been comparing amount of RI produced when the interpolated list consists of an old response to be learned to a new stimulus (K–B), or a new response to be learned to an old stimulus (A–K). The purpose of these experiments is to determine whether the notions concerning the Müller-Schumann law, which were put forward in an earlier part of this paper, have any applicability to RI. The traditional finding has been that a K–B interpolated list produces less RI than does an A–K interpolated list. This has been taken to mean that the A–K interpolated list disrupts the A–B association (either because of competition of response or unlearning), whereas the K–B interpolated list has no such effect. In discussing transfer we suggested that associative difficulties in transfer would be equivalent for the A–K and K–B designs if differences in item learning were ruled out. Similarly, it could be the case that in RI the K–B paradigm leads to less interference than the A–K paradigm since with K–B the response item remains during interpolated learning. This may have the effect of making the B item more available at recall for K–B subjects, and lead to little or no forgetting compared to both control and A—K subjects who have no opportunity to overlearn the responses. If a matching test is used, however, differences in item availability between A—K and K—B groups should be removed, and the prediction would be: no difference in RI for these groups. To test this hypothesis two RI experiments were performed, one using an A—K and one a K—B interpolated list, with a matching test at the point of recall. The results were in a sense too good, since the K—B interpolated list produced *more* RI than the A—K list; only equivalence was predicted. There were some features of the experiment which could explain why K—B was actually poorer than A—K, and the results seem promising in relation to our hypothesis.

It is evident that trace theory as yet has little to say about forgetting except that it may be of different kinds, namely, trace and associative disturbances. We know little of the conditions which produce these different kinds of forgetting, and therefore our understanding of the forgetting process is limited. We assume that these two types of forgetting are produced by material learned either before or after the critical material. In this sense we subscribe to an interference theory of forgetting. The vast literature on retroactive and proactive inhibition concerns experiments done almost exclusively with aided recall, a technique which we believe measures both individual trace and associative interference. Our proposal would be to use the matching and recognition techniques as well as the aided recall techniques systematically. We would like to know what conditions produce item forgetting, what produce associative forgetting, and what produce both. By condition we mean the kind of variable which has been used in traditional RI and PI studies, such as type of interfering material, temporal interval, and so on. This kind of information is necessary before we will be able to make meaningful generalizations about what is going on in forgetting.

The preceding section has dealt with the effects of trace preservation, trace unavailability, or associative disturbance, but there are other conditions which may lead to failure of recall. Classical theory and S-R theory both view the associative response as automatic. That is, A—B having been learned, when later A is given, B will occur provided forgetting is not involved. Yet the typical experiment entails specific instructions to the subject to learn because he later will be tested, and in the test he is always told to respond with the correct associate. Perhaps, therefore, such instructions produce a set to recall and perhaps such a set is needed for recall. (Such a set or intention to recall should not be confused with the set or intention to learn, discussed earlier.)

This was precisely the question Lewin raised in his controversy with Ach many years ago. In considering the evidence of Ach and Lewin we have come to the conclusion that there was an important flaw in most of the experiments. If one wants to know whether trace a will spontaneously redintegrate trace b, without the presence of a set, it is important to know whether trace a is itself aroused when stimulus A is presented (or, in phenomenal terms, whether A is first recognized). Höffding and later Köhler, Koffka, and others have made the point that when testing for the retention of an association A–B by aided recall, the test stimulus A must first contact or arouse the trace of itself left from the learning exposure (a). It is not the new stimulus A which is connected with trace b but the trace of the previously seen A. This logical point has important implications, because failure of recall could be due either to some disturbance in the a-b trace connection, the unavailability of the b trace, the absence of a set to recall B, or to the fact that stimulus A does not contact trace a. Although as noted earlier the recognition process (arousal of a by A) does generally occur successfully, there are circumstances where it might not. If, for example, test stimulus A is quite different from the prior A, the arousal of trace a might fail to occur. Thus failure to respond to a somewhat different stimulus in a stimulus generalization design would here be explained as failure of recognition and not as a diminished or insufficiently strong association. (See Rock, 1962, for a full discussion of this issue.) As a rule, however, trace a is aroused by stimulus A and recall depends upon the excitation of trace b by the associated trace a or the redintegration of the total memory by a part.

On the basis of this analysis it occurred to us that where, in the earlier experiments, the evidence went against spontaneous recall of B, it might have been due to conditions which prevented recognition of A. Koffka also arrived at this conclusion. We have therefore designed some new experiments in which recognition is known to occur. Thus with the assurance that trace a was aroused we wanted to know whether trace b will be spontaneously redintegrated or whether a set to recall b is necessary. Thus far the evidence favors spontaneous recall—i.e., against Lewin's hypothesis (provided no contrary set is operating); but we suspect that our subjects are not only recognizing A but also correctly localizing their remembrance of A—i.e., they realize it was an item seen in the earlier learning task. This realization may explain why they give the response.

Thus far in the discussion we have been referring to the case where only one association to A, namely B_1, is involved. Suppose, however, there exist other associations to A, namely B_2, etc. Tolchin and Ceraso (1961) have shown the tremendous importance of a set to recall in a transfer design when such multiple associations are involved. Subjects are required to learn a list made up of parts of compound nouns such as railroad and football. But these compound nouns are rearranged in the list to be learned—e.g., rail ball and foot road. Presumably such a list should be difficult to learn because of the prepotent associations of the compound nouns. The study showed, however, that it was primarily subjects first given a chance to inspect the compound nouns who showed the disturbance—i.e., subjects first given a set to think of the compound noun $(A-B_2)$. Without such a set there may be no disturbance at all in learning the list $(A-B_1)$. We are now considering the possibility that in such cases set is in essence a directing mechanism. If a stimulus A has more than one B associated with it we must assume the existence of several a-b traces, e.g., a-$b1$, a-$b2$, and so on. Set may then be conceived of as the mechanism which insures that the a trace corresponding to A-B_1, for instance, is aroused, rather than any of the other a traces. But once any given a trace is aroused, there will be spontaneous redintegration of b (assuming forgetting does not occur for some of the other reasons discussed above). Although there is some similarity between this notion and the competition of response notion, we believe it solves the problem discussed in regard to that hypothesis, namely, why both responses are not aroused. In the present case the question is why all the different *a* traces are not aroused. The proposed answer would be that arousal of *a* depends upon both stimulus A and a set to arouse a particular trace *a*. At any rate we consider our work on this problem of set in recall as only just begun.

SUMMARY

We have sought to point up the difficulties and limitations of the S-R theory and to make explicit the assumptions underlying a cognitive theory of human associative learning and retention. The cognitive theory we have outlined is an extension of pre-behavioristic classical association theory which dealt with the contents of experience. It differs from earlier association theory in its primary concern with the successive rather than the compound (or simultaneous) associations, in its stress on explanatory constructs such as the representational memory trace, and in its acknowledgment of the necessity for grouping of material when multiple items are presented.

The learning of individual items is a very typical form of learning and often entails nothing more than perceiving items. The preservation of the trace of an item is easily revealed in a recognition test. S-R theory has difficulty explaining the learning of items in terms of S-R connections when the item is clearly an indivisible whole to begin with. S-R theory also has difficulty explaining the so-called "recognition response."

The learning of association entails, in addition to forming traces of the items themselves, forming a connection between them; at least this is the case for discriminative associations where multiple associations must all be learned together. Where only a simple association is required (two items), mere contiguity seems sufficient and intention is unnecessary. For the learning of discriminative associations, on the other hand, intentional grouping seems to be necessary, the difficulty lying in the need to learn which item goes with which. Intention to learn has been mistakenly identified with the question of reinforcement. In the typical verbal learning paradigm, reinforcement is not even applicable. Furthermore, the designation of one item as stimulus and the other as response is inappropriate, if these are meant to be taken literally. It was argued that an unbiased description of the learning procedure is that the learner is being exposed to stimuli. If this is correct, then the principles of conditioning are not strictly applicable to verbal learning. A theory to account for the facts of transfer of training was presented in which no asymmetry of the two terms of an association is assumed. Some possible causes of difficulty in learning a list of paired associates were advanced and contrasted with the S-R notion of stimulus generalization as the major source of difficulty. It was pointed out that stimulus generalization during learning is linked to the assumption that associations are formed gradually (incrementally) and that this assumption has recently been called into question. The notion of the learning of associations on a single trial is compatible with cognitive theory.

In serial learning the bow-shaped curve has been explained by S-R theorists in terms of the pile-up of inhibition of trace-conditioned remote association at the middle of the list. However, there is no compelling evidence that remote associations exist and, even if they do, that they are based on trace conditioning. The cognitive theory stresses the distinctive positions of the ends of the list, for which hypothesis there is now considerable support. Recently evidence has been presented that serial learning in large part is based on the association of an item with its position rather than the sequential association of each item with the next.

S-R theories of human forgetting are derived from theories developed to explain extinction on the animal level, but forgetting is not the same as extinction. In any case the competition of response notion is inapplicable when the time allowed for recall is not restricted to a few seconds, because mere blocking could no longer be the cause. Proactive inhibition has been shown to occur even with longer recall time, and competition of response is the only explanation of PI to be put forth by S-R theorists. Unlearning, presumably based on the emitting of the first-list response during the learning of the second list, has been advanced by S-R theory to explain retroactive inhibition. But unlearning cannot be applied to proactive inhibition. Cognitive theory seeks to explain forgeting in terms of failure in the activation of the memory trace. Two basic reasons for forgetting would be (1) destruction of the individual trace (which we believe is *not* a major cause) or unavailability of the trace (which we believe is a frequent cause and can be experimentally demonstrated by the use of a matching test in comparison with aided recall) and (2) loss of the trace connection between the previously associated items. Some evidence now exists in support of the second factor. Two other factors in recall were discussed—namely, the need for the test stimulus to activate its own prior trace before the associated trace can be redintegrated, and the possible role of a set to recall a particular item.

REFERENCES

Asch, S. E., and Ebenholtz, S. M. The principle of associative symmetry. *Proc. Amer. Phil. Soc.*, 1962, *106*, 135–163.

Asch, S. E., Ceraso, J., and Heimer, W. Perceptual conditions of association. *Psychol. Monogr.*, 1960, *74*, No. 3 (Whole No. 490).

Barnes, J. M., and Underwood, B. J. "Fate" of first-list associations in transfer theory. *J. exp. Psychol.*, 1959, *58*, 97–105.

Deich, R. The learning of a single association in one-trial. Paper read at EPA, Philadelphia, April, 1961.

Ebenholtz, S. An analysis of the relative roles of position learning and sequential associations in the serial learning process. Unpublished Doctoral Dissertation, New School for Social Research, 1961.

Epstein, W., Rock, I., and Zuckerman, C. Meaning and familiarity in associative learning. *Psychol. Monogr.*, 1960, *74*, No. 4 (Whole No. 491).

Eysenck, H. J. Serial position effects in nonsense syllable learning as a function of interlist rest pauses. *Brit. J. Psychol.*, 1959, *50*, 360–362.

Hull, C. L., Hovland, C. I., Ross, R. T., Hall, M., Perkins, D. T., and Fitch, F. B. *Mathematico-deductive theory of rote learning: A study in scientific methodology.* New Haven: Yale Univ. Press, 1940.

Jacobson, S. On the nature of interference: What is interfered with by retroactive inhibition. Unpublished research paper, New School for Social Research, 1961.

Köhler, W. On the nature of associations. *Proc. Amer. Phil. Soc.*, 1941, *84*, 489–502.

Köhler, W. *Gestalt psychology.* New York: Liveright, 1947.

Lepley, W. M. Serial reaction considered as conditioned reactions. *Psychol. Monogr.*, 1934, No. 46 (Whole No. 205).

Meehl, P. E. On the circularity of the law of effect. *Psychol. Bull.*, 1950, *47*, 52–75.

Müller, G. E., and Schumann, F. Experimentelle Beitrage zur Untersuchung des Gedachtnisses. *Z. Psychol.*, 1894, *6*, 81–190.

Murdock, B. B. The retention of individual items. *J. exp. Psychol.*, 1961, *62*, 618–625.

Osgood, C. E. The similarity paradox in human learning: A resolution. *Psychol. Rev.*, 1949, *56*, 132–143.

Peterson, L. R., and Peterson, M. J. Short-term retention of individual verbal items. *J. exp. Psychol.*, 1959, *58*, 193–198.

Postman, L., and Riley, D. A. A critique of Köhler's theory of association. *Psychol. Rev.*, 1957, *64*, 61–72.

Reiff, R., and Scheerer, M. *Memory and hypnotic age regression.* New York: International Universities Press, 1959.

Rock, I. The role of repetition in associative learning. *Amer. J. Psychol.*, 1957, *70*, 186–193.

Rock, I. A neglected aspect of the problem of recall: The Höffding Function. In J. Scher (ed.), *Theories of mind.* New York: Macmillan (Free Press), 1962.

Rock, I., and Engelstein, P. A study of memory for visual form. *Amer. J. Psychol.*, 1959, *72*, 221–229.

Rock, I., and Heimer, W. Further evidence of one-trial associative learning. *Amer. J. Psychol.*, 1959, *72*, 1–16.

Schulz, R. W. Generalization of serial position in rote serial learning. *J. exp. Psychol.*, 1955, *49*, 267–272.

Sheffield, F. D. The role of meaningfulness of stimulus and response in verbal learning. Unpublished Ph.D. dissertation, Yale Univ., 1946.

Tolchin, G., and Ceraso, J.   Set and associative inhibition. Paper read
    at EPA, Philadelphia, April, 1961.
Underwood, B. J.   Interference and forgetting. *Psychol. Rev.*, 1957,
    64, 49–60.
Wishner, J., Shipley, T. E., Jr., and Hurvich, M. S.   The serial-position
    curve as a function of organization. *Amer. J. Psychol.*, 1957, *70*,
    258–262.

THE DEVELOPMENT OF
COGNITIVE STRUCTURES[1]

RILEY W. GARDNER

The Menninger Foundation

INTRODUCTION

THE DISCUSSION OF THE DEVELOPMENT OF cognitive structures that
follows is based at a number of points on two groups of studies of
individual differences in cognitive structures and of relationships
between different forms or aspects of structure conducted at The
Menninger Foundation during the past several years. The first
group dealt with individual differences in a variety of cognitive
structures in adults. The second dealt with relations between
these and other structures in children.

Before going further, let me point out that the ensuing discussion refers primarily to the specific class of structures comprised
of enduring *arrangements* of cognitive processes that shape the
expression of intentions under particular types of environmental
conditions. Several forms or aspects of structure in this sense will
be considered, including cognitive controls, defense mechanisms,
and intellectual structures. Findings concerning relations between
structures within this general class and between members of this
class and other aspects of cognitive structuring will also be considered. The term, *cognitive control*, was originally applied by

[1] The Menninger Foundation studies referred to in this chapter were made
possible by research grants from the United States Public Health Service.
The current and proposed work is supported by Research Grant M-5517.

147

George Klein (1954) to a group of enduring arrangements, patterns, or programs of cognitive functions whose formation and operation may be relatively independent of conflict between drives, and which therefore seem to be different from defensive structures in at least one important way. It is entirely possible, however, as indicated in several earlier publications (e.g., Gardner, Holzman, Klein, Linton, and Spence, 1959), that, following the first stages of structure formation, every cognitive structure serves both defensive and nondefensive purposes. The terms cognitive control, defense, intellectual structure, and so on, may actually, therefore, be most appropriately considered as useful rubrics referring to different facets of the structural complexity of any bit of cognitive behavior.

The specific studies referred to were designed and the results interpreted within the broad general framework provided by psychoanalytic theory, including the many recent developments in the ego-psychological aspects of this theory. We have employed this general theoretical framework because we feel that ultimate understanding of cognitive structures per se and of the interaction of various cognitive structures in development will be accomplished only within a conceptual framework that makes full provision, from the outset, for the importance of unconscious factors to structure formation, for the unconscious conflicts that lead to the formation of particular kinds of structures, and for the integral relationship between cognitive structures and the organization of the total personality.

Hartmann (1951, pp. 35–36) has summarized some of the relevant recent developments within psychoanalytic theory as follows:

The most incisive change which took place in Freud's model of psychic personality can be pictured as adding to its description as a series of layers its representation as a (more or less) integrated whole, subdivisible in centers of mental functioning—these substructures being defined by their functions, and their demarcation being based on the fact that empirically he found greater coherence among some functions than among others. . . . This facilitates a multidimensional approach and, so far as psychoanalytic psychology and therapy goes, it has been rather generally accepted as being more useful in giving account of the dynamic and economic properties of mental life.

The importance of understanding relationships between cognitive structures has been emphasized by Rapaport (1959), Hartmann (1951), Lois Murphy (1957), and others. The following further statement by Hartmann (1951, p. 40) seems particularly apt:

One day we shall probably be able to formulate more systematically the rational element of our technique, that is, "planning" the predictable outcome of our interventions, with respect to these structural implications.

This will in part depend on progress in a familiar field of analytic research: a deeper understanding of the choice and of the quantitative aspect of defense mechanisms, of their chronology, typical and individual, but above all else, of their genetic and economic interrelatedness with other functions of the ego. To touch at least on one of the genetic problems involved, we can assume that many defense mechanisms are traceable to primitive defensive actions against the outside world, which in part probably belong to the ego's primary autonomy, and that only later, in situations of psychic conflicts, do they develop into what we specifically call mechanisms of defense. Also, we can say of many of them that after having been established as such, they become in a secondary way invested with other functions (intellectualization, for example). This makes for a complicated overlapping of their role as resistances with various other functions they represent.

Beginning with Freud's (1937) re-emphasis upon the importance of inherited factors in the determination of defense structures, and continuing through the elaboration by Hartmann (1939) and others of the importance of constitutional characteristics of the conflict-free apparatuses involved in defensive and other cognitive functions, the ego-psychological movement has contained an important place for genic, as well as experiential factors in the complex of interactions that lead to the emergence of various types of cognitive structures.

In our earlier publications (e.g., Gardner *et al.*, 1959), we ourselves have emphasized—in considering the relationship between cognitive controls and defense structures—that some controls, which may be heavily determined by genic factors, may serve as essential preconditions for the development of certain defense mechanisms.

Lest my emphasis upon the adequacy of this general theoretical framework for dealing with the problem of cognitive structuring and its development appear overly exclusive, let me emphasize that we have been particularly interested in relationships between defenses, controls, intellectual abilities, and other structures and the vast array of valuable information concerning specific cognitive functions provided by a large group of earlier experimenters who neither employed this theoretical framework nor conceived of their studies in terms of their relevance to the problem of individual differences in cognitive structures. The work of Köhler and Lauenstein on memory formation, for example, provided valuable new information concerning assimilation effects in the registration of sequential stimulation. The work of Jean Piaget, both on the development of intellectual structures and on the development of the attentional structures involved in perception, serves as another representative example. But valuable as it is, earlier work on *general* laws of cognition provides only steppingstones for an approach to the organization of cognitive structures within the individual. As Gordon Allport (1937, p. vii) pointed out so effectively:

As a rule, science regards the individual as a mere bothersome accident. Psychology, too, ordinarily treats him as something to be brushed aside so the main business of accounting for the uniformity of events can get under way. The result is that on all sides we see psychologists enthusiastically at work upon a somewhat shadowy portrait entitled "the generalized human mind." Though serving well a certain purpose, this portrait is not altogether satisfying to those who compare it with the living individual models from which it is drawn. It seems unreal and esoteric, devoid of locus, self-consciousness, and organic unity—all essential characteristics of the minds we know.

With the intention of supplementing this abstract portrait by one that is more life-like, a new movement within psychological science has gradually grown up. It attempts to depict and account for the manifest individuality of mind. This new movement has come to be known. . . . as the *psychology of personality.*

As I shall attempt to elucidate in the remarks that follow, our investigations of relationships between different types of cognitive structures in adults, and the formation of these structures during development, seem to indicate that the problem is even more complicated than Allport suggested. Not only the general laws of adult cognitive behavior, but also the general developmental curves for cognitive functions, seem to tell us little or nothing of their relationship in the cognitive organization of a single individual.

STUDIES OF THE COGNITIVE
ORGANIZATIONS OF ADULTS

Before plunging into a description of a large developmental study of relations between different facts of cognitive structuring, let me provide a background by outlining some of the aspects of cognitive organization we earlier explored in adults.

One of our enduring interests has been in the ways people categorize their experience. Recently, we have focused our attention on relationships between the differentiation adults impose upon heterogeneous arrays of objects, persons, events, etc., the level of abstraction at which they *prefer* to function in such categorizing situations, and their capacity to abstract. You will recognize the last of these three aspects of concept formation as one which has in the past received consistent attention from psychologists interested in the laws of concept formation and of the development of concept formation. Relevant to these studies are, of course, the brilliant pioneer work of Vygotsky (1934), the contributions of Inhelder and Piaget, whose recent monograph on the development of comprehension and abstraction (Piaget and Inhelder, 1959) caps years of study, the recent work of Bruner and his associates (Bruner, Goodnow, and Austin, 1956), and the contributions of a large number of other investigators.

Relevant, too, are the significant contributions to our understanding of concept formation by our friend and valued consultant in this recent work, Martin Scheerer. Not only in his earlier work with Goldstein (Goldstein and Scheerer, 1941), but also in his later publications (e.g., 1949, 1959), his devotion to the general problem of concept formation is worthy of special note. In this area, as in many others, his contributions to the literature, his discussions with his students, and his consultations with our research group, were all marked by his keen eye for the dissimilarities among superficially similar phenomena, as well as the similarities linking superficially different phenomena. These qualities of his thinking were evident, for example, in his paper on performance analysis (Scheerer, 1946), in which he carefully and thoroughly detailed the value of thoughtful participation by psychologists in the procedure they employ, and of thoughtful reflection on the processes involved. Reference to our recent studies of conceptual differentiation and its relations to abstraction brings to mind Martin Scheerer's typically astute delineation of the two main forms of generalization (e.g., Scheerer, 1954), for the problem of generalization must be at the core of any adequate developmental conception of concept formation. Like Lashley and Wade before him, but perhaps with even broader awareness of the implications, he distinguished sharply between "generalization by default" and true generalization based on adequate discrimination. In addition to his contributions to the literature on various aspects of cognition, including the problem of cognitive embeddedness, with its obvious relations to the important work of Witkin and his colleagues (e.g., Witkin, Dyk, Faterson, Goodenough, and Karp, 1962), he brought to psychology a unique approach to cognitive functions. Rarely does one see psychological phenomena so well appreciated in their own terms or considered with such painstaking care and with such powers of delay and of analysis and synthesis effectively combined. In referring to Martin Scheerer in relation to our discussions of concept formation, we mean, of course, to detract nothing from his contributions to perception and to other major areas of psychology. His participation in our thinking about the cognitive structures involved in memory formation and in memory reproduction, to take but two examples, were fully as stimulating as his participation in our thinking about concept formation. To encapsulate these brief remarks about Martin Scheerer's influence on our work in a single observation, one might refer to his unflinching intellectual honesty in facing and in thinking creatively about psychologists' profound ignorance of psychological processes. He would be the first to point out that a superficial verbal description of a cognitive phenomenon, or of a dimension of individual consistencies in cognition, masks our ignorance of the processes involved. And he would be the first to suggest an ingenious method of testing one of the numerous process hypotheses that could be ventured.

Let us return now to the studies of adult individual consistencies in concept formation referred to earlier, and then proceed to some of the other areas we have explored and the developmental studies that have occupied us recently. Our recent studies of adult concept formation (Gardner and Schoen, in press) have impressed us once again with the remarkable complexity of the structures involved in cognitive behavior. Individual differences in conceptual differentiation, which we have studied in a number of contexts over the years (Gardner, 1953; Gardner *et al.*, 1959; Gardner, Jackson, and Messick, 1960), are relatively stable over time (Gardner and Long, 1960e) and show considerable situational generality—provided, of course, that both the stimulus conditions and the intention invoked in the subject are appropriate to this particular principle of cognitive control. But, surprisingly enough, this dimension of individual differences in conceptual differentiation is independent not only of the level of abstraction at which the person momentarily chooses to perform in relatively free categorizing tasks, but also of his capacity to abstract, at least as measured by various indices of intelligence, including similarities tests designed to assess one aspect of the capacity to abstract. In addition, the level of abstraction at which the individual prefers to function in these situations is remarkably independent of his capacity to abstract, assessed in the ways just referred to. Note here the complexity of the cognitive structures involved in a relatively limited segment of the vast area of concept formation. Rapaport, Gill, and Schafer (1945) have pointed out that concept formation may be the ultimate basis of thought functioning, and that it finds representation in a vast array of psychological phenomena ranging from largely drive-determined arrangements of ideas that are unconscious to certain conversion symptoms. The studies referred to above touch only three facets of a much larger realm of behavior involving concept formation.

Our recent work has also included a series of studies of the controls of attention, not because we feel that attention is the central or dominant variable in cognitive functioning or personality organization, but because attention and the controls of attention, which have been severely neglected in American psychology, represent the point of contact between the individual and both external and internal reality.[2] Our explorations of attention have been devoted to three general areas: the selectiveness with which the individual can attend, e.g., to relevant stimuli in the face of impelling irrelevant stimuli of various kinds; the extensiveness of the individual's scanning in free scanning situations leading to decisions about the relative characteristics of stimuli (Gardner, 1961a; Gardner and Long, 1962a, b); and the intensity of attention, as it affects assimilation in the registration and recall of sequential stimuli (Gardner and Lohrenz, 1961). We recently performed further studies of the differential effects on perception of selectiveness on the one hand and extensiveness of scanning on the other in a single set of test situations (Gardner and Long, 1962b). Our results once again demonstrate the multiplicity of cognitive structures involved in superficially similar performances. We find, for example, that, using speed in finding embedded figures in Witkin's test as a criterion measure of the selectiveness of attention, we can predict performances in other situations in which (1) the relevant stimulus is embedded in a larger context that, as it were, "competes" with it for attention; (2) the relevant stimulus is the surround rather than the embedded item, which in this case becomes the irrelevant stimulus; or (3) the relevant stimulus appears among irrelevant stimuli that do not combine with it to form a superordinate Gestalt organiza-

---

[2] Implications of this work for individual differences in the quality and contents of consciousness have been elaborated upon elsewhere (Gardner, in press).

tion, and in which organized part-whole relations do not obtain. We find, also, that measures of the extensiveness with which adults scan certain stimuli allow prediction, to a modest degree, of the experienced apparent magnitude of stimuli. Here, our work (Gardner and Long, 1960a, 1960b, 1962a, b) directly touches the studies of relations between attention and perception performed over a period of twenty years by Piaget and his associates and summarized in a recent monograph (Piaget, 1961). Even, however, when we obtain measures of the extensiveness of scanning and of the selectiveness of attention to relevant vs. compelling irrelevant stimuli from the same test judgments, these dimensions of individual consistency remain both logically and statistically independent of each other.

What, then, are the relationships between these two aspects of attention deployment—provided, of course, that our working hypotheses for certain laboratory situations ultimately prove tenable —and the individual consistencies in conceptual differentiation and levels of abstraction referred to earlier? Our findings suggest that all of these cognitive variables are essentially independent, in both adults and children.

We have also been intensely interested in the relationship of individual consistencies in field-dependence, or field-articulation, massively explored and documented by Witkin and others (see Witkin *et al.*, 1962), and a dimension of individual consistencies in assimilation among new percepts and related memories of earlier percepts, which Holzman and Klein (1954; Holzman, 1954) referred to as "leveling-sharpening." Their work has been extended in a number of subsequent studies (e.g., Gardner *et al.*, 1959, 1960; Gardner and Lohrenz, 1960; Gardner and Long, 1960c, 1960d, 1960e; Holzman and Gardner, 1959). Adequate measures of assimilation are difficult to achieve. We feel, however, that the procedures we have employed more recently are clear enough in their implications to provide tentative answers to one or two crucial questions concerning relationships between different cognitive structures representing a single general type of structure.[3] We find, for example, that performance in the criterion

[3] Clinical and experimental problems in the measurement of various con-

tests of field-articulation developed by Witkin and his associates allows prediction of certain aspects of learning and recall, but only in particular types of learning situations (Gardner and Long, 1961; Long, 1962). Knowledge of individual differences in a criterion test of leveling-sharpening allows prediction of other, nonoverlapping, aspects of performance in the same kind of test situation (Gardner and Long, 1960c). In other learning and recall situations—e.g., when the similarity of items is low—no such relationships obtain for either criterion. Once again it is apparent that cognitive controls are enduring patterns of cognitive functioning that mediate the expression of particular intentions when the individual is confronted with particular stimulus conditions (cf. Gardner *et al.*, 1959).

In a recent series of experiments, we employed procedures that seem to pinpoint the meaning of these earlier results. We have developed two superficially similar tests in which designs are presented to subjects sequentially in such a way as to invoke the operation of both cognitive control principles, field-articulation and leveling-sharpening. The first of these tests seems to maximize the effects of leveling-sharpening on the registration of similar sequential stimuli, the second to maximize the independent effects of selective attention upon the recall of similar stimuli. Both tests, however, were designed to involve both sets of controls. Only the balance of assimilation-selectivity is different in the two situations. Under these two sets of conditions, the two cognitive controls *appear* to have similar effects upon reproduction of the designs. The hypothesized difference between the effects of the two criterion variables on performance is appropriately tested by means of an analysis of variance that reveals that interaction between the criteria as predictors of performance in the two situations. In a recent sample, this interaction is significant. It could probably be made still more significant by increasing the unique properties of the two tests. These results are not unusual in our laboratory. We have performed other studies of the relationship between field-articulation and leveling-sharpening as determi-

---

trols and a continuing program of research in measurement conducted in our laboratory are described elsewhere (Gardner, 1962).

nants of learning and recall that confirm these findings. We have, over a period of years, also explored relations between these and other cognitive controls and kinesthetic and visual aftereffects (Gardner, 1961b). Once again, although assimilation theory and aftereffect theory could potentially account for many of the same performances, measures of individual differences in these cognitive variables are related neither to each other nor to any of the cognitive control variables we have dealt with.

Let me turn now to some of the other areas of adult cognition that we have concerned ourselves with over the years. I shall refer first to an aspect of cognition that has very different implications from those of the three control principles I have referred to thus far. We have described our findings concerning this aspect of cognitive organization in terms of a dimension of individual consistencies in tolerance for unrealistic experiences (Klein, Gardner, and Schlesinger, 1962). You will readily see that this dimension of cognitive functioning implies no specific set of cognitive processes, but rather represents a general characteristic of the ego-as-a-whole in the constant interplay between unconscious determinants of behavior on the one hand and the dictates of external reality on the other. I mention this body of work briefly here only to indicate the varied approaches we have taken to the cognitive organization of the individual. Our purpose in continuing to sample widely different forms or aspects of cognitive structure ranging from the specific to the general is to achieve a more adequate sampling of the still larger panorama of cognitive structures. As in our studies of individuality in other aspects of cognitive organization, we find that individuals are consistent in this aspect of their cognitive functioning in a wide variety of situations. A study by Snyder and Scheerer (1961), who used similar procedures, produced very similar results. Knowing the degree to which a person's perception is altered by proximal cues at variance with what he knows to be true, we can predict his approach to the Rorschach test and related situations with reasonable accuracy.

In our recent studies, we have also attempted to evaluate several other general aspects of the individual's cognitive organization. Following Rapaport, we are attempting to assess the relative autonomy of the individual's total array of cognitive structures from drive-determined, primary-process thinking on the one hand and from external reality on the other (Rapaport, 1951, 1958). This variable probably bears a curvilinear relationship to tolerance for unreality. In our recent studies focused on relations between various facets of cognitive structuring, we have also attempted clinical assessments of the basic integrity and psychological health represented by the total pattern of the individual's defensive and intellectual structures. Among the intriguing preliminary results with the latter measure is its relation to performance in the Color-Word test.

I have referred thus far primarily to a cluster of specific and more general aspects of the cognitive organization of individual adults that we have conceptualized as principles of cognitive control. But my initial remarks implied that we are particularly interested in *relations* between various control structures and between these and distinctly different forms or aspects of cognitive structure. In one study, we explored, with generally predictable results, relations between various dimensions of cognitive control and the intellectual abilities defined by Thurstone and his successors (Gardner *et al.*, 1960). We are now exploring relations between a cluster of cognitive control principles and performance in the Wechsler intelligence tests by groups of normal adults and by groups of adults whose psychopathology is of sufficient intensity to have required hospitalization. In these current studies, we are focusing with particular care upon relations between cognitive controls, intellectual structures, defense structures, and general properties of cognitive organization. In working with a patient group, we are, of course, also exploring relations between complex patterns of cognitive structuring and types and severities of symptomatology. These recent studies are based on a group of earlier studies aimed at relations between particular aspects of control in adults and particular defenses. To mention a few of these, we have demonstrated a special type of relationship between leveling and generalized repressiveness (Gardner *et al.*, 1959; Holzman and Gardner, 1959), and between extensiveness of scanning and the strength of the defense of isolation in adults (Gardner and Long, 1962a). Although we were not surprised at these results, they may in some ways increase our understanding of the cognitive processes involved in the employment of defenses. Let me point out here that although certain defenses are relatively easy to observe in the clinic, and although defenses have vast implications for the cognitive functioning of the individual, we as yet know extremely little about the actual cognitive processes involved in these enduring aspects of personality organization.

A STUDY OF THE DEVELOPMENT
OF COGNITIVE STRUCTURES

This very brief description of a part of our work with adults may provide a general background for consideration of a current study of relations between various aspects of cognitive structuring in a group of 60 children 9 to 13 years of age. These children were studied in infancy by Escalona, Leitch, and others; at preschool age, during the latency period, and again at prepuberty by Lois Murphy and her associates, of whom Alice Moriarty has been principally involved in the joint study I refer to here. After outlining this study, let us deal briefly with some of the preliminary results relevant to the general problem of the nature and the development of cognitive structures. Five major types of information about cognitive structuring are included in this study. First, of course, are assessments of the various aspects of cognitive control explored in our earlier studies of adults. Second are assessments of the major defenses of the children, evaluated as separate entities because of their unique characteristics and their unique implications for specific cognitive functions. These defense structures are being assessed independently (1) in a "blind" analysis of responses to a battery of clinical psychological tests and (2) on the basis of observations made during the clinical testing session. The third major block of information included in this study of relations between developing cognitive structures consists of 47 carefully selected ratings made on the basis of observations of the children. The fourth block is comprised of scores for performances in the subtests of Wechsler's Intelligence Scale for Children. The fifth block contains summary scores for the new research Rorschach technique developed by Wayne Holtzman and his associates (Holtzman, Thorpe, Swartz, and Herron, 1961).

In addition to these and several additional forms of current information concerning the children, several of which will be reduced to their major dimensions before relations between the blocks are considered, we have comparable behavioral ratings and clinical test materials on these children at the preschool level, and a variety of tests, observational ratings, and other measures of these children's behavior during infancy. Once the major aspects of current cognitive structuring identifiable in our data are isolated, we will test a series of hypotheses concerning relations between infancy, preschool, and prepuberty behaviors.

With this thumbnail sketch of the overall design of this developmental study in mind, let us turn to just a few of the intriguing findings that are beginning to emerge.[4] First of all, it appears, in children as in adults, that a wide variety of cognitive structures is involved in cognitive behavior. Second, comparison of the performances of younger and older children, and of both groups with adults, brings out some impressive facts. One often hears, for example, about a general progression during development from psychological diffuseness to psychological differentiation, and this is certainly true of the development of a number of complex functions, particularly generalized capacity or ability functions, such as those involved in response to intelligence tests. These have long been known to be heavily determined by genic factors. Our results point up, however, that the progressive structurization of other cognitive functions moves in at least two different sets of directions. Some of these functions rather obviously move not toward differentiation, but toward synthesis, i.e., a simplification by virtue of progressive organization along smaller numbers of parameters. There is evidence in our data that some

---

[4] Results of an intercultural study illuminating the effects of social norms on the formation of certain of the cognitive structures investigated are described elsewhere (Mercado, Diaz Guerrero, and Gardner, 1963).

cognitive functions that serve different masters, as it were, early in development, are later integrated under single organizing principles. In statistical terms, certain specific arrangements of functions that are unrelated to each other at relatively early ages are significantly related to each other at later ages and in adulthood. This last group of results would not be surprising, perhaps, were it not for the limited sample of cognitive control principles we are dealing with here. They are compatible with the findings of Cohen (e.g., 1959) concerning performance in intelligence tests. He points out that certain of the functions sampled by Wechsler's intelligence scales come under the organization of a smaller number of principles as one progresses up the developmental scale. An analogous progression is true of certain subgroups of the other cognitive structures we are exploring. A third general observation is that structures like those involved in defenses and tolerance for unrealistic experiences in no way imply a progression toward either maximal or minimal differentiation or synthesis, although employment of a defense may *implicate* qualitatively different structures at various points in development.

It is often assumed that children are more tolerant of unreality than adults. There is impressive evidence that their phenomenal worlds, at least, are less attuned to verifiable features of external reality than are those of adults. We know from Piaget's studies (e.g., 1936, 1962), for example, that the young child has not yet achieved the kinds of decentered logical operations characteristic of the adolescent or adult. We know from psychoanalytic observations that the child has not developed reality-attuned control structures, including defenses, that are adequate to effective limitation of the participation in consciousness of primitive, unrealistic aspects of mental functioning. But when we assess the Rorschachs of these children in terms of their tolerance for unreality, we are confronted with what may seem a basic incongruity, if we accept the assumption stated first. These children's records do contain, as an extensive literature would suggest, more direct expressions of relatively primitive aggressive and other wishes than the records of culturally and socioeconomically comparable adults. At the same time, however, the records of children at prepuberty contain many more specific representations of intolerance for the unreality implied by their productions than do even pathologically unconventional protocols of adults. Our preliminary assessment of their test productions suggests that these older children, at least, are at the same time less attuned to external reality, including social reality, yet are more troubled by unreality than many adults. This is, of course, a preliminary finding and needs further investigation before it can be made a firm statement. But it is typical of new hypotheses our data force us to entertain concerning cognitive development.

One thing at least is clear. No single principle or even type of principle can account for the various facets and hierarchies of cognitive structuring that emerge in the development of an individual. The components are of different kinds. Their interactions during the developmental progression toward a coherent comprehensive "cognitive style" are further complicated by a variety of additional factors, including the relative balance of genic and experiential factors in the determination of particular cognitive structures, the maturational stages at which different types of differentiation and integration take place, and the adaptive, defensive, and other facets of equilibration subserved by different cognitive structures.

To develop this general point further, and in so doing to return once again to the point Gordon Allport made about individuality, let me refer briefly to some results we obtained with adults which relate to the work of Comalli, Wapner, and Werner (1962). I refer now to two aspects of cognitive structuring that move not in different developmental directions, but in the direction of greater differentiation. The first of these is the general developmental progression toward greater articulation of experience so clearly described by Witkin and his associates.[5] The second is the similar-appearing progression toward greater differentiation in response to the Color-Word test, documented by the findings of Comalli, Wapner, and Werner (1962) and by our own recent results. Here

[5] Steven G. Vandenberg (personal communication) has shown that performance in the key laboratory tests of field-articulation is significantly determined by hereditary factors.

are two general progressions toward greater differentiation. But this fact tells us nothing of the relationship of these two forms of differentiation in *individual* human beings, either children or adults. In our recent large samples of adults and children, these two aspects of differentiation are simply not related.

SOME BASIC CRITERIA FOR FURTHER DEVELOPMENTAL STUDIES

In spite of its empirical richness, and in spite of the challenge to some long-held assumptions the data may provide, the kind of study described above can yield only partial answers and a limited range of further questions concerning the general problem of the developmental interrelationships of emerging cognitive structures. No single study will, of course, answer all the relevant questions. We are currently planning, however, a group of studies that may approach in a more effective way some of the major questions we are currently concerned with. There are, for example, crucial unanswered questions concerning the genic determinants of certain cognitive structures, including defense mechanisms. It is entirely possible that many of the relationships between the attitudes or behavior of parents and their children's behavior reported in the child development literature are secondary phenomena that mask genic relationships of several types. One criterion of a more adequate developmental study is, then, that greater attention be paid to isolation of the genic components involved in the emergence of particular cognitive structures. It would be foolhardy to assume that the different types or facets of cognitive structuring, or even the structures within some of the subclasses referred to above, are necessarily products of the same kinds of balance between genic and experiential determinants. From our experience thus far, and our clinical knowledge of structure formation, we would expect that various cognitive structures may ultimately be ranked in terms of genic vs. experiential determination, at least under generally "normal" experiential conditions.

What other major criteria of such developmental studies can be spelled out in advance? As one scans the literature on child development in relation to the clinical literature on the reconstruction of childhood experiences in psychoanalysis, he is impressed by two rather startling facts. First, even when other family members have been included in developmental studies, the father is almost universally absent. The importance of the father to identity formation impressed itself on psychoanalysts many years ago. Freud raised the general problem of identity formation early and capped a series of contributions with his book, *The Ego and the Id* (1923). The course of formal child development research is thus in striking contrast to developments within psychoanalytic theory, in which, as Anna Freud (1954) pointed out, early emphasis on the importance of the father to the emerging identities of children gradually yielded to a more balanced view which also gives full cognizance not only to the mother-child interaction but to the mother and the child as unique in their own right (cf. Brody, 1956).

The second impressive fact is that very few developmental studies have dealt with the family as an interactional *unit*. To omit both the father and the family-Gestalt from studies of the development of cognitive structures is to perpetuate errors that, in combination with the lack of genic information, may ultimately require considerable reinterpretation of results previously reported in the child development literature. More adequate studies of the development of cognitive structures must therefore include observation of the family in operation as a unit and assessment of individual variations in the *experiencing* of the family as a unit from the productions of individual members *about* the family as unit. In this connection, the work of Ackermann and his associates (e.g., 1955, 1958) and the contributions of F. H. Allport (e.g., 1955, 1962) to a conception of individual and group structures may prove particularly useful.

Having posed these objections to at least some of the present literature on child development, have we said enough about approaches to the family as it determines the development of cognitive structures? At least one other area of great importance suggests itself as too frequently ignored in studies of the development of personality organization. One need not confine himself to the literature on psychoanalytic theory to encounter concepts at least closely related to imitation, identification, incorporation, introjection, and so on, as important maneuvers in the young child's coming to terms with the adults he lives with and who control his very existence. The following general, perhaps obvious, hypothesis suggests itself: The structural characteristics of the parent figures are among the most important aspects of what Barker (1960) has called the "autecology" of the child, particularly in the child's earliest and most formative years. In earlier publications (e.g., Gardner *et al.*, 1959), we ourselves have suggested that the individual not only employs a distinctive total cognitive style, but enjoys using the structures involved for their own sake. I would add here that he not only takes pleasure in the employment of his unique cognitive style, but that he *represents* this cognitive style to his children and at least encourages them to conform to his style. I am suggesting, therefore, that both direct imitation and the several forms of opposition to parental orientations occur only in terms of the structural characteristics of the parent figures. Not only the enduring properties of any parent's cognitive style, but also his inherent narcissistic investment in his own cognitive style make it necessary for the child to achieve a personal equilibration in terms of these primary characteristics of his environment and the demands and restrictions upon him which they imply. If this general hypothesis is true, we can hope to understand the emergence of cognitive structures and relations between various aspects of cognitive structuring in the child only if we include assessment of the relevant cognitive structures in both parent figures. An effective study of the interaction of family members must take cognizance of the members' *structural* characteristics. As suggested earlier, these parental characteristics can themselves be considered only basic components of a more adequate investigation of the effects of experiential determinants upon the emergence of cognitive structures.

The contentions above are in accord with the general point of view concerning part-whole relations in personality organization recently expressed by Murphy (1960, pp. 204–205):

There is no sphere of psychology in which there is more frequent reference to the conception of wholeness than the field of personality study. Justly protesting against studies which attempt to define and measure traits *without reference to their context* in the individual make-up, psychologists have tended to refer to the "personality as a whole." The result has been a continuation of the confusion against which we have tried to protest. If it is misleading to dissect and independently discuss the traits of personality as if they existed in a vacuum, it is likewise misleading to define wholeness without reference to the observable phases of personality and the observable relations that exist between these phases; they must have some existence as *parts* if they are to be described. If our general analysis is sound, personality at any given moment is constituted of specific tendencies and an elaborate nexus of relations between these tendencies.

What are some of the other criteria of more effective developmental studies? Foremost among these is the requirement that our current knowledge of important cognitive structures be effectively drawn upon and transformed into concrete representation in such studies.

A number of recent investigators (e.g., Murphy, 1957; White, 1959, 1960) have emphasized the importance of major relatively conflict-free aspects of cognitive development and organization. These investigators, stimulated, as were Piaget, Rapaport, and others, by spontaneous tendencies in the infant to explore and to begin to master the environment, have postulated that such variables as a movement toward mastery, toward feelings of competence, etc., are major expressions of the inbuilt characteristics of the budding ego. Like many of the other recent developments in psychoanalytic ego psychology and related areas, these points of view help to balance and supplement the original focus of psychoanalytic theory on drives, inbuilt restraining structures, and maturational modes (Rapaport, 1960) as the major inherited determinants of ego development. It may be that still further additions will be necessary before adequate conceptual balance is achieved in formulations concerning relations between dynamic and relatively nondynamic aspects of cognitive organization.

A further area of importance is that of the developmental progression toward a stabilized identity. Erikson's work (e.g., 1950, 1956), which has effectively placed the original psychoanalytic conception of developmental stages in a broader social framework, can be considered another of the major recent contributions adding balance and scope to our conception of stages in the development of identity.

I have not referred here to other points of view concerning the structure of intellect (e.g., Guilford, 1959) and personality organization (e.g., Cattell, 1957; Eysenck, 1957) that could well be represented in such a study, although the massiveness of some of these approaches would make it difficult to include them in full-scale fashion. To the degree that such a developmental study included young children, it would of course be of major importance to include key tests drawn from those Piaget and his associates have used to identify the four major stages of intellectual development.

These, then, are some of the *general* criteria around which we propose to design further studies of the development of cognitive structures. Hopefully, these studies will provide clearer answers to a limited group of the broad array of unanswered questions concerning the formation of the various types or aspects of structure that together comprise the cognitive style of the individual.

REFERENCES

Ackermann, N. *The psychodynamics of family life. Diagnosis and treatment of family relationships.* New York: Basic Books, 1958.

Ackermann, N., and Behrens, Marjorie L. Child and family psychopathy: Problems of correlation. In P. H. Hoch and J. Zubin (eds.), *Psychopathology in childhood.* New York: Grune & Stratton, 1955. Pp. 77–96.

Allport, F. H. *Theories of perception and the concept of structure.* New York: Wiley, 1955.

Allport, F. H.   A structuronomic conception of behavior: Individual and collective. *J. abnorm. soc. Psychol.*, 1962, *64*, 3–30.

Allport, G. W.   *Personality. A psychological interpretation.* New York: Holt, Rinehart, and Winston, 1937.

Barker, R. G.   Comments on the papers by Dr. Taylor and Dr. Toman. In M. R. Jones (ed.), *Nebraska symposium on motivation.* Lincoln: Univ. Nebraska Press, 1960. Pp. 95–96.

Brody, Sylvia.   *Patterns of mothering.* New York: International Universities Press, 1956.

Bruner, J. S., Goodnow, Jacqueline J., and Austin, G. A.   *A study of thinking.* New York: Wiley, 1956.

Cattell, R. B.   *Personality and motivation structure and measurement.* New York: World Book, 1957.

Cohen, J.   The factorial structure of the WISC at ages 7–6, 10–6, and 13–6. *J. consult. Psychol.*, 1959, *23*, 285–299.

Comalli, P. E., Jr., Wapner, S., and Werner, H.   Interference effects of Stroop color-word test in childhood, adulthood, and aging. *J. genet. Psychol.*, 1962, *100*, 47–53.

Erikson, E. H.   *Childhood and society.* New York: Norton, 1950.

Erikson, E. H.   The problem of ego identity. *J. Amer. Psychoanalyt. Assn.*, 1956, *4*, 56–121. Also in Identity and the life cycle. *Psychol. Issues*, 1959, *1*, No. 1, 101–164.

Eysenck, H. J.   *The dynamics of anxiety and hysteria.* New York: Praeger, 1957.

Freud, Anna.   Psychoanalysis and education. N.Y. Acad. of Med., May 5, 1954.

Freud, S. (1923).   *The ego and the id.* (Transl. and ed. by J. Strachey). New York: Norton, 1961.

Freud, S. (1937).   Analysis terminable and interminable. *Collected Papers*, vol. 5, pp. 316–357. London: Hogarth, 1950.

Gardner, R. W.   Cognitive styles in categorizing behavior. *J. Pers.*, 1953, *22*, 214–233.

Gardner, R. W.   Cognitive controls of attention deployment as determinants of visual illusions. *J. abnorm. soc. Psychol.*, 1961a, *62*, 120–127.

Gardner, R. W.   Individual differences in figural after-effects and response to reversible figures. *Brit. J. Psychol.*, 1961b, *52*, 269–272.

Gardner, R. W.   Cognitive controls in adaptation: Research and measurement. In S. Messick and J. Ross (eds.), *Measurement in personality and cognition.* New York: Wiley, 1962. Pp. 183–198.

Gardner, R. W.   Personality organization and the nature of consciousness. Paper read at Conference on Problems of Consciousness and

Perception, Wayne State Univ., Detroit, February 9–10, 1961. To be published in a book of conference proceedings. In press.

Gardner, R. W., and Lohrenz, L. J. Leveling-sharpening and serial reproduction of a story. *Bull. Menninger Clin.*, 1960, *24*, 295–304.

Gardner, R. W., and Lohrenz, L. J. Attention and assimilation. *Amer. J. Psychol.*, 1961, *74*, 607–611.

Gardner, R. W., and Long, R. I. Errors of the standard and illusion effects with the inverted-*T*. *Percept. mot. Skills*, 1960a, *10*, 47–54.

Gardner, R. W., and Long, R. I. Errors of the standard and illusion effects with *L*-shaped figures. *Percept. mot. Skills*, 1960b, *10*, 107–109.

Gardner, R. W., and Long, R. I. Leveling-sharpening and serial learning. *Percept. mot. Skills*, 1960c, *10*, 179–185.

Gardner, R. W., and Long, R. I. Cognitive controls as determinants of learning and remembering. *Psychologia*, 1960d, *3*, 165–171.

Gardner, R. W., and Long, R. I. The stability of cognitive controls. *J. abnorm. soc. Psychol.*, 1960e, *61*, 485–487.

Gardner, R. W., and Long, R. I. Field-articulation in recall. *Psychol. Rec.*, 1961, *11*, 305–310.

Gardner, R. W., and Long, R. I. Control, defence, and centration effect: A study of scanning behavior. *Brit. J. Psychol.*, 1962a, *53*, 129–140.

Gardner, R. W., and Long, R. I. Cognitive controls of attention and inhibition. *Brit. J. Psychol.*, 1962b, *53*, 381–388.

Gardner, R. W., and Schoen, R. A. Differentiation and abstraction in concept formation. *Psychol. Monogr.*, in press.

Gardner, R. W., Holzman, P. S., Klein, G. S., Linton, Harriet B., and Spence, D. P. Cognitive control. *Psychol. Issues*, 1959, *1*, No. 4.

Gardner, R. W., Jackson, D. N., and Messick, S. J. Personality organization in cognitive controls and intellectual abilities. *Psychol. Issues*, 1960, *2*, No. 4 (Whole No. 8).

Goldstein, K., and Scheerer, M. Abstract and concrete behavior: An experimental study with special tests. *Psychol. Monogr.*, 1941, *53* (Whole No. 239). Pp. 1–151.

Guilford, J. P. *Personality.* New York: McGraw-Hill, 1959.

Hartmann, H. (1939). *Ego psychology and the problem of adaptation.* (Transl. by D. Rapaport). New York: International Universities Press, 1958.

Hartmann, H. Technical implications of ego psychology. *Psychoanalyt. Quart.*, 1951, *20*, 31–43.

Holtzman, W. H., Thorpe, J. S., Swartz, J. D., and Herron, E. W. *Inkblot perception and personality.* Austin: Univ. of Texas Press, 1961.

Holzman, P. S.   The relation of assimilation tendencies in visual, auditory, and kinesthetic time-error to cognitive attitudes of leveling and sharpening. *J. Pers.*, 1954, 22, 375–394.

Holzman, P. S., and Gardner, R. W.   Leveling and repression. *J. abnorm. soc. Psychol.*, 1959, 59, 151–155.

Holzman, P. S., and Klein, G. S.   Cognitive system-principles of leveling and sharpening: Individual differences in assimilation effects in visual time-error. *J. Psychol.*, 1954, 37, 105–122.

Klein, G. S.   Need and regulation. In M. R. Jones (ed.), *Nebraska symposium on motivation: 1954*. Lincoln: Univ. of Nebraska Press, 1954. Pp. 224–274.

Klein, G. S., Gardner, R. W., and Schlesinger, H. J.   Tolerance for unrealistic experiences: A study of the generality of a cognitive control. *Brit. J. Psychol.*, 1962, 53, 41–55.

Long, R. I.   Field-articulation as a factor in verbal learning and recall. *Percept. mot. Skills*, 1962, 15, 151–158.

Mercado, S. J., Diaz Guerrero, R., and Gardner, R. W.   Control cognicitivo en niños de Mexico y los Estados Unidos. Paper read at VII Congreso Interamericano de Psicologia, Mexico City, December 22, 1961. Also, Cognitive control in children of Mexico and the United States. *J. soc. Psychol.*, 1963, 59, 199–208.

Murphy, G.   Organism and quantity. A study of organic structure as a quantitative problem. In B. Kaplan and S. Wapner (eds.), *Perspectives in psychological theory*. New York: International Universities Press, 1960. Pp. 179–208.

Murphy, Lois B.   Psychoanalysis and child development. Part II. *Bull. Menninger Clin.*, 1957, 21, 248–258.

Piaget, J. (1936).   *The origins of intelligence in children.* New York: International Universities Press, 1952.

Piaget, J.   *Les mécanismes perceptifs.* Paris: Presses Universitaires de France, 1961.

Piaget, J.   The stages of the intellectual development of the child. *Bull. Menninger Clin.*, 1962, 26, 120–128.

Piaget, J., and Inhelder, Bärbel.   *La genèse des structures logiques élémentaires.* Neuchâtel: Delachaux & Niestlé, 1959.

Rapaport, D.   The autonomy of the ego. *Bull. Menninger Clin.*, 1951, 15, 113–123. Also in R. P. Knight and C. R. Friedman (eds.), *Psychoanalytic psychiatry and psychology*. New York: International Universities Press, 1954. Pp. 248–258.

Rapaport, D.   The theory of ego autonomy: a generalization. *Bull. Menninger Clin.*, 1958, 22, 13–35.

Rapaport, D.   The structure of psychonalytic theory. A systematizing attempt. In S. Koch (ed.), *Psychology: A study of a science.* Study

I. *Conceptual and systematic.* Vol. 3. *Formulations of the person and the social context.* New York: McGraw-Hill, 1959. Pp. 55–183. Also in *Psychol. Issues,* 1960, *2,* No. 2 (Whole No. 6).

Rapaport, D.   Psychoanalysis as a developmental psychology. In B. Kaplan and S. Wapner (eds.), *Perspectives in psychological theory.* New York: International Universities Press, 1960. Pp. 209–255.

Rapaport, L., Gill, M., and Schafer, R.   *Diagnostic psychological testing,* Vol. 1. Chicago: Year Book Publishers, 1945.

Reiff, R., and Scheerer, M.   *Memory and hypnotic age regression. Developmental aspects of cognitive function explored through hypnosis.* New York: International Universities Press, 1959.

Scheerer, M.   Problems of performance analysis in the study of personality. *Ann. N.Y. Acad. Sciences,* 1946, *46,* 653–678.

Scheerer, M.   (With the collaboration of Ludwig Immerglück and Morris Buchman). An experiment in abstraction. *Confinia Neurologica,* 1949, *9,* 232–254.

Scheerer, M.   Personality functioning and cognitive psychology. *J. Pers.,* 1953, *22,* 1–16.

Scheerer, M.   Cognitive theory. In G. Lindzey (ed.), *Handbook of social psychology.* Cambridge, Mass.: Addison-Wesley, 1954. Pp. 91–142.

Scheerer, M.   Spheres of meaning: An analysis of stages from perception to abstract thinking. *J. indiv. Psychol.,* 1959, *15,* 50–61.

Scheerer, M., and Huling, M. D.   Cognitive embeddedness in problem solving: A theoretical and experimental analysis. In B. Kaplan and S. Wapner (eds.), *Perspectives in psychological theory.* New York: International Universities Press, 1960. Pp. 256–302.

Snyder, Rebecca, and Scheerer, M.   Interrelationships between personality, skeleto-muscular, and perceptual functioning. In W. H. Ittelson and S. G. Kutash (eds.), *Perceptual changes in psychopathology.* New Brunswick: Rutgers Univ. Press, 1961. Pp. 166–210.

Vygotsky, L. S. (1934).   *Thought and language.* New York: M.I.T. Press and Wiley, 1962.

White, R. W.   Motivation reconsidered: The concept of competence. *Psychol. Rev.,* 1959, *66,* 297–333.

White, R. W.   Competence and the psychosexual stages of development. In M. R. Jones (ed.), *Nebraska symposium on motivation.* Lincoln: Univ. Nebr. Press, 1960. Pp. 97–141.

Witkin, H. A., Dyk, R. B., Faterson, H. F., Goodenough, D. R., and Karp, S. A.   *Psychological differentiation: Studies of development.* New York: Wiley, 1962.

ORIGINS

OF COGNITIVE STYLE[1]

HERMAN A. WITKIN

State University of New York,
College of Medicine at New York City

THERE HAS BEEN A MARKED UPSURGE of interest in problems of cognition during the past fifteen years. The sources of this revival have been numerous, and as the areas of the papers in this volume suggest, the channels in which it has found expression have been very diversified. Some of the channels have taken the form of roaring rivers, others of small rivulets. One channel that by now has reached river size is concerned with the study of cognitive styles, that is, the characteristic, self-consistent ways of functioning shown by the person in the cognitive sphere. Considerable research has gone into both the identification of cognitive styles and the understanding of their relation to personal functioning. It is obvious, however, that much remains to be done.

First of all, there are the important tasks of sharpening the definition of some of the cognitive styles now in vogue, and of developing better "marker" tests for their identification. The obvious overlap among some of the styles described in the literature points to the need for "codification" of cognitive styles. Greater attention needs to be given to the patterning of cognitive styles in individuals, particularly to the effect of different kinds of

[1] The research described in this paper has been supported mainly by a grant (M-628) from the United States Public Health Service, National Institutes of Health.

patterning upon the expression of a given cognitive style and to the characterization of persons, with regard to cognitive style, in multidimensional terms. For many cognitive styles, their connection with personal functioning requires further elucidation.

While these issues, bearing upon the essential nature of cognitive styles, remain to be resolved, there is a next research step that is becoming clearly apparent and that will command more attention as work on these issues advances. This next step is the investigation of the development of cognitive styles. How do differences among people in modes of cognitive functioning arise? How early in the individual's development do his characteristic cognitive styles appear? How stable are these styles over time, both during growth and in adulthood?

The most recent work of our laboratory has been concerned with the development of cognitive styles. In view of the great complexity of the problems involved in this domain, the work we have done up to this point must be considered only first steps. What I am going to do is to discuss selected portions of the cross-sectional and longitudinal studies in which my colleagues and I have been engaged for the past eight years (Witkin, Dyk, Faterson, Goodenough, and Karp, 1962). As much as anything, I want to use this work to illustrate one kind of approach to the study of the origins of cognitive styles and some of the related developmental issues. I will try to point out some of the difficulties and promises of this approach and to identify directions for further work that seem to be needed.

It is worth noting that cognitive styles may offer a very useful medium in which to investigate broad issues of psychological development. Because cognitive styles are salient yet specific dimensions of behavior, rather readily identified and measured, and also tying in with broad networks of psychological characteristics, they provide us with "tracer elements" which may be used in pursuing the course of individual development.

Let me start by bringing you up to date on our view of the cognitive style, field-dependence-independence, with which we have been especially concerned. As our work has progressed, our initial view of this dimension of perceptual functioning has been modified and extended. Perhaps the best way to begin this attempt to represent the essential nature of the dimension is by describing the test situations we devised for its identification.

I would like to mention here what I consider to be a critical feature of our early research methodology. Considerable attention was given at the outset to working through the basic perceptual processes involved, as a prelude to the development of this battery of perceptual tests. This entailed, in particular, intensive study of the "situational" (as contrasted to intra-individual) factors contributing to variations in perceptual functioning. From these studies came the knowledge—about stimulus conditions, experimental procedures, instructions, etc.—needed for devising an effective, reliable test battery to evaluate individual differences in perception. This early investment in the development of measurement procedures has paid off by giving us solid anchorage points for all our subsequent studies.

One of the situations used in our very early work evaluates the person's manner of determining the position of his body in relation to the upright in space. We call it the body-adjustment test. The person sits in a small chair which can be tilted clockwise or counterclockwise, and there is a small room around him which may also be tilted clockwise or counterclockwise, independently of the chair. In a typical dilemma in which the subject finds himself in this test, the chair is tilted 22° and the room 35°, and his task is to adjust his chair to a position where he perceives himself as upright. As you may know, people differ greatly in how they execute this task. Some people, in order to perceive their own bodies as straight, require that they be more or less aligned with the surrounding field, even though this may mean being tilted as much as 35°, or in some cases even more. At the other extreme are people who are able to bring the body close to the true upright, regardless of the position of the surrounding field.

Another kind of situation we developed early in our work, to identify individual differences along the same perceptual dimension, is the rod-and-frame test. Here again the issue is perception of the upright. The rich visual field ordinarily available to the person is completely eliminated, and substituted for it is the simplest field it is possible to have and still represent the vertical and horizontal—a square frame. This frame, coated with luminous paint so the subject can see it in the dark, can be tilted clockwise or counterclockwise about its center. Pivoted at the same center is a rod, again coated with luminous paint, which can also be tilted clockwise or counterclockwise. These are the only two objects visible to the subject in the completely darkened room. Both are presented in tilted positions, and the subject's task is to make the rod upright while the surrounding frame remains at its initial tilt. Again, people vary as to how they carry out this task. At one extreme are people who adjust the rod more or less to the axes of the tilted frame; at the other extreme are people who bring the rod close to the true upright, adjusting it independently of the context that the frame provides.

Finally, we have a situation quite different from the ones just considered, the embedded-figures test, which is a variant of the Gottschaldt. The subject's task is to locate a simple figure embedded in a complex design; his score is the amount of time taken to discover the simple figure in each of a series of 24 complex designs. Although perception of the upright or of body position is not at issue here, there is an essential similarity between the structure of this task and the structure of the tasks presented by the body-adjustment and rod-and-frame tests. In all three there is a particular object of perception with which the subject is asked to concern himself; the object is contained in a complex field which is so organized as to affect the manner in which the object is perceived.

We early observed that when the same people were put through these three test situations, and others similar to them, they tended to perform in a self-consistent manner. Thus, the person who tends to tilt his body far toward the tilted room in the first situation is likely to tilt the rod far toward the tilted frame in the second, and to take a long time to locate the simple figure in the complex design in the third. This self-consistency is evident despite variations in many specific features of the tasks involved. It was also clear very early in our work that the individual's characteristic way of perceiving is quite stable over time. This observation, together with the finding of marked consistency across situations, suggested that the perceptual styles with which we were dealing were not transient ways of coping with a particular situation. I will have a good deal more to say about stability later when I discuss some of our developmental studies.

It is also of interest that from the very outset we found women as a group more affected than men by the context in which an item occurs in their perception of that item. The sex differences in perception, first found with Brooklyn College students, have now been observed with many other groups of various ages, educational levels, and socioeconomic backgrounds. They have also been observed in other geographic areas, including Holland, Italy, England, and Hong Kong. Clearly these sex differences rise above whatever cultural variations exist among these countries. They are certainly not a uniquely "Brooklyn" phenomenon.

As to the nature of the cognitive dimension involved, it is clear that in all the tasks considered the basic requirement is to separate some item (rod, body, or geometric figure) from the context in which it is contained. We use the label *field independent* to refer to performances which reflect ready ability to perceive objects apart from the context in which they occur, or to overcome an embedding context, or to deal with a field analytically. We use the term *field dependent* to refer to performances which reflect dominance of perception of an item by the organization of the prevailing field, or relative inability to separate item from field, or to overcome embedding contexts. Let me emphasize that there is no presumption that we are dealing with two types. In all the perceptual situations used to evaluate field dependence we find a continuum of performance, with most people falling in the middle of the range.

A recent study by Karp (1962) shows clearly that the field-dependence-independence dimension cannot be interpreted in terms of general capacity for figure-ground separation. Rather it involves, quite specifically, ability to overcome an embedding context and it is manifested in tasks which require the breaking-up of an organized context or field. Karp used two kinds of tasks, both of which required that a simple figure be found in a more complex field. In one kind of task the field was simply distracting—for example, lines passing randomly across the figure to be located. In the second kind, the complex field had an organized character. In a factor analysis, Karp found that these two kinds of tasks loaded different factors.

The field-dependence dimension has now been identified in many perceptual situations, suggesting even more pervasive self-consistency than we had observed. For example, the same essential kinds of individual differences in mode of perceptual functioning described for the body-adjustment, rod-and-frame, and embedded-figures tests have now been observed in classical perceptual situations, such as illusions, constancies, reversible perspective. It has also been possible to pick up this dimension in tasks involving different sense modalities. There is a study by White (1953) in which an auditory embedded-figures test was used. In this test the subject first listens to a series of notes and then to a melody which may or may not contain these notes. Subjects who had difficulty determining whether the series of notes was present in the melody could not easily separate item from context in a visual embedded-figure task. Axelrod and Cohen (1961) used a tactile embedded-figure test. The subject, blindfolded, feels the contours of a simple figure, which he must then trace in a complex embedding figure. The correlation between scores on this test and scores on a visual embedded-figures task was .78. It is clear that the field-dependence dimension cuts across sense modalities.

This picture of pervasive self-consistency has been further extended by the demonstration that the tendency to experience in a more or less analytic fashion characterizes the person's intellectual activity as well as his perceptual activity. There is now considerable evidence that people we call field-independent do significantly better at problems in which the essential element required for solution must be isolated from the context in which it is presented and used in a different kind of relation to the rest of the problem material. An example is provided by studies of the relation between field dependence and performance in the *Einstellung* situation.

The subject in a typical *Einstellung* problem is given (or told about) three jars of known capacity, and by manipulation of the contents of these jars is required to obtain a given quantity in one of them. The known maximum capacities of the jars are the only measures available to him. The first few problems can be solved by one method only. Thus, the jars being designated X, Y, and Z, X-Z-2Y would be the only possible solution (that is, if X is filled and from its contents Z is filled once, and Y twice, the remainder in X will represent the amount required). A set is induced by the repetition of the solution. The effect of this set is measured by performance on two kinds of problems. The first, designated the "critical" problem, may be solved by the method used in the set-inducing problems (X-Z-2Y) or by a shorter method, such as X-Y or X + Y. The second, or "extinction" problem, may be solved by the shorter method only.

We may consider the set-breaking process in terms of ability to overcome embeddedness. The elements X, Y, and Z are used repeatedly in a given pattern (such as X-Z-2Y) during the establishment of the set. To break the set, the elements must be considered apart from this previously adopted organization and arranged in a new organization. In this way we may expect that persons who are field-independent would show greater capacity for breaking the set in the *Einstellung* situation. We would further anticipate, since only the extinction problem provides an effective test of set-breaking ability, that the expected relation would be found with performance on the extinction problem, and not necessarily with performance on the critical problem. These expectations have received support from a number of studies; see, for example, Guetzkow (1951), Fenchel (1958), and Goodman (1960).

There is another study by Goodenough and Karp (1961) showing a similar relation between perceptual and intellectual functioning that I want to cite because its results are important for a problem to be considered later on. The study was motivated by accumulating evidence of a significant relation between total IQ scores and performance in our perceptual tests. The possibility arose that the individual differences with which we were dealing might be a function of differences in general intelligence. Even at the time, let me say, we had reason to believe the situation was probably not as simple as that; several studies had shown higher correlations of perceptual test scores with the performance part of standard intelligence tests than with the verbal part.

The factor-analytic study by Goodenough and Karp was carried out with groups of 10-year-old and 12-year-old boys, using the perceptual tests described earlier, as well as other tests of field dependence, a special series of cognitive tasks designed to test particular hypotheses, and the subtests of the WISC.

As in previous factor-analytic studies of the Wechsler scales, three main factors emerged: a verbal factor, best represented by the vocabulary, information, and comprehension subtests; an attention-concentration factor, represented by the digit-span, arithmetic, and coding subtests; and an analytic factor, as we now call it, represented by the block design, picture-completion, and object-assembly subtests. Our perceptual tests were loaded on the same factor as block design, picture completion, and object assembly—that is, the analytical factor; it did not appear on the verbal or attention-concentration factors. A job analysis of the tasks presented by block design, picture completion, and object assembly suggests that they require the same kind of analytic functioning as do the perceptual tests. Apparently, children with a more field-dependent or field-independent way of perceiving are not different in overall tested intelligence. They are different on those parts of intelligence tests which feature analytical ability but not on parts which require verbal ability or capacity for sustained attention.

It now appears that the significant relations previously reported between total IQ scores and measures for the body-adjustment test and the other perceptual tests is "carried" primarily by those subtests of standard intelligence tests which in structure are similar to the perceptual tests of field dependence. In other words, the cognitive style we have been studying is tapped by some of the subtests of standard intelligence tests.

I would cite just one more study of the relation between perceptual and intellectual functioning. It now seems pretty clear that there is high overlap, or perhaps even identity, between what we call field dependence and Guilford's adaptive-flexibility dimension. Factor-analytic and correlational studies have shown a very high relation between performance on our perceptual tests and performance on tests of adaptive flexibility. An example of the latter tests is the following insight problem: "A man went out to hunt a bear one day. He left his camp and hiked due south for ten miles, then went due west for ten miles. At this point he killed a bear. He then dragged the bear back to his camp, a distance of exactly ten miles. What was the color of the bear he killed?" The answer is white, because only in the region of the pole are such geographic relations possible. The solution of this problem requires overcoming the dominant organization of the problem material and restructuring it. Studies have shown that people who are relatively good at this kind of problem are likely to be field independent in our perceptual tests.

With evidence such as this, it became apparent that the style of functioning we first identified in perception, where the person must deal with an immediately-given stimulus configuration, manifests itself as well in intellectual activities, where we are dealing more with symbolic representations. Because it has a too specifically perceptual connotation, the label *field-dependence-independence* did not seem appropriate for this broader dimension. Accordingly, we adopted the designation "analytic-global field approach" to represent this broader dimension of cognitive functioning, involving at one extreme a tendency to experience items as discrete from an organized context, and at the other extreme a tendency to experience items as fused with context.

This cognitive dimension has been still further extended by the demonstration that people whose experience is relatively analytical tend to show greater structure of experience as well. Let me point out that our studies of the structuring dimension are at an early stage relative to the analytical dimension. Let me emphasize too that we do not presume a sharp separation between these two components of experience. I am sure that in real life they never truly exist apart; it is more a matter of focusing, for purposes of research strategy, on one or the other by creating tasks that, on the one hand, require the breaking up of an organized configuration, or, on the other hand, demand that inherently unstructured material be organized in some fashion. The evidence now available suggests that children who are strongly influenced by the organization of the prevailing field in their perception of an item within it tend to leave "as they find it" stimulus material that is unorganized, and so experience it as poorly structured and vague.

We consider analysis and structuring as complementary aspects of articulation of experience. The person who experiences in articulated fashion has the ability to perceive items as discrete from their background, or to reorganize a field, when the field is organized; and to impose structure on a field, and so perceive it as organized, when the field has relatively little inherent structure. Our impression now is that the cognitive differences we have been dealing with are, in the broadest sense, in the extent to which experience is relatively articulated or relatively global. It is the tendency toward one or the other way of experiencing that seems responsible for pervasive self-consistency in the individual's cognitive functioning. We now consider the field-dependence-independence dimension with which our studies began as the analytical component of this broad cognitive style, "picked up" in perception.

The situations discussed thus far have been concerned mainly but not entirely (the body-adjustment test described at the outset is an exception) with the nature of people's experience of situations external to themselves—for example, complex designs containing simple figures, a rod within a tilted frame. As a still further extension of our pursuit of the cognitive style basically at issue here, we have more recently given greater attention to the nature of the person's experience when the main source of the experience lies "on this side" of the integument rather than in the field "out there." This distinction, let me stress, implies no more than the fact that there may be differences in where the primary source of an experience lies. That "inner" and "outer" may never be viewed as separate, but are rather in continuous interaction, is reflected, for example, in the observation made earlier, that perception of body position is influenced by the relation of the body to the surrounding visual field.

The studies I want to turn to now focused particularly on nature of experience of the body and nature of experience of the self. In a sense they continued the work begun with the body-adjustment situation, where the issue is also manner of experiencing the body.

We can conceive of the body, and of the self more generally, as sources of experience, and we may imagine that such experience may be viewed from the standpoint of extent of articulation. We may also consider that the development of experience of the external world and of body and self are closely linked. I would like to outline very briefly some of our thinking on this point.

It seems reasonable to believe that very early in his development the child experiences himself and his environment mainly as a more or less amorphous, "continuous mass." It is very hard to obtain direct evidence on this, of course; but it seems likely that even if the young infant at the very outset does experience feelings from within and from the surface of his body as already somehow special, segregation of self from field is still rather limited. We may imagine that one of the very early developments in the crystallization of experience is the growing awareness of the difference between inner and outer within the original body-field matrix. Boundaries between body, the early representation of self, and the outer world are formed and continue to become stronger during the course of development. Along with the formation of boundaries, the child develops an awareness of the various parts of the body and their interrelatedness. The developing sense of self is rooted in, but obviously not limited to, sensations generated by body functions and activities—for example, hunger, satisfaction of thirst, change in position, pain. Various other kinds of experience, such as emotions, ideas, memories, come to be perceived as emanating particularly from within and are distinguished from experiences which have their primary source "out there." The registration of activities and attributes which the child experiences as somehow belonging to him do not remain discrete, as the pull of an eye muscle, a flash of anger, or a feeling of contentment, but early form a "complex" invested with special feelings and experienced as a bounded inner core.

An important factor in the development of the child's experience of himself is a movement away from the initial inevitable state of unity with mother toward some degree of separation. In the course of this evolving relation with the mother and other people, the child identifies and internalizes particular values and standards—internal frames of reference, we may call them—which help him determine his view of himself. The child develops a growing sense of what he is like, whether objectively correct or not, and how he is different from and similar to others. We refer to the outcome of this double trend in the development of the self as the achievement of a sense of separate identity. So the formation of the self, we would say, involves the more or less simultaneous development of an inner core of experience and the segregation of this core from the field. There is a progression from an initial unstructured state, with segregation of self from environment at best limited, to a more structured state with greater segregation of self. In this sense the self becomes more differentiated as it develops. The achievement of a relatively differentiated self thus implies that in the area of experience where a person's own activities and attributes are the source, experience is relatively articulated rather than global. As you can see, we are casting the concept of the self in cognitive terms.

Not only do the experienced self and the experienced world emerge from an initially more or less continuous body-field matrix, but we would say further that segregation of self from field, and the further crystallization of experience within each of these "segments," proceed in such a way during development that progress toward greater articulation in one area is likely to depend upon and foster the achievement of articulation in the other. Depending on the child's initial make-up and the nature of the forces operating during his development, progress toward articulation of experience may be rapid or slow. Moreover, a tendency for experience to be relatively more articulated or less articulated will be manifested whether the experience has its primary source in one's own activities, attributes, feelings, or in objects and events outside. We may therefore expect that from the standpoint of extent of articulation there would be some degree of consistency in the person's way of experiencing neutral external objects, the body and the self.

The studies we have done on the nature of experience of the self, in the expectation that with regard to extent of articulation such experience would be related to the nature of experience of the external field, have been of two main kinds: first, studies of the body concept, and, second, studies of sense of separate identity. Perhaps some of the broadly stated notions about the development of experience just outlined will become more meaningful through an account of some studies based on these notions.

In our work on nature of the body concept, our expectation was that children who show greater articulation of experience of the world would have a more articulated body concept. By "articulated body concept" we mean that the body is experienced as having definite limits or boundaries and the parts within as discrete, yet interrelated, and formed into a definite structure. In other words, the concern is with the more cognitive rather than libidinal aspects of the body concept, and with a particular cognitive characteristic, articulation.

The results of the body-adjustment test discussed earlier may be considered as providing inferential evidence about articulation of the body concept. Consider the person who, when tilted 35° (being then aligned with the surrounding tilted room), does not feel the enormous tug to one side and says that he is sitting perfectly straight, that this is in fact the way he sits when he eats his dinner. In such a performance the person is certainly giving some indication of a lack of adequate segregation of body from field, an important component of articulation.

We have gone to other methods to pursue the study of articulation of body concept, particularly to the figure-drawing technique. We had used this figure-drawing technique in our earlier work with adults (Witkin, Lewis, Hertzman, Machover, Meissner, and Wapner, 1954), but the scale developed by Machover considered information not only about the body concept but about a variety of other aspects of functioning as well—nature of controls, drive level, manner of handling drives, etc. There were many ingredients in the pudding. The objectives of our more recent research led us to seek ways of evaluating figure-drawing productions of children specifically from the standpoint of what they showed about articulateness of the body concept. Our expectation, based on the view of development of the body concept briefly outlined earlier, was that children whose field-dependent performance in our perceptual tests reflects a more articulated way of experiencing would give evidence of a more articulated concept of the body in their figure-drawing productions.

It will be of aid in describing the scale for evaluating drawings along the articulation dimension to examine the sample drawings shown in Figs. 1 and 2. These drawings were all made by 10-year-old boys from a neighboring elementary school, in response to the request to draw a person, and then to draw a person of the opposite sex. The four pairs of male and female drawings in Fig. 1 come from boys whose performance in our perceptual tests showed an analytical way of experiencing. The drawings show such characteristics as these: The body is typically drawn in proper proportion. The parts of the body are presented in some detail and fairly realistically. There is clear representation of sex and sex differences. Aside from indication of sex through body characteristics—such as breasts, beard, hair formation, etc.—the sex of the figure is also indicated by such externals as clothing. We also find attempts at role representation, suggesting a sense of the uses to which the body may be put. The characteristics cited reflect on level of articulation of the figures drawn. Many other things could be said about each set of drawings referring to other aspects of functioning, but these are not of concern to us now.

In Fig. 2 we see pairs of drawings from children whose perceptual performance was field dependent. These drawing reflect very poor proportioning of the body; in one case the head is about as large as the rest of the body. There is also very little representation of details of the body. Sexual characteristics are shown minimally, or not at all, so that in some pairs it is difficult to tell which is male and which is female. In most cases there is no attempt at role representation.

The rating scale for evaluating articulateness of body concept considered three areas of the drawings: form level, identity or

FIG. 1. These four pairs of drawings were made by four 10-year-old boys whose perception was field independent. In each pair the figure on the left was drawn first. (From Witkin *et al.*, 1962.)

FIG. 2. These four pairs of drawings were made by four 10-year-old field-dependent boys. (From Witkin *et. al.*, 1962.)

role and sex differentiation, and level of detailing. How these areas were used in the five-point scale that was developed may be seen from the criteria used in assigning a rating of 1, for example, the category representing the greatest articulation. This rating was given to drawings which showed a high form level (for example, representation of waistline, hips, shoulders, chest or breast, shaped or clothed limbs); appendages and details represented in proper relation to body outline, with some sophistication in mode of presentation; appropriate, even imaginative detailing (for example, successful profiling, such as young girl in evening clothes, well-dressed man with cigarette)—in other words, the role of the figure is indicated. A rating of 5, at the opposite extreme, was given on the basis of criteria such as these: a very low level of form and integration (for example, ovals, rectangles, sticks stuck onto each other); no evidence of role or sex identity (for example, same treatment of the male and female with, at most, difference in hair treatment; no facial expressions; little shaping or clothing). The three intermediate steps of the five-point scale were defined with reference to these two extreme categories.

It will be noted that the use of the figure-drawing test does not follow the usual projective interpretation of such productions. The scale is based on evident graphic features of the figures placed on paper.

We have found satisfactory interjudge reliability for this scale. In one study the correlation of ratings made independently by two judges was .84. In another study, in which the raters were four psychiatrists, the correlations of ratings for pairs of judges ranged from .83 to .92.

Relating scores for the figure-drawing test to composite perceptual index scores for the body-adjustment, rod-and-frame, and embedded-figures tests, we have found for four separate groups of children correlations of .71, .44, .57, and .76 (P < .01 in all cases). Thus, as expected, children with a more articulated way of experiencing the field in our perceptual tests produce figure drawings suggestive of a more articulated body concept.

Even superficial inspection inevitably provokes the question of whether the children who made the drawings in Fig. 2 were simply intellectually dull, whereas those who made the drawings in Fig. 1 were much brighter. In fact we do find that figure-drawing test scores relate significantly to total IQ, but the availability now of three IQ's of the kind described earlier permits a more probing analysis of the relation between IQ and body-concept measures from the figure-drawing test. Such an analysis shows that the observed relation between figure-drawing and total IQ scores is primarily a function of performance on those subtests of standard intelligence tests which were earlier found to load the analytical factor (block design, picture completion, and object assembly). This is clearly evident when we compare, for example, the relative relation of what we may call the analytical and verbal IQ's to figure-drawing test scores for three groups of children (Table 1).

TABLE 1.   RELATION OF FIGURE-DRAWING SCORES TO ANALYTICAL
AND VERBAL WECHSLER FACTOR SCORES

	Analytical Factor Scores	Verbal Factor Scores
10-year boys	.54[a]	.33
12-year boys	.79[a]	.17
12-year boys	.53[a]	−.10

[a] P < .01.

Findings such as these show clearly that whereas the children whose drawings appear in Fig. 1 may be expected to be quite different from the children who made the drawings in Fig. 2 on the triumvirate of Wechsler subtests loading the analytical factor, they could not be told apart on the subtests which identify the verbal factor (vocabulary, information, comprehension). It would seem that the measures derived from the perceptual tests, the figure drawings, and the analytic subtests of the Wechsler all fall along the same cognitive dimension.

There have been other studies which have related articulateness of the body concept to articulateness of experience of the world, but which have used more experimental means to evaluate the body concept (see, for example, Epstein, 1957; Silverman, Cohen, Shmavonian, and Greenberg, 1961).

I would like to turn now to studies we have done of experience of the self, based on the concept of sense of separate identity.

The self may be regarded as an object of experience. It is also possible to consider that there are differences among people in how the self is experienced. On the one hand, the self may be spontaneously experienced as a clearly separate entity, or, on the other hand, as "fused" with or only vaguely separated from the field, including others. In addition to differences in the segregation dimension, we may also think of differences in experience of the self in terms of degree of inner structure. The self may be experienced as a vague "blob," or as distinctly structured. In other words, we would believe that the articulation concept may be applied to the area of experience where the self is the source of experience.

Our approach to the study of experience of the self reflects our specific concern with the articulation dimension and is based on some of the concepts of development briefly reviewed earlier. It was postulated that progress toward differentiation of the self entails a growing awareness of needs, feelings, and attributes recognized as one's own and the identification of these as distinct from those of others. The outcome of this development was referred to as a "sense of separate identity." This concept implies experience of the self as segregated. It also implies experience of the self as structured; in other words, internal frames of reference have been formed and are available as guides for definition of the self. To the extent that inner frames of reference fail to develop, we might expect that definition of attributes of the self are subject to determination from without, from moment to moment. To do research with such a conceptualization it is necessary to ask in what observable ways may we expect a developed sense of separate identity to manifest itself. Our thought has been that ready and continuing use of external frames of reference for definition of one's feelings, needs, attitudes, characteristics would be suggestive of a relatively limitedly developed sense of separate identity. On the other hand, the ability to establish and, within limits, to maintain attitudes, judgments, sentiments without continuous reference to external standards, and in the face of contradictory expressions from others, might be considered presumptive evidence of a developed sense of separate identity.

Defining sense of separate identity operationally in this way, many studies by ourselves and others, using a great variety of approaches, have shown that persons with a relatively articulated way of experiencing the world tend to give evidence of a more developed sense of separate identity. Let me tell you about one such study, our own, both to represent the results on hand and to make a bit more concrete the meaning of the sense-of-separate-identity concept.

This study was concerned with particular aspects of the child's relation to an adult in authority while taking a test—the TAT. Using the sense-of-separate-identity concept as a guide, we hypothesized that in the TAT type of test situation, where the task is defined in very general terms and the role of the examiner is left deliberately vague, children with contrasting cognitive styles would relate to the examiner in characteristically different fashion. Children with a relatively global field approach, being less able to define their own role in relation to the task, would seek guidance from the examiner as to how to proceed; they would lack confidence in their ability to perform the task, and consequently would react with tension and anxiety during the test. In contrast, children with a relatively analytical field approach would define their roles for themselves and would not need to seek guidance from the examiner; they would proceed with greater confidence and would show less tension and anxiety. The data used to evaluate the child's attitudes and feelings in order to check this hypothesis consisted of the remarks he made during the test, supplemented by the examiner's extensive notes about the child's behavior, made as the test was going on. The content of the TAT stories was not considered. This analysis showed that children with contrasting modes of field approach differed significantly, as expected, in the extent of reliance on their own standards or those of the experimenter, and in their accompanying feelings toward the task.

There have been many other studies based on this same model, and yielding similar results, but using quite different kinds of situations to evaluate extent of reliance on external sources for determination of attitudes, judgments, feelings, self-attitudes. Rudin and Stagner (1958) determined fluctuations in subjects' self-descriptions with change in social situation. Linton (1955) considered the effect of a confederate's judgment upon the subject's estimate of light movement in the autokinetic situation. She also determined the influence of a planted communication upon a previously stated attitude. Bell (1955) employed a questionnaire based on Riesman's inner- vs. other-directed concept. Sangiuliano (1951) employed the Eysenck-Furneaux tests of secondary suggestibility. The results of these and numerous other studies all lead in the same direction: persons with a global way of experiencing are more likely to use external sources for self-definition.

In the studies cited, nature of experience of the self has been inferred from particular kinds of behavior. There lies ahead the very difficult but necessary task of devising methods for more direct assessment of the nature of self-experience.

The studies we have been considering, and many others as well, have yielded a variety of measures, tapping many sources of experience, which we consider to reflect extent of articulation of experience. These measures tend to be significantly interrelated, often quite highly. The evidence thus suggests consistency in a person's characteristic ways of experiencing neutral external objects, the body and the self. Greater or more limited articulation seems to be a quality running through much of a person's experience. Or, drawing on earlier terminology, we might express the same relation by saying that greater articulation of experience of the world is associated with greater self-differentiation.

We now believe that the cognitive dimension first identified in perception, and traced since then along the lines described, may be defined most broadly in terms of the extent to which the individual's experience, both of himself and of the outside world, tends to be relatively articulated or relatively global.

Let me interpolate here a few facts and ideas from areas of our work which I do not have time to go into here, but which are necessary background for the several studies on origins to be described.

We consider a more articulated way of experiencing to represent greater progress toward differentiation during development. Our studies suggest that children who in this way give evidence of more developed differentiation in the cognitive sphere are likely to show greater differentiation in other areas as well. For example, studies we have done of controls and defenses suggest that persons with a more articulated way of experiencing have a more developed defensive structure, with a tendency to use specialized defenses such as intellectualization and isolation. In contrast, persons with a global way of experiencing are likely to have a less developed defensive structure, and to use more global defenses, such as primitive denial and massive repression.

We have already seen that persons who differ along the dimension with which we are concerned are not necessarily more intelligent or less intelligent; the important thing is the composition of their intelligence. A similar picture is found when we consider pathology and adjustment. The evidence indicates quite clearly that there is no relation between mode of field approach and effectiveness of integration or adjustment. Pathology is found at both extremes—in fact, more at the extremes than in the middle range. There are, however, important differences in the *kind* of pathology observed at each extreme, and the pathology at each end is of the nature we may expect to find in the setting of a more differentiated or less differentiated personality. This evidence on pathology is consistent with the differentiation concept. Many patterns of integration, both effective and impaired, may occur at any level of differentiation, so that presence or absence of pathology as such is not directly related to differentiation level. However, we may reasonably expect different kinds of pathology to follow upon impaired integration of a highly differentiated or a limitedly differentiated personality. But the issue of the relation between pathology and mode of field approach is a world in its own right and beyond our present time limitations.

The results of our cross-sectional and longitudinal studies leave little doubt that the trend in development is from a relatively global to a relatively articulated way of experiencing. It is also clear that already at five years—the earliest age we have looked at thus far—there are marked individual differences in performance on tests of articulation of experience; and the results of our longitudinal studies suggest marked relative stability in this dimension during the time of growing up. The extent of stability is illustrated by findings on the body concept. We have been following one group of children since they were 10 and we are now seeing them at age 24. The figure drawings these children made at 10 and again at 17 were evaluated by the scale described earlier. The test-retest correlation was .73 ($P < .01$). In terms of this measure of articulation there is marked stability over a seven-year period, a period of generally rapid growth and change. The drawings as a group showed greater articulation at 17 than at 10, as might be expected; but within this group change, the child who at age 10 showed a global body concept, compared to his peers, did so at 17 as well.

The evidence on stability from our longitudinal studies suggested individual differences in pace of development of the early established, deep-seated cluster of characteristics with which we have been concerned. With this observation the question arose as to the sources of these individual differences. Considering the nature of the characteristics, we can speculate about the possible role of constitutional factors and of early life experiences. Obviously, a very large research program is required to settle these issues. Guided by an interaction approach to the relation between constitutional and experiential factors, we made a start on such a program by carrying out two kinds of studies.

First, we investigated patterns of relations to the family, particularly to the mother, of children who present a picture of greater or more limited differentiation. As you can see, the concept of differentiation had become central in our thinking by the time we undertook these studies of parent-child relations. A second line of work has been longitudinal in nature. As already mentioned, in one investigation we have been following a group of children, now 24, since they were 10. In a second study, we pushed farther down in age. With the help of Lois Murphy and Sybille Escalona we were able to restudy, when they were 6 to 8 years old, the children studied by Escalona and her collaborators during infancy. The data collecting for this study is done, but the analysis of data is still going on so I cannot say very much about it.

I can say more, however, about our study of mother-child relations, undertaken as an exploratory investigation which might yield insights for a later, more definitive, study of the family as a unit. We chose to start with the mother, in part on practical grounds (her availability for study) and in part on conceptual grounds (her probably important role in the development of the particular characteristics of the child on which we had focused).

As suggested earlier, we considered that crystallization of experience probably proceeds out of an initial diffuse "perceptual mass," and involves, as an early step, the separation of the "me" from the "not me"; this separation depends in part upon movement away from an initial state of unity with mother. It is possible that the nature of the child's relation to the mother may be influential in the further crystallization of experience. We may speculate, for example, that hampering separation from mother may interfere with the early act of crystallization that segregation of body-self from mother-field entails, and this, in turn, may interfere with the further development of articulated experience.

Out of the whole vast complex of interrelations between mother and child the areas that seemed most important for development of the characteristics of concern to us were, first, the opportunity the mother gave the child to separate from her; and second, the mother's contribution to the child's development of internalized standards, or frames of reference—or her role in the development of self-differentiation in the child.

Again we considered an interaction approach as most appropriate for viewing the relation between mother and child. The logic of the interaction approach leads inevitably to longitudinal studies, starting before the child even appears on the scene. For practical reasons we could not, when we began this work, do that kind of ideal study. Instead, we began with a cross-sectional study, recognizing its limitations, but we were able to supplement this study later on by the two longitudinal studies mentioned. Our thought was that the findings of the cross-sectional study, exploratory in nature, would suggest hypotheses which could be specifically tested in the longitudinal studies.

In one cross-sectional study with a group of 10-year-old boys and their mothers, we sought evidence on the nature of the mother-child interaction by exploring this interaction from the standpoint of each participant. The mother's views were obtained through an interview with her, conducted without any knowledge of the results of the study of the child himself. The child's viewpoint was explored through his fantasies about parental role projected in TAT stories.

The interview with the mother sought to explore the mother-child relation both in the immediate present and in longitudinal perspective. On the basis of the total impact of the evidence in the interview record the mothers were divided into two groups: (1) Mothers whose relation to their children seemed to have encouraged, permitted, or even pushed the development of differentiation in the child; we have called these "IFD" mothers, or mothers whose interactions with their children have fostered the development of differentiation. (2) Mothers who seemed to have interacted with their children in ways which hampered the child's progress toward differentiation; these we have called "IID" mothers. Though a great deal of ground was covered in the interviews, the emphasis was on the mother's handling of the separation issue and her role in imparting standards for internalization to the child.

These ratings are patently global, but an effort was made to anchor them to a set of clues for judgment, based upon fairly specific behavior. Let me mention just a few of the clues that were used as guides (although not in any weighted fashion) to judge that a mother hampered differentiation. One was that the mother's behavior was not in the direction of helping the child achieve increasing responsibility and self-sufficiency. The handling of the allowance is an example of a specific item of behavior considered here. We had mothers, for instance, who gave their children an allowance which they were allowed to spend on their own. There were other mothers who gave their children no allowance at all. I remember one child who said, when asked about his allowance, "Who, me? I'd only spend it." Another criterion was that the physical care of the child was inappropriate to his age. We had mothers of these 10-year-old boys who still bathed their children, who helped them dress, and when their childlren did not eat fast enough, distracted and spoon-fed them. Other criteria considered in judging a mother as having interacted with her child in a way that hampered the development of differentiation included: she markedly limits the child's activities; she regards her child as delicate, needing special attention and protection; she expresses strong approval of social conformity and propriety; she limits the child's curiosity; she does not encourage her son to assume a masculine role.

Because the categories developed for evaluating mother-child relations were based on evidence obtained from interviews with mothers, they are inevitably "slanted" toward the mother. They must be regarded, however, as referring to mother-child interactions.

The classification made of the mothers according to the method described agreed significantly, in the expected direction, with their children's performance on our perceptual tests and other tests reflecting articulation of experience of the world. Significant correlations were also found between the ratings of mothers and measures for their children of extent of differentiation in the areas of articulation of body concepts and sense of separate identity. We have been able to repeat this study twice now with the same results. The relationship between characteristics of mothers and children in the areas with which we are concerned is a rather strong one. Thus, in one validation study the correlation between children's composite scores for the perceptual tests and ratings of mothers was .65 ($P < .01$).

It cannot be too strongly emphasized that the evaluations made from the interviews are not to be regarded as reflecting a good-bad dimension of mothering. Mothers in the IFD group, who themselves typically showed a sense of separate identity, were better equipped to help their children develop control over impulses and a sense of their own identity. At the same time, some of the characteristics which enabled these mothers to contribute to the development of differentiation in their children tended, in particular cases, to interfere with the help they could give their children in working out an effective adjustment. Some IFD mothers seemed to have contributed to their children's emotional aloofness and tendencies to be overintellectual, overcontrolled, and perfectionistic. On the other hand, some mothers, classed as IID, who did not provide experiences which would help their children develop differentiation, nevertheless seemed to contribute to social adjustment of a specific kind.

The results thus far have come from studies of mother-child interactions as described by the mother. These results were essentially confirmed when the interactions were studied from the child's standpoint. The child's view was assessed primarily through his projection of parental role in the TAT. The TAT study was undertaken with the premise that mothers who interact with their children in the contrasting ways described would be experienced differently by their children, specifically as more supportive or less supportive. We expected that children with a more articulated way of experiencing and who in other ways show a relatively high level of differentiation would tend to portray parents as more supportive than less differentiated children. Within the medium of TAT fantasy productions, support or lack of support may each be expressed in a variety of ways. Eight categories were devised for evaluating the child's view of parental role in terms of extent of support. Our expectation that children with a more articulated way of experiencing would see parents as more supportive was confirmed.

The findings from the studies of the mothers and their children tend to support each other in still another way. A significant correspondence was found between the nature of the children's fantasies about their mothers on the TAT and the impression formed of the mothers themselves when they were actually seen "in the flesh" on interview. There is thus a network of findings which tend to confirm each other. Our results on mother-child relations have also received support from an independent study by Seder (1957). This confirmation is of particular interest since Seder followed a different approach from our own, considering quite specific elements of behavior in contrast to our global evaluations.

I would like to indicate some of the further research steps that now appear necessary.

Obviously, more specific identification must be made of the components of the large complex of factors that went into the global ratings of mother-child relations on the basis of the interview with the mother. We have made a start in this direction with specific studies of the mother as a person, i.e., what the mother is like aside from her role as mother.

As we examined the characteristics of the mothers, in a *post hoc* study of the interview records, with regard to both their interactions with their children and their attributes as persons, it became apparent that included were many which in the children we had regarded as indicative of greater or more limited differentiation. For example, mothers who had been judged as interacting with their children in ways that interfered with differentiation seemed not to have a developed sense of self. They lacked, for example, a clear definition of their roles as wives and mothers. They lacked realization of their children's needs as individuals, and particularly of changes in these needs from one stage of development to another. On the other hand, in this *post hoc* study we formed the impression that mothers judged to have fostered differentiation had more clearly defined their roles, were more aware of their children's needs apart from their own, and had formulated ways of implementing goals and standards for their children. This led to two notions: First, the extent of the mother's own differentiation formed part of the global rating of the mother; second, more undifferentiated children are likely to have mothers who are themselves less differentiated. The rationale for the second hypothesis was, briefly stated, that a mother who has not developed a clear sense of her own identity as a person apart from others is less likely to be able to guide her children toward separation from her.

What we did, as a first preliminary step toward checking these hypotheses, was to evaluate the mothers by two of the techniques we had used with the children themselves to judge extent of differentiation: the embedded-figures and figure-drawing tests. The use of these tests not only permitted us to evaluate mothers aside from their relation to their children, but it also had the advantage that, compared to the complex clinical judgments involved in ratings of interviews with mothers, the measures derived from these tests are based on more limited and therefore more readily identifiable information.

Our first expectation that the extent of the mother's own differentiation was part of the global rating made of her on the basis of the interview was partially confirmed. The interview ratings correlated positively but not significantly ($r = .20$) with the mothers' embedded-figures test scores. However, interview ratings of the mothers agreed significantly ($r = .53$, $P < .05$) with the ratings of the mothers' figure drawings made according to the scale described earlier for evaluating articulation of body concept.

Our second hypothesis, that more undifferentiated children are likely to have mothers who are themselves less differentiated, did not receive much support from the mothers' embedded-figures test results. There was a marginally significant correlation of the mothers' embedded-figures test scores with the children's composite perceptual test scores, but not with other measures of the children's differentiation. The results for the mothers' figure drawings gave stronger support to our hypothesis. Ratings of these drawings generally correlated at a significant level with measures for their children of extent of articulation of experience and other measures of differentiation. As one example, the mothers' figure-drawing ratings correlated .63 ($P < .01$) with their children's figure-drawing ratings.

I might mention parenthetically that examination of individual mother-children pairs showed that when the relationship was not in the direction expected from our hypothesis, it was a matter of a relatively differentiated mother having a relatively undifferentiated son. We had only one case of a limitedly differentiated mother (as judged by the criteria we used) having a highly differentiated child.

A second necessary direction of further work concerns the issues of causal relations and of process. The evidence from the cross-sectional studies just described does not speak on the whole cause-effect problem. The mothers and children in these studies had been "in business" together for ten years when we entered their lives. All we can say, as we observe their relations and feelings toward each other, is that this is what their current interactions are like. Only longitudinal studies can reveal the processes which have these interactions as their end products. The cross-sectional studies already done have, however, yielded hypotheses, as expected, concerning the nature of these processes which may be checked in the longitudinal studies.

For example, we now think that the early interaction between mother and child in relation to the child's body is critical for development of the dimension with which we are concerned. We would consider particularly important the nature and amount of body-to-body contact between mother and child. A given amount and kind of bodily contact and handling is undoubtedly important for the development of an articulated concept of the body. But if a given mother's need for physical contact is strong, and her baby is especially in need of such contact, physical unity may be prolonged and separation delayed. Obviously, just as some babies may have a strong need for contact, others may resist physical closeness, so what the baby is like is extremely important. Again, we would consider that the nature of the mother's attitudes toward the body—the child's, her own, others'—would affect development along the articulation-of-experience dimension. If the mother has essentially negative feelings toward the body, and so, for example, has deep concern about the baby's handling of his genitals, bodily exploration may be discouraged in the child. The result may be interference not only with the formation of an articulated body concept but with the development of articulation of experience of self and world.

Notions such as these, suggested by our cross-sectional studies, will be tested in the data for the children studied in infancy by Escalona and her collaborators and restudied by us in the 6–8-year period.

In the face of mounting evidence of their intimate interrelations it has been increasingly difficult to maintain the traditional separation of cognition and personality. The studies described have contributed further evidence against such a separation. This is apparent in the finding of a common underlying basis for such disparate segments of an individual's behavior, as, for example, his manner of determining the position of a rod within a frame in a darkened room, the speed with which he finds simple figures embedded in complex designs (segments ordinarily considered to fall in the area of perception), the way in which he conceives of his body, the extent to which he experiences himself as a person "in his own right" (segments ordinarily subsumed under personality).

Earlier work, from many laboratories, had shown that, to paraphrase Gordon Allport, cognition must be viewed as embedded in a personal life. The studies of growth described here suggest, in addition, that cognitive development must be viewed as embedded in a personal history.

REFERENCES

Axelrod, S. and Cohen, L. D.   Senescence and embedded-figures performance in vision and touch. *Percep. mot. Skills*, 1961, *12*, 283–288.

Bell, Elaine G.   Inner-directed and other-directed attitudes. Unpublished Ph.D. dissertation. Yale Univ., 1955.

Epstein, L.   The relationship of certain aspects of the body image to the perception of the upright. Unpublished Ph.D. dissertation, New York Univ., 1957.

Fenchel, G. H.   Cognitive rigidity as a behavioral variable manifested in intellectual and perceptual tasks by an outpatient population. Unpublished Ph.D. dissertation, New York Univ., 1958.

Goodenough, D. R., and Karp, S. A.   Field dependence and intellectual functioning. *J. abnorm. soc. Psychol.*, 1961, *63*, 241–246.

Goodman, Beverly.   Field dependence and the closure factors. Unpublished study, 1960.

Guetzkow, H.   An analysis of the operation of set in problem-solving behavior. *J. gen. Psychol.*, 1951, *45*, 219–244.

Karp, S. A.   Overcoming embeddedness in perceptual and intellectual functioning. Unpublished Ph.D. dissertation, New York Univ., 1962.

Linton, Harriet B.   Dependence on external influence: Correlates in perception, attitudes, and judgment. *J. abnorm. soc. Psychol.*, 1955, *51*, 502–507.

Rudin, S. A., and Stagner, R.   Figure-ground phenomena in the perception of physical and social stimuli. *J. Psychol.*, 1958, *45*, 213–225.

Sangiuliano, Iris A.   An investigation of the relationship between the perception of the upright in space and several factors in personality organization. Unpublished Ph.D. dissertation, Fordham Univ., 1951.

Seder, Judith A.   The origin of differences in extent of independence in children: Developmental factors in perceptual field dependence. Unpublished A.B. thesis, Radcliffe College, 1957.

Silverman, A. J., Cohen, S. I., Shmavonian, B. M., and Greenberg, G. Psychophysical investigations in sensory deprivation: The body-field dimension. *Psychosom. Med.*, 1961, *23*, 48–61.

White, B. W.   Visual and auditory closure. *J. exp. Psychol.*, 1953, *48*, 234–240.

Witkin, H. A., Dyk, R. B., Faterson, H. F., Goodenough, D. R., and Karp, S. A.   *Psychological differentiation: Studies of development.* New York: Wiley, 1962.

Witkin, H. A., Lewis, Helen B., Hertzman, M., Machover, Karen, Meissner, Pearl B., and Wapner, S.   *Personality through perception.* New York: Harper, 1954.

SUMMATION

RONALD TAFT

University of Western Australia

NO ONE IN THIS SYMPOSIUM on cognition has offered us a definition of this concept. We could do little better than refer to Martin Scheerer's definition in Lindzey's *Handbook of Social Psychology*. He says that cognition is the process of gaining information and understanding of the world. He goes on to say that the task in studying cognition is to discover the processes which underlie it, to determine the conditions for its occurrence and its function in behavior. This statement is a prophetic anticipation of the scope of the papers which have been delivered at this conference.

One advantage of being a student of cognition as opposed to some other branch of psychology is that one can readily derive hypotheses and obtain data from introspection and observation of everyday occurrences around one. This is perhaps why the cognitive orientation of psychology is so typically grasped by humanistically oriented people. It seems to me that almost all psychologists who emphasize a cognitive standpoint are humanists; but, as we have seen in the last three days, it is possible to be a humanist and at the same time a tough-minded experimenter—a very fine combination in my opinion.

As I have just said, one can pick up hypotheses and thoughts about cognition from everyday experience. I picked up one yesterday from Beatrice Wright, when she was asked in my presence what she got out of her trip around the world. Beatrice replied, "Well, the world became more meaningful and at the same time more confusing." I think this represents my own reactions to this conference; the subject of cognition has become more meaningful and at the same time more confusing.

Perhaps as listeners and participants in a conference centering on aspects of a single topic, our own cognitive processes go through ontogenetic stages analogous to those described by Werner. Thus, commencing with an initial state of general open-mindedness, or diffusion, together perhaps with some articulation in those regions relevant to our own special interest, we proceed to a state of increasing differentiation. At the same time, to dispel feelings of confusion, we actively attempt to organize sections of the material communicated to us in an endeavor to attain eventually an overall integration of the material. Most conferences, by the nature of their planning, provide little opportunity for anything but the proliferation of confusion due to differentiation without encouragement or opportunity for integration.

Why integrate anyway? Maybe it is just the cognitive style of the scientist, or perhaps my own personal style, to try to integrate material into as few common units as possible. First, then, considering the papers phenotypically in terms of topics, they seem to reduce to three major concerns.

Dr. Lyons stands alone, with his treatment of the experimenter-subject interaction. He, of course, addressed himself primarily to methodological questions which, although not absent from the others, were not of primary concern to them. Asch and Rock dealt mainly with memory processes; and the other speakers—Wapner, Phelps, Korchin, Gardner, and Witkin—were concerned with cognitive performance and achievement in relation to individual differences in personality, organic defects, states of the organism, developmental stages, and so on. They addressed themselves to the subject of cognition as an intervening variable and as a piece of behavior worthy of study for itself; they considered cognition both as a response to a stimulus and as a stimulus to further behavior. It struck me, in considering the work of these latter five speakers, that there was a considerable amount of replication in their methods and data. I say this not in any critical way, but with a slight sense of disappointment that it has not been possible within the confines of this conference to have a little bit more consideration of comparative results. I hope that in the near future the literature will report the studies by the various students of these topics virtually side by side, comparing findings and discussing differences. I gather, for example, from the fact that Dr. Gardner had very little of a critical nature to say in his discussion of Dr. Witkin's paper that their two series of studies to a very large extent support each other.

Now for comments on some of the common features in the conference. Is there a theme? It seems to me that this conference might well have been called "Europe's gift to American Psychology." There are many figures present ideologically, even though they were not here physically, notably, of course, Scheerer, Werner, and, I think, Lewin—there is a great deal of Lewin in practically every speaker, although his name was barely mentioned. And certainly Goldstein was present. The influence of many others was strongly present in one or more of the papers— very obviously Freud, Stern, Wertheimer, Koffka and Köhler, Schilder, Hartmann, Erikson, Piaget, and many others; just to put in a plug for a fellow-Britisher, I think Henry Head was very much here too. In a sense this conference has given to those of us who are interested in the history of psychology a feeling of turning back the clock, regression without retrogression. We have somehow managed to survive the onslaught of behaviorism and mathematicianism (to coin a phrase) and somehow got back to the person-oriented stream in psychology which was so greatly boosted in the U. S. A. by the immigration of European workers in the 30's.

The main characteristics of this work are quite clear to all of you, but as it is my duty to integrate the conference, I shall try to bring them out to you. The obvious feature running through all the papers is an emphasis on *holism*. This is represented in two ways: (1) the integration of the cognitive material itself and (2) the quasi-closed system consisting of the subject who is being observed and the context in which he is being observed. An emphasis on organized wholes is clear in practically every one of the papers; for example, development is being observed as a sequential emergence of unit formations, that is, of organized structures. Or let us think back on the discussion yesterday on the subject of rote association. Dr. Rock pointed out that one can present apparently unrelated nonsense syllables to a subject and he learns a paired association. A critic might ask where is the integration in that? The answer is that associations of this kind are low-level special cases of organized structures. Where do we get these organized structures from? Well, we learn them, at least to some extent, although autochthonous factors may be operating too. To the extent that we learn to pair these new and meaningless sounds, we are developing a new organized system of a low order. Now we come to holism in the second sense represented in the experimental context. This was not stressed sufficiently in the papers, although it formed the focus of Dr. Lyons' paper and more particularly in his references to Duncker's work on embeddedness. I must say parenthetically that the report by Scheerer and Huling on the role of unit formation in problem solving (learning to remove the string from a sign in order to solve a problem) is a delightful example of the organismic approach to the understanding of behavior in a context. Dr. Witkin referred to the fact that cognition is embedded in the personality and we could go further and say that personality is embedded in the unit made up of the person in his situation. Well, that is the first common theme that one can see through all the papers, the emphasis on holism.

The second is the interest in the *mediating processes* between stimulus and response. This has been remarked on by a number of the speakers. Worthy of comment here—I'll have more to say later about this—is that, despite the interest in process, there has been very little reference to models. The speakers have been far more interested in describing the process in terms that can be communicated through common experience and everyday language than through the medium of psychological constructs. It is clear also that apart from our interest in cognition as a process mediating between stimulus-and-response situation in behavior, most of the speakers have an interest in cognition for its own sake as well. In other words, cognition is a response—more than just an intervening variable, it is a response with the same legitimate status as any other behavior.

Another common element we have seen in many of the papers, if not all, is an *interest in pathology*. For instance, the brilliant exposition by Dr. Phelps of the effect of brain damage on the integrative process; clearly integration was the key construct to handle the effect of that pathology, as it has been in many other types of pathology. We have had several papers in which the effect of differences between schizophrenics and normals or between particular sorts of schizophrenics have been noted. Pathology, in the context of the papers, takes peculiar forms! It takes the form of extreme youth and extreme age, as well as alcoholism, everyday forgetting and anxiety states. All of these variables appear to influence cognition. It would be interesting to know just what they affect. Do they affect the receptive aspect of the behavior, do they affect the integrative, or do they affect the response side? The emphasis in this conference has been largely on the integrative aspects of the effect.

A number of the papers concerned themselves with the *ontogenetic development* of cognition, although there was little consideration given to etiology except by Witkin. There was a heartening interest in the role of self in this cognitive development, with an implied isomorphism between articulation of the objects themselves and differentiation between self and environment. It was pleasing to note, in this reference, that the *role of the sense of personal identity* in cognitive behavior was not neglected. This represents a healthy turning back to earlier workers, such as Claperède and, later, Koffka, who appreciated the role of self in the articulation of the cognitive field. Reiff and Scheerer used this focus to good advantage in their distinction between "remembrances" and "memoria" in their book on hypnotic age regression; and as Dr. Rock pointed out, it is difficult for a non-ego-oriented S-R theory to handle the former.

With the fairly consistent interest, on the part of the speakers, in *cognitive strategies*, there is an implication that further consideration should be given to *intention*. Scheerer himself writes about the role of "abstract intentionality," the use of conceptualizing as an instrument in the service of the organism. This represents a type of strategy; and most of the papers, especially that of Dr. Gardner, considered the role of characteristic control structures in the person's strategies for realizing his goals. Wherever there are intentions, there are usually beliefs about the utility or disutility of different strategies for the attainment of those intentions. The relevant strategies concern not only overt action, but also cognitive behavior.

Despite this emphasis on cognitive strategies, there was little attention paid to the characteristic goals which might be involved in the intentions. Such considerations are to some extent outside the scope of the conference, but it undoubtedly makes a difference to cognition whether the intentions are the achievement of some material need, the enhancement of the ego, or some stylistic purpose such as self-expression, efficiency for its own sake, or some other conception of elegance. More consideration might well be given to the effect of the type of purpose on the cognitive styles adopted.

Some of the speakers made a distinction between performance and achievement, thinking of performance presumably in terms of its process. Clearly most of the speakers have been far more interested in performance than in achievement, but the latter has not been ignored entirely; for instance, in Dr. Witkin's work he relates articulation to performance on an intelligence test, but as these performances are scored they are treated as achievements. Achievement implies a task or intention. The task (*Aufgabe*) is set not only by the experimenter in the experimental instruction but also by the subject in the intentions that he brings with him to the testing situation. And here we are reminded of the most important paper by Dr. Lyons on the consideration of the experimental situation as a subject for study in itself. It is disturbing to notice so much reporting in the psychological literature, especially in the personality and social psychological area, which gives no recognition whatsoever to the fact that the subjects bring certain expectations, intentions, background into the lab whenever they are asked to take part in a certain experiment. Just consider the typical report—"The subjects for this experiment were 128 males between the ages of 18 and 21." Where did those subjects come from, what did they think they were doing there, what were they trying to do for and to the experimenters, and what were they trying to do to the material? Such questions are usually given no attention in the reports in the journals. And while on the topic, to revert to the importance of context in the experiment, it also should be mandatory for a person reporting an experiment in the area of personality and social psychology to give at least some hint of who the experimenter was, apart from discussing what the intentions of the subject might have been. I had occasion to work on an experiment in cognition which produced results opposite to those in a similar study reported in the literature. My efforts to explain the differences came up against a dead end, because the sex of the experimenter in the earlier study was not clearly stated. If E was a male, one particular interpretation of the results could be applied; but if E was female, it could not. There should be more awareness of the questions raised by Dr. Lyons of the effect on a subject's behavior of intentions, role perceptions, and the experimental context.

Now let us consider some of the topics and emphases which might well have been stressed more at a conference such as this, but have been comparatively neglected.

It is curious that the pupils and associates of Martin Scheerer, himself a pupil of Cassirer, should have passed so lightly over the role of *meaning* in behavior. Scheerer's distinction between schematic activity, spheres of meaning, and conceptualization could provide a framework for describing the ways in which cognition mediates between the situation and behavior at different levels of complexity and abstractness. Many of the points that have been raised could have been handled in terms of meaning concepts. For example, a question was asked in Dr. Wapner's paper concerning the notion of constancy. Constancy can be treated as a case of invariance of meaning, as Scheerer, I believe, would have done it in terms of levels of symbolic generalizations, either through schema or spheres of meaning or conceptual analysis, and it is these symbolic generalizations that may be considered to give constancy to the personality too. A typical cognitive approach to personality would make a special point of the role of meaning in both cognitive and personality constancy.

Another type of content which has been absent from here—and I don't say this in a specially critical way because it is just a matter of one's own interests—there has been practically no reference to *cognition of people*. Nearly all of the examples given have concerned cognition of objects, in most cases "artificial" objects set up in a laboratory. In many ways, studies of cognition of people can inform studies of cognition of nonhuman objects, as well as vice versa, because of both the similarities in process and the differences. For example, would the organization of traits, as studied in Dr. Asch's classical experiment, show developmental trends similar to those reported here for other cognitive material? It would be interesting for some of the work reported at this conference to be applied now with much greater effort to the cognition of people.

Finally, I would just like to refer to a point that I already briefly mentioned and that is the role of *models*. In some of the papers, especially Dr. Gardner's paper, there was certainly an almost explicit statement of the fact that he was relying on a Freudian or neo-Freudian model. Dr. Wapner clearly was deriving his work from the sensory-tonic model which has not been worked out in anything like the detail of some of the other models that are available. As I have said before, I think that the Lewinian topological model has been implicit in most of the presentations, though it has not been referred to specifically. But there are many other models that could be considered appropriate to this field: physiological, mathematical, and computer, for example. As Dr. Witkin stated, there would be advantages if workers in cognition, such as those represented here, gave more consideration to some of the measurement problems in this area, especially questions related to the cognitive dimensions implied in their experimental measures. In this context, I should mention the cognitive model adopted by Sarbin, Taft, and Bailey in which cognitive structures, or "modules," are described in terms of a dimensional model and are set in the context of a syllogism analogy to cognition.

It is interesting that information theory and its typical concepts have had no place in this conference, devoted as it is to the study of knowing. The communication model would appear to be the one par excellence to apply to cognition, but it has not become a part of the Gestalt-derived traditions represented here. More attention needs to be given to the development of some satisfactory model of cognition that integrates the influences of the cognizer's intentions, his structures, and the information value of the data available.

If we were to ask at this point what does the future hold for studies of cognitive performance, the answer might be dependent on the possibility of developing models for integrating, at least partially, this work with aspects of the other four major orientations in psychology today: personality differences, the nature of psychological dimensions, motivation, and learning. There is still a long way to go, but already giant strides have been made. It is clear from this symposium that Martin Scheerer, through his writings and his associates, is continuing to make his contribution toward the development of the needed integrative concepts.

PUBLICATIONS

OF MARTIN SCHEERER

ARTICLES AND CHAPTERS IN BOOKS

Ernst Cassirer's philosophy of symbolic form. *Philosophie und Schule,* 1931, 157–165.

A critical review of current approaches to psychology of language. Teubner: *Neue Jahrbuecher für Wissenschaft,* 1933, 379–384.

(With B. Katzenstein) Child psychology III. The child and his world in the first sound moving picture of Kurt Lewin's. *Z. F. Paedag. Psych.,* 1933, 117–122. Ditto: Child psychology I., 1932, 454–455.

Current research problems in psychology. Teubner: *Neue Jahrbuecher für Wissenschaft,* 1933, 84–90.

(With K. Goldstein and E. Boring) A demonstration of insight—the horse and rider puzzle. *Amer. J. Psychol.,* 1941, *64,* 437–438.

Facts about memory. *Amer. Mercury,* April, 1944, 481–487.

Problems of performance analysis in the study of personality. *Ann. N.Y. Acad. Sciences,* 1946, *46,* 653–678.

(With the collaboration of L. Immerglück and M. Buchman) An experiment in abstraction. *Confinia Neurologica,* 1949, *9,* 232–254.

Measures of impairment of intellectual function: The Goldstein-Scheerer test. *Military Clinical Psychology,* 1951, TM 8–242, AFM 160–45, 116–151.

(With Kurt Goldstein) Tests of abstract and concrete behavior. In A. Weider (ed.), *Contributions toward medical psychology.* New York: Ronald, 1952, pp. 702–731.

Personality functioning and cognitive psychology. *J. Pers.,* 1953, *22,* 1–16.

Cognitive theory. In Gardner Lindzey (ed.), *Handbook of social psychology.* Cambridge, Mass.: Addison-Wesley, 1954. Pp. 91–142.

(With J. Lyons) Line drawings and matching responses to words. *J. Pers.,* 1957, *25,* 251–273.

From perception to thought and from thought to perception. International Congress. *Psychol. Bull.*, 1957, Theme 12, 311–314.

On the relationship between experimental and non-experimental methods in psychology. *Psychol. Record*, 1958, *8*, 109–116.

(With M. Huling) Cognitive embeddedness in problem solving. Paper presented at APA meeting, 1958. *Amer. Psychologist*, 1958, *13*, 372.

Spheres of meaning: An analysis of stages from perception to abstract thinking. *J. indiv. Psychol.*, 1959, *15*, 50–61.

(With M. Huling) Cognitive embeddedness in problem solving: A theoretical and experimental analysis. In B. Kaplan and S. Wapner (eds.), *Perspectives in psychological theory*. New York: International Universities Press, 1960. Pp. 256–302.

The unsettled and unsettling problem of chronic schizophrenia. In L. Appleby, J. M. Scher, and J. Cumming (eds.), *Chronic schizophrenia*. Glencoe, Ill.: Free Press, 1960.

(With Rebecca Snyder) Interrelationships between personality, skeleto-muscular, and perceptual functioning. In S. B. Kutash and W. H. Ittelson (eds.), *Perceptual Changes in Psychopathology*. New Brunswick: Rutgers Univ. Press, 1961, pp. 166–210.

BOOKS AND MONOGRAPHS

Die Lehre von der Gestalt (*The Theory of "Gestalt"*). Berlin: W. de Gruyter, 1931.

(With K. Goldstein) Abstract and concrete behavior: An experimental study with special tests. *Psychol. Monogr.*, 1941, *53*, 1–151.

(With K. Goldstein and Eva Rothman) A case of Idiot Savant, an experimental study in personality organization. *Psychol. Monogr.*, 1945, *58*, 1–63.

(With R. Reiff) *Memory and Hypnotic Age Regression*. New York: International Universities Press, 1959.

BOOK REVIEWS

M. Sherif and H. Cantril, "The psychology of ego involvements: Social attitudes and identifications." *J. abnorm. soc. Psychol.*, 1948, *43*, 106–112.

H. Schaeffer-Zimmern, "The unfolding of artistic activity: Its basis, processes and implications." *J. abnorm. soc. Psychol.*, 1950, *45*, 562–564.

E. Kretschmer, "Der sensitive Beziehungswahn, etc." *Amer. J. Psychol.,* 1952, *65,* 152–153.

D. Rapaport, "Organization and pathology of thought." *J. abnorm. soc. Psychol.,* 1952, *47,* 268–274.

E. Schachtel, "Metamorphosis." *Contemp. Psychol.* 1961, *6,* No. 1, 1–4.

INDEX OF NAMES

219

INDEX OF SUBJECTS